contents

Gospel influenced Musicor songstress Marie Knight whose classic 'That's No Way To Treat A Girl' is high in the chart, though her various other worthy 45s like 'You Lie So Well' didn't quite make it.

production credits

Written and edited by Kev Roberts.

Additional editing by Dave Carne.
Photograph and illustration captions
by Kev Roberts and Dave Carne.

Book and cover design by Dave Carne
at CHC, 015396 23619.

Printed and bound in Great Britain by:
Hi-Tec Print Limited, 01909 568533

Published by: Goldmine/Soul Supply Ltd,
P.O Box 4,Todmorden,OL14 6DA, UK.
www.firstnet.co.uk/goldsoul

Sources of additional information:

The In-Crowd (Bee-Cool), Billboard Book of Top 40 Hits
(Billboard), Behind The Hits (Bob Shannon), Joel Whitburn,
Soul Music (Hugh Gregory), Sound Of The City (Charlie
Gillett), Soul Harmony Singles (Beckman, Hunt and Kline).

Photographs and illustrations courtesy of:

Kev Roberts, Tim Brown, Martin Koppel, Raymond 'Ginger'
Taylor, Pete Whitney and Dave Carne, Blues and Soul, The
LA Black Music History, Derek Allen, Rob Smith, Richard
Searling, Dave Leedham and Ian Levine.

First published ©2000 by Goldmine/Soul Supply Limited

Made in the United Kingdom.

A CIP catalogue record for this book is available
from the British Library.

ISBN 0-9539291-0-8

foreword

I had been producing records independently for around 18 months in the early early 60's when I came to work for Motown. During that time I had written and produced a song for Ike and Tina Turner with another recording quickly following for their backing group the Ikettes. Things were starting to roll, especially following a song I had written for Stevie Wonder entitled 'Castles In The Sand'.

At that time Brenda Holloway, a new young beautiful and talented songstress with Motown was having an incredible impact on my desire to become a popular songwriter and producer. I thought that the only thing that stood in my way was sufficient opportunity to realise my dream.

Shortly after I secured a position as a producer with Motown, Berry Gordy Jnr. invited me to move to Hitsville, USA in Detroit from my base of operations in Los Angeles and I jumped at the opportunity! Within weeks I was there in the studio, producing a song on 'Smokey' Robinson! After Smokey's record came out I started to work with Marvin Gaye, The Four Tops, Diana Ross, The Supremes, The Marvellettes, The Originals, Kiki Dee, Jimmy Ruffin and Eddie Kendricks.

Now besides being one of America's top five producers I also ranked number one in Britain - thanks! At this point my work as both a songwriter and producer with these great artists had already sold over 35 million records worldwide! Later, lost in all of my success with Motown was a song that Berry had originally intended to release on me as an artist, it was entitled 'Do I Love You (Indeed I Do)'. Prior to producing all these other artists I had been doing a bit of songwriting around the Los Angeles area and often became the vocal vehicle for my own material.

Now standing backstage at the Fox Theatre in Detroit, Michigan one night in 1966 a decision was made that changed my life in more ways that I could have imagined. It was decided between myself and Berry that, rather than becoming a recording star myself, I would instead concentrate on being a writer and producer for Motown stable of awesome talents.

Berry then ordered that all of the masters with my voice on be destroyed and overdubbed another artist (Chris Clark sic.) on my backing track!

Somehow, and I don't know how, a copy surfaced in England and was played in the clubs... The rest is, one might say, history!

It seems to me that England is made up of people who are by nature explorers, discoverers and pioneers. I should therefore have not been surprised to find that 'Do I Love You' has been caught up in the phenomenon called 'Northern Soul' which has been secretly bubbling under in the North of England for quite sometime but is now seeping slowly into the rest of the world.

How did I become such an integral part of such an occurance? It has to be supernatural, it has to be God because I knew nothing of it until just a few years ago!

A producer/promoter from London called me up enquiring whether I had any idea where he might get his hands on an original recording of 'Do I Love You' - of course I didn't! I had NO idea an original still existed! Though today I consider it to be one of my life's great achievements!

Since this discovery, I have done countless interviews for the print and electronic medias with regard to this unique musical uprising known as 'Northern Soul' and my own part in it. What have I learned about it personally? Northern Soul is a love affair, some callously suggest that it is just American music that never made it. But if you are in love with it you know that it is music that has found a true home in the hearts of those who have found it to be for them a 'treasure'.

I'm honoured to be included in this book and happy that Kev has asked me to write this foreword to his work which chronicles the experiences, history and most importantly harmonies of this grand odyssey known affectionately in England as Northern Soul.

Frank E. Wilson

Writer and Artist behind 'Do I Love You (Indeed I Do)'.

the author

Kev Roberts started collecting records in 1968. Becoming a disc jockey in 1972, he was one of the originals at the legendary Wigan Casino, before embarking on a successful music and radio career, spending 2 years living and working in New York at the end of the 70's.

His launch into the music business realised many production credits including Mai - Tai, Edwin Starr, Bizzare Inc, Altern 8, Linda Lewis plus hits as diverse as Mistura and Andy Stewart. Radiowise, he has worked for many ILR stations including a long stint at Magic 828 in Leeds. Kev was a key partner in the development of Soul music on CD, compiling over 100 titles for Goldmine/Soul Supply, Sony, BMG, Connoisseur Collection amongst others.

Currently, he holds several directorships and media interests, and through his consultancy business has created new radio brands and many compilation albums.

Married to Sam, with two children, he cites Soul, travel, radio, Italian food and Sheffield Wednesday as his personal vices!

The author, Kev Roberts, aged just 16 on his first night as a DJ at the legendary 'Heart Of Soul'... Wigan Casino.

This book is dedicated to my many inspirational past masters...

In the United Kingdom from the 60's: DJ's Paul Harrison, Laurie and Tony Prince and in the 70's DJ's Ian Levine, Tony Jebb, Alan Day and Sgt., Army Bill Kemp. Stateside, from the 70's: DJ's Hy Lit, Jerry Blavat and Don Steele and from the 80's DJ's John Hook, Dick Heatherton (Joey's brother) and Jeff Thomas

And of course to my friends and influences...

Ann Bond, Derek Allen, Rob Smith, Glenn Bellamy, Richard Searling, Tim Brown, Ian Levine, Nigel Coghill, Paul Lightly, Paul Fairburn, Wayne Kennedy - and Stateside, Dave Nives, Fred Kaplan, Rob Roth, Tony Gioe, Bob Miller and Martin Koppel.

Feel free to e-mail kev@btclick.com

As a young man growing up in a small mining town in the North of England, I became fascinated by the club scene. I became even more enthusiastic after hearing the 'local' hits of the day. Tunes such as 'The Horse', 'Just Like Romeo and Juliet', 'Girl Watcher', mixed with homegrown favourites like 'Green Door', 'A Little Bit Hurt' and 'Trampoline'.

The vibe during these times was a mixture of cool, trendy and violent - all rolled into one.

The thought of a visit to the local bop to hear 'Spirit In The Sky' topped off with giving someone a real hiding repulsed me. Instead I played the wallflower, hanging on to the DJ's coat tail. I was the nerdy anorak who became self obsessive at 'being someone'. The entrepreneurial side grew as the need to own these out of print 45's took over my personality, much to the dismay of my first sweetheart (the unfortunate cutie will be spared the blushes). The 'seriousness' of the Soul business is one of image. I can now fully understand the nature of the beast. In the UK there is an overload of emotional baggage attached to the rare Soul scene, largely due to the intensity of owning a record, discovering a track, or simply being at the gig, which your friends are not aware of. Either way, it's your secret, a little piece of history no one can take away.

The Top 500 became a reality after frequent 'music scheduling' meetings at radio stations which resulted in playing 'Now Is The Time' by Jimmy James and never listing 'A Man Like Me' which is just as popular..

During my stint at EMAP's Magic 828 the phone calls to my show invariably requested 'The Snake', 'There's A Ghost In My House', 'Here I Go Again' or 'You Didn't Say A Word'.

'irrepressible sounds that influenced a generation'

Stuart Maconie, Radio and Television Journalist

Above, left: An early 'big-money' sound. Leon Haywood's 'Baby
Gloucester's Graham 'Docker' White most likely,
for first playing it, sadly both these

The music represented here is feel good and classic. Floods of calls from housewives in Batley or Seacroft demanding more 'Northern Soul' comes as no surprise. The novices like it, even though they can't tell the difference between 'Band Of Gold' and 'That's Not Love'.

The secrecy of the scene and lack of radio exposure has on one hand been dismissive of future interest. The cultishness of it however has allowed it to move forward, and certainly in record collecting terms the movement has never been healthier.

The resulting '500' and add-ons was developed from a basic game-plan backed up with a 'million' overviews. The job of compiling the most loved songs of 'our' scene is a difficult one, for instance I have spoken with a variety of fans who are loosely connected with the current spectacular revival. The choices of long established fans ranged from 'You're Ready Now' to 'The Champion', whilst dance enthusiasts often cite 'Elijah Rockin' With Soul' or 'Psychedelic Soul'. 70's nighter goers reveal the liking for 'Help Me' or 'Thumb a Ride', while collectors and current nighter regulars dwell on George Pepp, Don Gardner or Al 'Mr. Soul' Scott.

What actually constitutes a Northern 45 is open to conjecture. My gut reaction is to focus on what has been played and popular at 'Northern Soul' all nighters rather than what is technically 'Soul' music.

Northern Soul legends... Fred Smith, James Carmichael and Earl Nelson (Jackie Lee) - between them, both as writers and producers and artists in their own rights, responsible for literally dozens of Northern classics.

Below: 'Could Become Bigger Than The Torch', Russ (here assisted in the early days only by Kev) was never a man given to understatement! What would he have said if he knew what we know now?

The Northern Soul Paradox...

The obscurity and uniqueness of Northern Soul has a monster following, for many newcomers and especially our international friends it is often confusing. Let me offer some insight into some of the paradoxes of the world of Northern Soul and its fans.

1. Classic Northern tracks do not necessarily have to be performed by black artists.

2. The typical 'fan' may often also listen to other forms of music - not only including 'Modern' or current Soul (by black artists) but also 60's hits, reggae and modern Soul influenced pop artists such as Lisa Stansfield, Simply Red and The Lighthouse Family. Over the years this broader spectrum of interest has led to other musical influences in the allnighter sound.

3. Many Northern 'hits' are spoken of as being 'Soul' classics, yet are performed by pop artists like Holly St. James, Joanie Sommers, Timi Yuro and Lynne Randell.

In the final analysis this chart is derived from overall long term POPULARITY!

Without resorting to a psycho seasoned oldies theory, I have carefully selected the 'chosen ones' from a well researched piece of 'scene data' going back some 30 years.

For instance, The Tams' 'Hey Girl Don't Bother Me', could easily be at the top of the pile, if it were based on real sales. The fact is, whilst incredibly popular, the track has received very little play since the 60's and early 70's, although it remains a 'loved treasure'.

Above: And you thought he was white! Now back in favour - Ron Holden's storming 'I'll Forgive And Forget' for Challenge records was one Wigan 'stomper' that actually wasn't 'white pop'!

Right: Meanwhile Lada Edmund Jnr. though promoted as a white artist Stateside was in fact black! The lady featured right who was used to promote the single DID NOT sing it at all! The brilliant 'Larue' was also produced by none-other than Shrine supremo Eddie Singleton!

At the very top of our pile Frank Wilson, a 45 only discovered in 1977 yet the mystique, the label interest, sheer brilliance and incredible enduring popularity of this side warrants such an accolade.

We all have our favourites, the pioneers champion 'Mr. Bang Bang Man', 'That's What I Want To Know' and 'She Blew A Good Thing'. Traditional club kings/queens rave over 'They'll Never Know Why', 'I Need You' and 'Come On Train'. Hardcore followers claim 'It's Your Voodoo Working', 'I'm Losing Again' and 'Gonna Hang On In There Girl'. From the mod - era, through the 70's commercial exposure to the 80's underground and subsequent revival today, the variety of sounds has never been greater with Motown, 60's stompers, big beat ballads, modern movers, and early 60's R&B being aired at most venues.

Right: The man behind an early pioneer Northern sound 'The Right Track', Billy Butler's classic first played in the late sixties remains popular today.

9

'Dancing Was Our Weakspot', the mid-late 70's saw massive media intrusion onto the scene as TV crews and magazines descended on Station Road to find out what all the fuss was about. Sadly, apart from serious coverage by the likes of Blues and Soul, the media circus did little apart from deride us 'quaint pill-popping Northerners doing backdrops in our baggy trousers', it seems that no-one can begin to understand our scene - unless they are part of it.

Pictured above: A scene from Granada's 'This England' programme that at least showed the ecstasy 'Out On The Floor' (note cameraman bottom left) - it was of course was cut from the final documentary in favour of footage of cotton mills and old miners!

Left: Well known for their 'Girl Watcher' the O'kaysions also recorded a version of the Embers' superb 'Watch Out Girl'.

'Different strokes for different folks' agreed, as the scene has been bubbling along for over 30 years, let us all embrace and cherish such a magnitude of music. Whether you're a 'Barefootin', 'I Spy For The FBI' man or a 'Gettin' To Me', 'It's Torture' gal, the definitive list represents the ultimate underground of possibly the biggest youth culture movement ever.

A Note On Record Values

The prices listed next to each of the top 500, are the current national average retail prices as determined by top UK dealer Anglo American in Todmorden (www.raresoulvinyl.co.uk).

When referring to this book in future years, bear in mind that the values of the records listed herein will, most likely increase. Expert sources tell us, the records that are rare but not so popular with collectors at the moment and are priced around £30/40 are the most likely to increase.

Our prices are based on the original source issue, ie if recorded in the US, then the American first release is indicated and where only one value is listed this is because the demo and stock issue are of pretty much the same value. Values are intended to give you an idea on what they are worth and are certainly not the final word on record prices which constantly vary depending on current demand and availability.

Below: TV personality DALE WINTON is just one of an army of seemingly unlikely fans of Northern Soul who continue to follow the music behind the scenes and collects the many new CD releases now available.

It is interesting to note that Russ Winstanley's compilation of well known Northern tracks 'Soul Survivors' recently went <u>Platinum</u>!

'Northern Soul
*is a **timeless** movement that*
***never** ceases to amaze me.'*

Dale Winton, TV personality.

UNINSPIRING?...
'What Happened To Yesterday' (here seen on the Mr. Soul release) on the grubby black 'Genuine' label. Dull and uninteresting?...
NO!!!! it is a £1,500 legend that sends dancers and serious collectors alike into paroxisms at the very thought of this exquisite, and incredibly rare, piece of Soul music that was also released credited to Al Scott.

THE TWISTED WHEEL
MANCHESTER

EDWIN STARR
souvenir photo

SATURDAY JAN 30th
SPECIAL SCOOP ATTRACTION
DIRECT FROM AMERICA

the clubs

Many of our great arenas of the past such as The Wheel, Torch, Catacombs, Blackpool Mecca, Wigan Casino are of course legendary in as much as they were part of the youth culture of the time and were innovative in the style of music played.

Certainly in the late 60's and early 70's the emphasis was on keeping the dance floor happy , which may have resulted in rhythm being the operative word not necessarily 'Soul'.

During the 80's the large crowds started to disappear but the serious record collectors tended to have more say as to the future of the scene.

To anyone purchasing this book I am merely demonstrating that 'Soul' of course is the main reason we all discovered this exciting underground, but many if not all the collectors of Northern Soul are likely to have 'dance floor ' classics filed in their collections which probably constitute music by white artists as well as African American/Carribean.

WELCOME TO THE ALL TIME NORTHERN SOUL TOP 500!

Above:Until Dave Godin christened it in 1970 Northern Soul was usually termed 'Rare Soul' (a name still widely used even today). It is an interesting paradox that, though it saw its great first flowering at clubs like the Twisted Wheel, the Mojo and the Blue Orchid, in fact many of the earliest purely Soul venues beloved by Mods were in the South!

The Flamingo with its 'All Nighter' club (the first venue to use the term) in London's Wardour Street was perhaps the greatest of these.

Special thanks for their invaluable assistance and support are due to the following individuals and businesses:

Ian Levine, Mike Ritson, Stuart Russell, Bill Snow, Pete Smith, Derek Howe, Tom Smith, Roger Stewart, Derek Allen, Keith Minshull, Weldon McDougall III, Richard 'Popcorn' Wylie, Coachman Records, Dave Carne, Tim Brown, Martin Koppel, John Manship, Richard Searling, Pete Whitney, Dave Evison, John Atkinson and Rick Foster.

"I'M THE ONE WHO LOVES YOU"
(M. Davis)

VOLT

VOA-4014
(VO-0151)
Groovesville
Music, BMI
Time: 2:38

DARRELL BANKS
Produced by: Don Davis
May, 1969

VOLT RECORDS, 926 EAST McLEMORE, MEMPHIS, TENNESSEE 38106

Great unsung hero of Soul music, Darrell Banks whose sadly short career (he was shot dead in highly suspicious circumstances in 1970) produced a number of all-time Northern classics for Revilot, Volt and Atco.

14

Frank Wilson

Do I Love You (Indeed I Do)

Top 500 Position: **1**
Original Label: **Soul**
Current Value: **£15,000**

'A truly awesome piece of vinyl, and worth every penny of fifteen grand!'

Tim Brown,
Owner of one of the two known copies and MD of Goldmine/Soul Supply Records

The ultimate floorshaker that shook the UK in 1978 and has reached dizzy heights ever since. The most valuable, played and stunning 60's Soul dancer ever made. Recorded in 1965 for Motown's subsidiary SOUL label, the release was shelved as Frank concentrated on his work as a Motown producer.

The flipside 'Sweeter than the day before' was also recorded by Marvin Gaye and Chris Clark, who recorded her own version of 'Do I Love You'.

Frank remained a respected arranger/producer, working with the likes of The Commodores, The Supremes and Brenda Holloway, as well as other great independent label releases, including the Checkerboard Squares and Connie Clark.

There are only two known copies, both are in the UK!

so what's the story?

As one of the former owners of this legendary piece of vinyl I will attempt to shed a little light on the mystery surrounding Frank Wilson's anthem - 'Do I Love You (Indeed I Do)' Soul 35019.

The actual discovery was made by a former researcher Tom Dieperro, a Motown historian who worked for the company in the mid 70's. Low on Tom's list of priorities, the disc and its destiny were about to be turned upside-down when legendary Northern Soul dealer and record producer Simon Soussan finally met up with him. They both shared a love of Detroit and Motown in particular. Dieperro gave a clutch of oddball 45s, including Frank Wilson to Soussan for his collection.

The initial play was enough to send Simon into a frenzy and with his marketing know-how immediately sent acetates to the UK DJs under the guise of Eddie Foster. Understandably it became Northern's biggest ever find and caused much debate as to it's real identity (Simon being notorious for discovering Northern classics and giving them false identities).

The secret was out in 1978 when Soussan offered his collection to Les McCutcheon (an entrepreneur from Weybridge, Surrey who later formed the band Shakatak amongst other chart successes). The fact that it was now owned by a relatively unknown player in Les Mac, and the fact that it's origin was Motown, made collectors give it something of a luke-warm reception.

Whether or not Les got cold feet or simply moved on to pastures new remains unclear but the disc was subsequently sold to Jonathon Woodliffe, a Nottingham DJ who briefly emerged as one of the UKs top collectors.

With a sudden change of heart Jonathon agreed to part company with the record to yours truly, who owned the disc for over 10 years, when my future partner in Goldmine/Soul Supply and reputedly the world's biggest Northern Soul collector offered me the (then) staggering sum of £5,000. At the time I thought that the Northern Scene had bottomed out and I couldn't see prices getting any higher so I agreed to the deal.

Tim Brown has now sold a second copy belonging to Martin Koppel for £15,000, this single voted by collectors and DJ's as the biggest Northern Soul single of all time now belongs to Scots DJ Kenny Burrell.

Ken ya lend us the bus fare te get home?.... Kenny Burrell, right, a popular face and DJ on the scene has recently fulfilled his dream of owning an original copy of 'Do I Love You (Indeed I Do)'... Unfortunately it cost him £15,000 to do it!

Dateline

1977   Tom Dieperro discovers the disc. Simon Soussan acquires the disc from Tom Dieperro in Los Angeles. 1978

1978   Les McCutcheon reputedly paid $500 to Simon for the single. Les loans the single to Russ Winstanley to play. Russ was the key DJ in turning the record into a monster. After a mishap at Wigan Casino the disc accidentally develops an edge warp. Les McCutcheon retrieves the disc from Russ and sells it to Jonathan Woodliffe for a reputed £250.

1979   Jonathan Woodliffe sells the disc to me in an exchange deal valued at £350 for 12", LP's and white demo Funk/Soul releases for his collection.

1989   I sell the disc, warp and all, to Tim Brown for the new world record of £5,000.

1990   The 'only other' copy turns up in Canada with Martin Koppel who acquires an original from former Motown collector Ron Murphy in Detroit. 1996 Tim Brown is offered an earth shattering £15,000 for the ultimate Northern Soul 45.

1999   Scottish DJ and collector Kenny Burrell actually does purchase the only other known copy for the princely sum £15,000 from Martin Koppel through Tim Brown!

Notes

- The single was scheduled for release on the U.S. Motown subsidiary label 'Soul' on November 23rd 1965 (Tim Brown's Birthday!).
- Marvin Gaye had recorded a version of the flip side "Sweeter As The Days Go By". Chris Clark also recorded "Do I Love You".
- The single gained a UK release in 1979.
- A source at Motown/Polygram revealed Wilson's about turn on his vocal debut and quickly convinced Berry Gordy to destroy all existing promo copies.
- Frank Wilson was a reputable writer and producer and has legendary status with Northern Soul collectors for his work with Connie Clark, Mary Love and the Checkerboard Squares amongst others. He is now a church minister in California.

Dobie Gray

Out On The Floor

Top 500 Position: **2**
Original Label: **Charger**
Current Value: **£10**

'My first experience with Northern Soul -this is it!'

Dobie Gray, Artist, USA

Born Leonard Ainsworth, Dobie is a veritable giant amongst Northern fans due to this disc. The groove encapsulates the 60's 'full on' with a stirring LA production and DG's controlled vocal and Spectoresque reverb.

In terms of 'feel good' they do not come much better than this. First released on the US Charger label, the disc was massively imported into the UK during the 70's, finally entering the UK charts in 1975 on Black Magic. Best known for his classic 'The In-Crowd', Dobie went on to record the ultra-rare 'What A Way To Go' for White Whale before topping the charts in the 70's with the country influenced 'Drift Away'.

Yeah, yeah, yeah babe it's out of sight!

Yvonne Baker
You Didn't Say A Word

Top 500 Position: **3**
Original Label: **Parkway**
Current Value: **£200 Demo**
£300 Issue

'This obscure disc I made, still sends a shiver through me even today'

Yvonne Baker, Artist, Philadelphia, USA

The James Bond intro was typical of many 60's 'groovers' of their day. Miss Baker, born Yvonne Mills, was already an experienced hand in the studio, realising a US No. 4 hit in 1962 with 'Let me In', as lead singer of the Sensations. In fact she later teamed up with the group again for a cover of Lorraine Chandler's 'I Can't Change'.

To the North of England this is Yvonne's unsurpassable classic, a moody John Barry type arrangement, precocious Dinah Washington type lead, and a dance beat to die for. When the beloved Casino opened its hallowed doors to this winner it confirmed the new venture's position as No.1. Bizzarely, this original version has never been released on CD or as a vinyl reissue, at least not legally! Apparently, the ownership of the master is as shrouded in mystery as the record itself!

19

Al Wilson

The Snake

Top 500 Position:	**4**
Original Label:	**Soul City**
Current Value:	**£6 Issue**
	£15 Demo

'Fast, funny, and as original as you can get'

Tom Smith, Beatin' Rhythm, Manchester, UK

A kooky 60's song produced by Johnny Rivers and executed to perfection by singer/drummer Al Wilson. The oddity of the disc stems from the pen of Oscar Brown Jnr and together with the basic groove alongside the Jim Webb type orchestration, the song and lyrics sit nicely for dancers and listeners alike.

Wilson hails from Meridian, Mississippi, which could be a contender as a twin town with... WIGAN!

Jimmy Radcliffe
Long After Tonight Is All Over

Top 500 Position: **5**
Original Label: **Musicor**
Current Value: **£20 Issue**
£30 Demo

'The pure emotion of the song is the most precious thing I have ever heard'

Pete Waterman, Record Producer, UK

Jimmy may no longer be with us, but his superlative 1964 recording of Bacharach and David's underrated song means much to all Rare Soul lovers... This is the side that rendered machismo and girl power to mush.

A stylish ballad originally recorded by Jimmy as a demo for its intended artist, Gene Pitney, 'Long After' is similar in style to Chuck Jackson and Roy Hamilton singles of the time.

Imagine the scenario at the all-nighter, you have spent too much money, argued with your best friend, the cloakroom girl AND the 'other half', to top all that the 45 you've bought for £100 is cracked! Jimmy's vocals suddenly appear at ten minutes to eight and Sunday is spent in lustful motion.

James Fountain

Seven Day Lover

Top 500 Position: **6**
Original Label: **Peachtree**
Current Value: **£30**

*'A hunk of Northern funk,
excuse me while I wriggle
on to the dance floor'*

Paul Hatton, Soul Fan, Hull, UK

Undoubtedly the 45 that broke the mould in terms of traditional Northern productions. A typical 70's bass drum and melodic piano kick starts a script from James that transforms into a wailing five star piece of Atlanta Soul.

The real credit goes to Ian Levine though, for vigorously challenging the Northern scene to 'look, listen and learn'. Well we did, and became wiser for it.

Label owner, the legendary William Bell, has found himself in the unusual but pleasurable position of releasing a single which bombed in the States but was revered in Europe.

Epitome Of Sound
You Don't Love Me

Top 500 Position:	**7**
Original Label:	**Sandbag**
Current Value:	**£30 Issue**
	£100 Demo

'The first of many classic turntable spins from the class of '74'

John Manship, Record Dealer, UK

I suspect a blue eyed Soul effort here, and what a performance. 'You told me that you loved me (told me that you love me) states the lead singer. Nothing too interesting there until you hear the most uplifting performance from Robert Paladino's Epitome of Sound. I can't help thinking the initial release might have caused a stir somewhere on the East Coast of America, largely due to an abundance of copies that were in several record stores in Philadelphia during the 70's.

Backed by the excellent 'Where Were You', in some quarters 'You Don't Love Me' is considered to be <u>the</u> Wigan anthem.

Garnett Mimms
Looking For You

Top 500 Position: **8**
Original Label: **United Artists**
Current Value: **£40 Issue**
£50 Demo

'Hearing it in 1970 and today tells me nothing has changed, it's fantastic!'

Derek Allen, DJ, Leicester, UK

In recent interviews the man from West Virginia is as surprised as any one at his 1966 recording's history. Though originally in R&B group The Gaitors, 'Cry Baby' launched his solo career in '63, but it is 'Looking' that has become the 'anthem'.

Again, totally easy on the ear, the simplistic arrangement confirms, great songs do not need complicating. The 45 has have pounded the speakers at most Northern gigs during the past 30 years, and I for one never tire of it. In keeping with the scene's tradition a disastrous cover version attempt was made in 1979 by the Echoes, co-produced by... Whatsisname!

Frank Beverly and the Butlers

If That's What You Wanted

Top 500 Position: **9**
Original Label: **Sassy/Gamble**
Current Value: **£50 Sassy**
                    £100 Gamble

'The intro testifies that this really is the business'

Rob Smith,
DJ, Collector, Record Dealer, Nottingham, UK

I remember distinctly the first time I ever heard this at Va-Va's in Bolton, where after a chance meeting with the late Les Cokell, I raced over to the turntables to see a Gamble label spinning at 45 rpm. The following week was spent humming it, and desperately trying to find a copy. Although on Kenny and Leon's outlet, the side's initial release was on Billy Jackson's Sassy label from where most DJ's secured it to play. The truly gifted front man of MAZE, Frank revels in a tip-top production, of which Philadelphia never mind Lancashire should be proud.

Following the initial hi-hats and horn intro, the next 8 bars suggest a heard of elephants are about to run through the auditorium while you're in full flight on the floor.

If you are looking for big time Northern Soul? - THIS IS IT!

Chuck Wood

Seven Days Too Long

Top 500 Position: **10**
Original Label: **Roulette**
Current Value: **£10 Issue**
£15 Demo

'Seven minutes is too long without this one'

Chris Williams, HMV, Stoke-on-Trent, UK

Chuck's finest hour reveals to all that here is a performer who sounds like he's auditioning for Otis Redding. A monster, walloping, racing, looping, bounding, Soul side from '67 (to quote the late James Hamilton) and known to bit part players as the flip to the UK release of 'Footsee', which peaked at No.9 in 1975. You can see the thinking back then, stick a fantastic record with massive credibility on the flip of a in-vogue piece of nonsense!

The record is marvellous and I urge everyone to own it. Chuck may have faded into obscurity but the legacy left by this outing will remind all of us what a totally brilliant track it is. Chuck, welcome to the Top 10!

Billy Butler
Right Track

Top 500 Position:	**11**
Original Label:	**Okeh**
Current Value:	**£15 Issue**
	£25 Demo

'Simply awesome'

Alan Day, DJ, Derby, UK

A super slick, but basic workout from Jerry Butler's brother.

Recorded for the US Okeh label in 1966, this (amazingly) B side was championed by the Soul City record store in London, who subsequently released the single. The hook is in the guitar and piano which bubbles along delightfully for dancers.

The man from Chicago who recorded many fabulous 60's sides finds himself an unlikely hero 3,500 miles away. Collectors trivia-during a reissue by Columbia (Sony) in 1973, they accidentally used the wrong master and pressed the instrumental version!

The Salvadors
Stick By Me Baby

Top 500 Position: **12**
Original Label: **Wise World**
Current Value: **£800**

'A mesmerising performance on such an obscure disc'

Martin Smith, Soul Fan, Herts, UK

The Salvadors, a Chicago group formed in '62 hit us with one of the great intros of all time, with eight bars of a dark, sinister piano, bass and drum melody. The really big venues associated with Northern Soul can rely wholeheartedly on such a side to get the night underway and it is easy to see why.

In rarity terms, the original vinyl 45 is extremely sought after, as very few copies have emerged after the initial finds over 27 years ago.

Played simultaneously at Blackpool Mecca and Wigan Casino.

The Tomangoes
I Really Love You

Top 500 Position: **13**
Original Label: **Washpan**
Current Value: **£500**

'Detroit has produced many things, most notably (in my house)… The Tomangoes'

Steve Crozier, Soul Fan, London, UK

Similar in style to our preceding number, the basis of the scene lives and breathes on such a side as this. The trademarks are all here, a super rare Detroit 45 with a great lead vocal by Geno Washington (the Atac/Do-De-Ri man, NOT the Ram-Jam band singer!), with an almost 'hey this will be popular, someday, somewhere' stamp on the label.

One thing you will discover about Northern Soul is that the roots are based around a production such as this, and while other distractions (ie, quirky pop dancers) diverted us from time-to-time on the dance floor, it is a 45 of this magnitude which gets us focused again on the big picture.

This is Northern Soul of the <u>highest</u> quality - Tomangoes, take a bow!

Tobi Legend
Time Will Pass You By

Top 500 Position: **14**
Original Label: **Amy**
Current Value: **£100 Demo**
£300 Issue

*'One of the world's
great enders'*

Clarence Bennett,
Soul Fan and DJ, Oldham, UK

Recording as Tobi Lark for Dave Hamilton's Topper label, the gal from Detroit realised 20 years post release that Bell records had issued a demo she recorded in 1968.

Under the guise of 'Legend' Tobi's finest hour was captured weekly at the Casino, known as one of the 'three before 8'. 8am being the closure time of the all-nighter.

The song also received long awaited publicity via M People who covered the song several years ago.

All in all the track is one of the true anthems and still carries enough charisma long into the millennium.

Tony Clarke
Landslide

Top 500 Position: **15**
Original Label: **Chess**
Current Value: **£30 Issue**
£150 Demo

'The drum roll instigates the perfect back drop'

Dave Nowell,
Soul Journalist, Blackpool, UK

Once again, if you are someone with a good memory you're likely to challenge the chart position.

All things being equal, it ought to be a Top 10 sound at the very least. Overkill is the key word here, as this explosive dancer from the late TC rocketed it's way into the arena in late '73.

The track hardly got a play in the 80's, but has since reactivated itself to be one of the true giants. If there was any argument as to the voted position, I would almost certainly be on the side of the challenge.

Passing away in 1970, Clarke recorded for Chess, MS, Chicory and Fascination and became an actor, appearing in 'They call me Mr. Tibbs'. 'The Entertainer' on Chess was his only hit.

Larry Williams and Johnny Watson
Too Late

Top 500 Position: **16**
Original Label: **Okeh**
Current Value: **£25 Issue**
£50 Demo

'Amphetamine driven Northern Soul'

Franny Moore, Soul Fan, Leigh, UK

The Northern traditionalists would possibly rate the track as No.1 contender, considering it's dance floor history and, while turntable spins have fallen of late, the nostalgia value in it is unequalled.

Duets are uncommon on the scene, but an exception is made in this case as two seasoned pro's 'tear it up' with a full blown rampant display that Little Richard would be proud of.

Larry sadly committed suicide in 1980, Johnny passed away recently. Williams in particular was a huge influence on the Beatles. What a shame they did not live to see a major Soul night spinning this marvellous gem. From the vaults of Okeh and recorded in 1967, Williams and Watson we salute you.

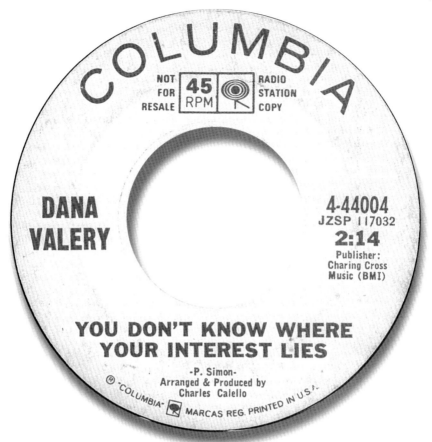

Dana Valery

You Don't Know Where Your Interest Lies

Top 500 Position: **17**
Original Label: **Columbia**
Current Value: **£125 Demo**
£350 Issue

'An adrenaline rush just hits you every time you hear it'

Dave Raistrick,
Record Dealer, Skegness, UK

Many years on, one could question this disc's validity in such an important chart. Dana singing a Simon and Garfunkel song has trademarks of lack of fulfilment Soul-wise, but again the tempo clicked instantly with dancers and it became a truly massive Wigan spin, 25 years on it seems DV has retained a level of credibility.

She later moved to record for Brunswick where 'You Babe' found favour with the UK Soul crowd once more - not bad for a blonde of Italian extraction!

Willie Tee
Walking Up A One Way Street

Top 500 Position: **18**
Original Label: **Nola**
Current Value: **£40**

'Easy does it as Willie tells the tale superbly'

John Abbey, Blues & Soul, UK

Willie Turbiton from New Orleans specialised in recording simplistic lyrics with stunning craft and guile, complimented by that unique Louisiana feel. 'Thank you John', 'Teasin' you' and later 'Please don't go' have their own following, but the winner is 'Walking' which bubbled under the US chart in '66, and remains a classic on both sides of the Atlantic.

The quaintness of tempo lies solely with the artist's vocal control, of which Mr. Tee is a master.

From the Wheel to Keele this masterpiece proudly sits on the top shelf in the Northern Soul Top 500.

Dena Barnes

If You Ever Walk Out Of My Life

Top 500 Position: **19**
Original Label: **Inferno**
Current Value: **£300 Issue**
£200 Demo

'A timeless piece of sugar coated Soul'

Kev Sowerby, DJ, Penrith, UK

Dena produced just one single for Harry Balk's Inferno label, though there are pressings of 'These Heartaches I Can't Stand', an alternative vocal to Duke Browner's 'Crying Over You' which actually have nothing to do with her!

At a funeral recently of a good friend, the song was broadcast to the congregation which many shed a tear. The moment was poignant, and while the masses grieved, my thoughts also turned to others who had embraced this classic Detroit 45 and made it 'their song'.

Still, it's only a 3 minute piece of black plastic and we should not take it too seriously, but hey, this Northern Soul business is like life and death, except it's far more important than that!

THERE'S A GHOST IN MY HOUSE
(Holland, Dozier, Holland & Taylor)

V. I. P.

Disc Jockey
Advance Sample
V.I.P.-25042
© 1966
Jobete BMI
H-LS-V-288M13
2:34
Produced By
Holland &
Dozier

NOT FOR SALE

R. DEAN TAYLOR

A TRADEMARK OF MOTOWN RECORD CORP. © 1967

R. Dean Taylor
There's A Ghost In My House

Top 500 Position: **20**
Original Label: **V.I.P.**
Current Value: **£20 Issue**
£30 Demo

'R. Dean's cowboy hat fell off at hearing which of his songs had made the UK charts'

Roger St Pierre,
Journalist, London, UK

Hailing from Toronto, Taylor was the all original session guy for Motown. He occasionally got to write for Mr. Gordy too, as co-author on 'Love Child' for The Supremes and the Canadian also had is own chart success with 'Indiana Wants Me' and 'Gotta See Jane'.

Hang on there RD, 3,000 miles eastbound your throwaway 1965 single for Motown subsidiary VIP is hot in England, in fact it was at No. 3 in the charts (1974)!

The tour, the acclaim, and back to reality. In real terms the 45 is only rarely played at the rarer events, however in the 70's, 'Ghost' pleased many a promoter with the level of spins it demanded.

Archie Bell and the Drells
Here I Go Again

Top 500 Position: **21**
Original Label: **Atlantic**
Current Value: **£6 Issue**
                      £10 Demo

'The first of many 'handclaps' within the scene... fresh sounding even now'

Carol England,
Soul Fan, Birmingham, UK

Archie Bell from Henderson, Texas was on a roll when a 'out of print' single from 1969 hit the shores of an unsuspecting old blighty. I say on a roll, because he had scored with 3 hits in a row for Atlantic during the late 60's. The 'Tighten Up' man was certainly surprised when 3 years later the single 'Here I go again' was unearthed by DJ's here.

Gamble and Huff had already marked our cards with their new sound, i.e. 'Moody Woman' with Jerry Butler.

In terms of ingredients it has the lot, swirling string intro, fast uptempo beat complimented by the unique vocal that we have come to cherish. Bell of course became a hit maker for the Philly machine, but the US totally missed out on this sensational Soul platter.

Rose Batiste
Hit And Run

Top 500 Position: **22**
Original Label: **Revilot**
Current Value: **£100 Issue**
£150 Demo

'A major felony has been committed... Run onto that dance floor!'

Tot Johnson,
Collector, Stoke-on-Trent, UK

Don Davis formed a label in Detroit called Revilot (the name is Toliver spelt backwards) with a partner Lebaron Taylor (aka Toliver). Together, they released a plethora of gems, aimed at taking on Motown. Unfortunately the gameplan failed but the legacy has been truly embraced by us Brits. 'Hit and Run' is arguably the finest single on the label, certainly the best dancer.

Rose in an interview recently, choked back the tears as she thanked the UK for discovering one of her long lost 45's.

Rose sweetie, thank you for a performance to savour!

The flipside 'I Miss My Baby', vocal to the classic 'Bari Track', is of course superb too!

Hidle Music
B.M.I.
Time: 2:15
0004-X
ST-45-0004-B
Produced by
H. B. Barnum

WHAT
(H. B. Barnum)

JUDY STREET

Judy Street
What

Top 500 Position:	**23**
Original Label:	**Strider**
Current Value:	**£100**

'The regionality of sales precluded a chart position'

John Anderson,
owner of Grapevine Records, UK

'What' by Judy Street is an HB Barnum production of late 1966 that almost charted in the UK. The unknown Californian had strong competition from several better known artists who have recorded it over the years (including Britain's Soft Cell, who had chart success with their homage to their own musical roots).

The 'What can I do, what can I say?' chorus is an instant winner and, although considered too poppy by many today, it has undeniably been one of the biggest Northern Soul dance sounds of them all!

Gloria Jones
Tainted Love

Top 500 Position: **24**
Original Label: **Champion**
Current Value: **£15 issue**
£40 Demo

'A great big beautiful romp'

Michelle Vincent, Soul Fan, London, UK

The history of Ms. Jones is well documented, the Soft Cell cover hit even more so. What else can we extract from a US non hit from '65? Well, one key factor to the disc's rating is timing, as initial plays in late '73 mixed perfectly with the 'stomp' sound Wigan was to become famous for.

I would certainly rank it at No.2 behind R. Dean Taylor as the Casino's biggest ever play. In terms of strength, the drum pattern sells it, working dancers to a frenzy, and a mere 2.12 of audio delivers all that's good about the 60's. Gloria recorded for Minit too shortly after her contract with Ed Cobb expired, but those sessions circa 65/66 were the best by a mile, so much so, she enjoys another chart placing later in the book.

Moses Smith

The Girl Across The Street

Top 500 Position:	**25**
Original Label:	**Dionn**
Current Value:	**£100 Demo**
	£40 Issue

'The unique vocal sets the song alight'

Rod Hemmings, Soul Fan, Australia

The artist is a mystery, his only other recording being for Cotillion. At least label boss Gilda Woods saw 'hit' written all over it, the problem for label and act though is one of bad timing.

Recorded in '67 in Philadelphia and with the smooth but tense delivery from Smith, I can't help thinking this must have caused a stir somewhere in the Delaware Valley upon release. No, not a fig, many radio contacts have the blank face on this one. So would the real Mr. Smith stand up, we are dying to know who you really are!

Barbara McNair

You're Gonna Love My Baby

Top 500 Position: **26**
Original Label: **Motown**
Current Value: **£60 Issue**
£100 Demo

'Still sought after by many'

Pete Smith, Record Dealer, Sussex, UK

When a Tobi Legend or Timi Yuro capture the scene's imagination, the songs themselves develop a longevity that many traditional dancers lack. Similarly Barbara was the showgirl at Motown, a sort of Rogers and Hammerstein version of Miss Ross.

With a Berry Gordy production in tow, one should expect a decent chart placing at least. Sadly, it bombed - even worse it's the B side! The UK release fared no better, but the association with Northern finally gave it the acclaim it deserves, albeit North Of Watford.

This wonderful orchestral performance was co-written by Babs herself, who's unreleased 'Baby A Go-Go' is a massive current sound gleaned from a master tape.

Rubin

You've Been Away

Top 500 Position:	**27**
Original Label:	**Kapp**
Current Value:	**£250 Issue**
	£150 Demo

'A delightful over the top performance'

Dale Winton, TV Celebrity

Two stories on this hot blooded piece of ferocity.

Firstly, when aired initially the track became massive and remained so for about a year. Then without notice the 45 was eliminated from most play lists due to the 'reissue' becoming available. Following a 20 year isolation period, apart from collector interest in the super rare 'stock' copy issue on Kapp, the song re-invented itself as the Felix cat food theme.

Obviously, the Northern Soul loving advertising agencies rate it as much as we do! Consequently the popularity now is at an all time high, and deservedly so. Rumours are rife about the identity of the artist, personally I will stick to my own illusion of who he really is.

43

Mel Britt

She'll Come Running Back

Top 500 Position:	**28**
Original Label:	**FIP**
Current Value:	**£600 Issue**
	£800 Demo

'Style and sophistication during a glut of stompers'

Ian Levine,
Filmaker, DJ, Producer, London, UK

Recently discovered living in Grand Rapids, Michigan, Mel has appeared in 'The Northern Soul Story' video.

First discovered by DJ Ian Levine 'the shuffler' as it was known, was an instant hit telling us a great deal about the DJ and Mel's finest hour too!

An extremely sought after disc, even after the influx of around a 100 copies in the seventies. The once common reissues are even scarce today!

Smooth and oh-so classy.

The Checkerboard Squares
Double Cookin'

Top 500 Position: **29**
Original Label: **Villa**
Current Value: **£300**

'The best instrumental ever'

Peter Whitney, Soul Fan, Cumbria, UK

In the early 70's, cover-ups were part and parcel of the scene.

One of the first major pseudonyms and in some circles still known as 'Strings-a-go-go', this massive instrumental kicks ass like no other (OK, maybe Mike Post's 'Afternoon Of The Rhino' is a contender) and complete with Frank Wilson style influence, the recording from Los Angeles relates to Detroit perfectly.

Thank heavens the production team relinquished any vocal suggestions! (The Del-Satins' version is a vocal overdub recorded in 1977) leaving us with a legacy of symphonic stomping SOUL.

The Carstairs
It Really Hurts Me Girl

Top 500 Position: **30**
Original Label: **Red Coach**
Current Value: **£25 Issue**
£75 Demo

'The first time I ever heard a wah-wah in a Northern single'

V. Truman, Soul Fan, Australia

Cleveland Horne and Ray Evans recorded a vintage single for Gene Redd's Red Coach label, it promptly bombed in the US.

A glimmer of hope appeared on the horizon, when in 1974 Ian Levine on vacation in Miami heard the track on a local Soul station. Levine intuitively acquired the single(on a promo at the time) and promptly aired it at his forthcoming gig at the Mecca. Surprisingly the patrons loved it, as the UK was still in the midst of stomp fever and a track of this styling was a considered to subtle and too modern!

Persistent plays by Levine got everybody hooked, including the group themselves who visited the UK recently, and played live at the same venue that first broke it!

Jerry Williams

If You Ask Me

Top 500 Position: **31**
Original Label: **Calla**
Current Value: **£30 Issue**
　　　　　　　£40 Demo

'My worst seller to-date in the States!'

Jerry 'Swamp Dogg' Williams,
performer, writer and producer, USA

Legendary writer-producer Swamp Dogg's 'If You Ask Me' coupled with strings and backing vocals drift in and out of Richie Rome's richly textured production.

A UK release in '75 almost realised a hit according to Pye (Disco Demand) label manager Dave McAleer. Fashion was to dominate the labels output, hence the success of Wigan's Chosen Few and The Javells.

In terms of real quality, the single is still being enjoyed by a new army of fans 25 years on.

Lou Johnson
Unsatisfied

Top 500 Position:	**32**
Original Label:	**Big Top**
Current Value:	**£20 Issue**
	£40 Demo

'Yep!... I'm satisfied!'

Derek Howe,
Retailer, Manchester, UK

Lou Johnson was one of Bacharach and David's favourite sons and, although he always remained second in the pecking order to Dionne Warwick. Recording many killer sides for Big Top in the early 60's, this became Lou's 'dance' tune - in the UK at least.

Absolutely perfect for DJ play in as much as use of the thunderous intro to ID the track which whips dancers into a frenzy.

If youth is on your side (lucky you!) you will have missed (for me) the greatest all-nighter ever at The Torch in Tunstall, Stoke-on-Trent, where a playlist would have consisted of maybe 150 winners. Unsatisfied would have been high in the chart even then and, mixed with a cocktail of pharmaceuticals, you most definitely left Hose Street well and truly 'satisfied'

JJ Barnes
Our Love Is In The Pocket

Top 500 Position: **33**
Original Label: **Revilot**
Current Value: **£80 Pink**
£100 Multicoloured

'One of United Sound's premier recorders'

Frank Garcia, Soul Fan, Detroit, USA

It is hard to find any other record that is as instantaneous as this 1966 outing recorded at the famous United Sound Studios.

Crikey! even Amen Corner recorded it!

The Darrell Banks version is of course brilliant too, but it is JJ on what is for me the most commercial Soul record of the 60's never to be a major hit!

Discovered at Stoke's legendary Golden Torch, DJ Tony Jebb gets most acclaim for plugging this masterpiece to death!

Don Thomas
Come On Train

Top 500 Position:	**34**
Original Label:	**NUVJ**
Current Value:	**£15 Issue**
	£25 Demo

*'A superb 70's sound
full of originality'*

Bryan Wakelyn,
Collector, Blackpool, UK

Virtually a new release at the time of discovery, but no real problem due to the originality of the waxing. Don Thomas hit the North big in 1975/76, why even UK label DJM picked it up for UK release.

Mixing with the likes of other 70's finds, 'Train' sat rhythmically in sync with other spins, and soon became one of the most requested on the manor. As for Don Thomas, well he slipped back into San Francisco obscurity, probably never knowing the new sexy wriggles his workout had created.

The M.V.P.'S
Turnin' My Heartbeat Up

Top 500 Position: **35**
Original Label: **Buddah**
Current Value: **£100**

'A song's pulse is paramount in a great Northern track, mine races to herculean proportions listening to this!'

Will Harris, BMG/Arista, UK

To any newcomer, the most difficult aspect to understand is the variety of tunes on offer, plus the differential between each track via a dance floor fill.

'Turning My Heartbeat Up' initially appears to have no credence with the scene for the following reasons- 1. It's a rock single from '72. 2. It's a tricky beat and non-traditional.

This is the 'show off' 45, the one where the movers and shakers go for it with energetic twists and turns, leaving onlookers jealous and unfulfilled as claps of appreciation are given to 'dancefloor nomads'. The cultured track deserved more internationally, but again the great Uncle Sam had too many releases of commercial intake to worry about another wannabee searching for stardom.

Sandi Sheldon

You're Gonna Make Me Love You

Top 500 Position:	**36**
Original Label:	**Okeh**
Current Value:	**£200 Issue or Demo**

'A total adrenaline rush'

Adey Pierce,
Record Dealer, Gloucester, UK

To trigger off your real interest in the scene, you need a record that is 'Northern Soul', on this occasion you've found it first hit.

A traditional classic usually needs to engage a 4/4 beat, strong vocal, big city production, all polished off with super gloss. Van McCoy delivers the request with consummate ease, adding to the theory that big time producers make the best records.

The track is quite outstanding and the unknown Ms. Sheldon can quietly be 'well chuffed' at her debut. Van, rest in peace, the legacy you have left us with this soulful adventure leaves a leviathan conquest.

The Vel-vets

I Got To Find Me Somebody

Top 500 Position: **37**
Original Label: **20th Century**
Current Value: **£100**

*'The 'woo' in the track
is just irresistible'*

Steve Jeffries,
Record Dealer, Leicester, UK

Special times at a club centre around invigorating sounds, and this 1967 outing from LA's Vel-Vets captures the very essence of spirit and togetherness.

The track hurtles out of the speakers like Hurricane Andrew and not once does it allow a smidgen of breath.

A trio of gals have simply been given a recording opportunity, and accepted the chance with relish, grasping the mic. and yelling 'n' screaming until producer Jackie Mills is satisfied with the end product. The rest is down to marketing, with which our 'scene' is generally un-interested.

Patti and the Emblems

I'm Gonna Love You A Long, Long Time

Top 500 Position: **38**
Original Label: **Kapp**
Current Value: **£250 Issue**
£75 Demo

'A race against time
for dance floor space'

Matt Jahans,
Capitol Soul Club, London, UK

Philly stood tall within the R&B spectrum, churning out countless hits from a variety of production outlets, some however didn't make it but still are quite breathtaking.

The group we focus on here were no strangers to success and one can be forgiven for thinking this is yet another smash for the city of brotherly love. It wasn't and mores the pity as lead singer Patty Russell takes charge of the Leroy Lovett / Frank Bendinelli production and delivers the package beautifully. Many memories are associated with this discovery of the early 70's and it is great to see the more youthful end of the market gagging to hear it at most venues.

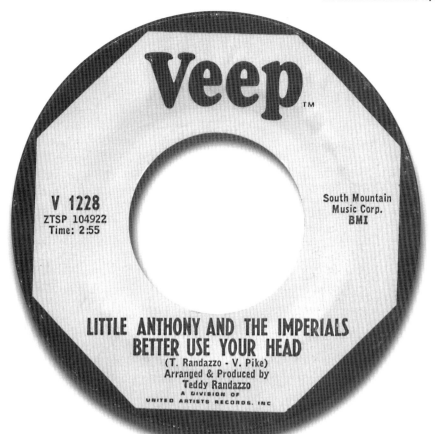

Veep ™

V 1228
ZTSP 104922
Time: 2:55

South Mountain
Music Corp.
BMI

LITTLE ANTHONY AND THE IMPERIALS
BETTER USE YOUR HEAD
(T. Randazzo - V. Pike)
Arranged & Produced by
Teddy Randazzo
A DIVISION OF
UNITED ARTISTS RECORDS, INC

Little Anthony and the Imperials

Better Use Your Head

Top 500 Position:	**39**
Original Label:	**Veep**
Current Value:	**£10**

'A top tune of '75'

Chas Lucas, Soul Fan, Southampton, UK

Consequential to popular belief, a proven winner on the Northern scene often has to realise a kind of distinctiveness. It can be a drum pattern, vibes, or the inevitable hook.

Song 39 is all about vocalising, and who better than Anthony Gourdine, with his unmistakable falsetto lead which scored a series of pop hits as far back as 1958.

Again, we Brits feast on the 'loser', this time the disaster(US wise) is 'Better Use Your Head' a fairly typical Randazzo/Pike production. Soaring to rapturous applause from day one, the soft texture of this Northern classic is summed up astutely by the record buyers, landing the group to a No. 42 position in 1976.

The Casualeers

Dance, Dance, Dance

Top 500 Position: **40**
Original Label: **Roulette**
Current Value: **£20 Demo**
£40 Issue

'Wreaking havoc on the Casino dance floor... Ahhhhhh heaven!'

Chris King, DJ, Nottingham, UK

There was only one venue that could accommodate such a disc and that was the big building in Station Road.

The Casualeers, a New York group, consisted of Arnold Davis, Isiah Love, Jimmy and Ollie Johnson. Production wise it has everything, including the all important 'stomp stomp' feel. Although pop in it's approach (largely due to input of 'Star Wars' themester Meco Monardo) the guys click instantly with the groove and the whole experience is one of joyous fulfilment.

Along with the R. Dean, Javells, and 'Footsee', 'Dance, Dance, Dance' was one of the the biggest songs of '74. The title reveals it's true intention, and we Brits take the challenge gleefully.

Jack Montgomery

Dearly Beloved

Top 500 Position: **41**
Original Label: **Scepter**
Current Value: **£150 Issue**
£100 Demo

'Detroit again, thanks a lot Don Mancha'

Dave Flynn,
DJ and Collector, London, UK

A tale of two sides, firstly the 70's spin being the flip 'Do you believe it'. From the mid-80's our no. 41 came in to play and quite rightly too. Mancha, although a bit part player in Detroit did produce a few excellent sides, but it's the simplistic 'BELOVED' that craves attention. Montgomery is in fact really the writer Marvin Jones, and with other collectables on Barracuda and Revue it is hard to understand why a more successful career was not forthcoming.

An interesting trivia note; Northern Soul fan and friend to the scene Dennis Coffey arranged the orchestration during the session, back in 1966.

Roy Hamilton

Crackin' Up Over You

Top 500 Position: **42**
Original Label: **RCA Victor**
Current Value: **£60**

'The song gets all over you like a rash, but you don't need any lotion after hearing it'

Eddy Edmundson, Soul Fan, Kendal, UK

Legendary, and requiring little introduction. One of the first major 'niter' sounds, circa 1971.

Total big city anthem from the man responsible for 'Unchained Melody', 'You'll never walk alone' plus a few corkers from the Northern archive.

Roy left us for that great 'gig' in the sky in 1969 and considering he started as a gospel act in 1948 no less. 'Crackin' Up' was one of his final recordings along with 'You Shook Me Up', a enormously popular floorfiller of recent years.

Ironically, a book published in 1999, traced the youth culture surrounding Northern Soul. The title? you guessed it...

Connie Clark

My Sugar Baby

Top 500 Position: **43**
Original Label: **Joker**
Current Value: **£250**

'Frank Wilson on a sojourn from Motown with Chris 'Connie' Clark'

Gary Mellor,
Collector, Swansea, Wales, UK

Written and produced by the legendary Frank Wilson in 1965, 'My Sugar Baby' is not dissimilar to 'Do I Love You' - perhaps unsurprising given Connie's own version under her real name - Chris Clark!

Connie - or rather Chris - remains with Motown to this day in a managerial capacity whilst the Reverand Wilson recorded his own version which sadly languishes in the Motown vaults.

Achieving monster status at the Casino long before anyone made the connection(s) this Joker release is many people's all-time favourite and remains one of the biggest sounds born of a golden era.

The Voices Of East Harlem

Cashing In

Top 500 Position:	**44**
Original Label:	**Just Sunshine**
Current Value:	**£15**

'A generous mix of Gospel and Blackpool'

Bob Hinsley, DJ, Bolton, UK

Wigan Casino had established itself as the new No.1 venue, with Blackpool Mecca pushing it's nose in the air by creating a brand new playlist of current releases mixed with exclusive 60's, in keeping with their one upmanship policy. Silly as it was, the scene became better for it, simply by accepting new but exquisite sides such as this Leroy Hutson/Curtis Mayfield production.

Sounding as fresh as ever, the 1973 release has crossed over to a posse of outlets and, it has the distinction of bridging the North/South divide perfectly. Piano driven, with a Windy City string effect all topped off with customary gospel wails, I'll have this for brunch any day!

Dee Clark

That's My Girl

Top 500 Position:	**45**
Original Label:	**Constellation**
Current Value:	**£30 Issue**
	£50 Demo

'A crazy flute driven ditty, that drives 'em wild'

Glenn Bellamy, Dealer, UK

Dee Clark was already established as a hitmaker on both sides of the pond and his 'Hot Potato' side for Constellation, was a 'nearly' song on the UK's dance floors 25 years ago.

The track kicking in at 45, is a strange one to say the least, modelling itself on a former pop hit 'Sugar Shack' by Jimmy Gilmer.

Internationally, the single has acquired cult status on both the Soul and Scooter scenes by receiving more plays than most in the last decade.

Born Delecta Clark in Arkansas, Clark was vastly underrated, and in true nostalgic style, we salute him for giving us a real monster Chicago single. He sadly died in 1990.

Bobby Hutton
Lend A Hand

Top 500 Position: **46**
Original Label: **ABC**
Current Value: **£20**

'Oh so classy'

Carol Smart, Soul Fan, London, UK

To everyone who has heard this Dee Erwin production first played from his album, I can't think of a single contact who does not rate this as one of the great Soul records of all time.

I did not of course use the word Northern, the reason, well I believe it to be the perfect 'Soul' record to dance to, even on the planet Mars!

Hutton, from Chicago, has grown in stature on our scene in recent times due to 'Come See (What's Left Of Me)' recorded for Philips in '69. 'Lend A Hand' though cannot be topped, and probably is the adhesive that held Northern and Modern fans together in more acrimonious times.

Ruby Andrews
Just Loving You

Top 500 Position:	**47**
Original Label:	**Zodiac**
Current Value:	**£80**

'A superb single from a cult artiste'

Roger Williams, Soul Fan, Wirral, UK

Originally recording as Ruby Stackhouse on Kellmac, Andrews' 45 was a heavy hitter in the 80's, spilling nicely into the revival scene of NOW. The track was released on the Zodiac label and bustled around the back of most guys record boxes, until the fateful day, someone plucked up courage to champion the track.

'Just Loving You' caught on instantly, and though we all have experienced Ms. Andrews' various recordings at some time or another, it is the 1969 track recorded in Mississippi that wins the day.

The Vibrations

Cause You're Mine

Top 500 Position: **48**
Original Label: **Okeh**
Current Value: **£40 Issue**
£60 Demo

*'A track that could cause
serious injury to
the dance maniacs...'*

Robin McKenzie,
Soul Fan, St Neots, UK

Led by Ricky Owens, who sadly died in 1996, this exceptional Soul group have recorded a couple of classics since their initial hit on Atlantic in 1963.

A strange quirk of fate evolves out of this 'pill poppin' niter anthem. Not wishing to glorify the drugs scene, the flip of the original 45 is called 'I Took An Overdose'. A sombre thought I know but, we have the ultimate dancer here from the real deal-1973.

The track knocks you sideways by the 4th bar and continues to race against time, leaving you collapsed in a crumpled heap of delight!

Julian Covey
A Little Bit Hurt

Top 500 Position:	**49**
Original Label:	**UK Island/ US Philips**
Current Value:	**£15/£20**

'Dump your holdall next to the Lambretta and Dance, Dance, Dance!'

Rino Sapere, Soul Fan, Italy

Covey, together with his band, The Machine, hails from Sherwood... near Nottingham! A popular R&B band of the mid-sixties they played most of the local clubs and gained a contract with Island.

'A Little Bit Hurt', was also released in the States on Philips and has proved to be a perennially popular tune both on the mainstream Northern scene and the Scooter scene of the seventies, eighties and nineties.

Keyboard driven, the hook and lead vocal combine to deliver an enthralling performance.

Dee Dee Sharp

What Kind Of Lady

Top 500 Position: **50**
Original Label: **Gamble**
Current Value: **£25**

*'Gamble and Huff
again!...That figures!'*

Rob Johnson,
Soul Fan, Dublin, Eire

The production is clinical and arranged by the legendary Bobby Martin and Tommy Bell. All that's required is a vocal of some repute, and who better than the former Mrs. Gamble.

The label owners were just starting to make serious noises in the industry but were still three to four years off the real big time, without any disrespect to their 1968 million seller 'Cowboys to Girls'.

The key motivation here lies with the fresh sounding 'Sigma Studios' input along with a major orchestral backdrop.

The unique piano riff, played by Leon Huff, scurries along to the end, with the vocalist asking 'Tell me, Tell me, Tell me, Tell me!'

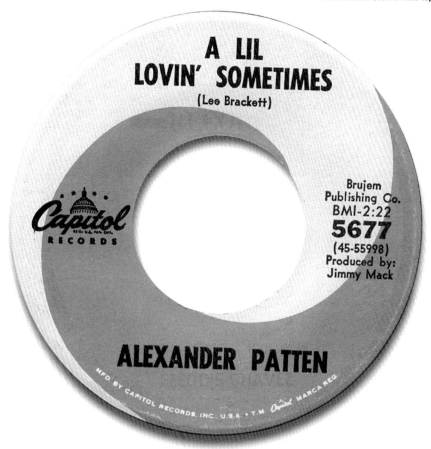

Alexander Patten

A Lil' Lovin' Sometimes

Top 500 Position: **51**
Original Label: **Capitol**
Current Value: **£50**

'I wanted this on a British demo so badly

Julian Bentley,
Soul Fan, Manchester, UK

True old school from California produced by James 'Tenafly' McKeachin who has a plethora of great productions to his credit (ie The Furys) and the distinction of being 'Al the DJ' assisting Clint Eastwood in the movie 'Play Misty For Me'

It took a new scene 6,000 miles away in Manchester, UK to discover the track on Capitol (British), which was amazing to say the least as I rate the US copy even harder to find.

In terms of quality, this really is the business, with the usual big city production amidst a tireless vocal from Patten. If you are discovering Northern Soul for the first time, get a load of this!

Chubby Checker

You Just Don't Know (What You Do To Me)

Top 500 Position:	**52**
Original Label:	**Parkway**
Current Value:	**£350**

'I thought we were supposed to do the twist not the cart wheel'

Dave Clark, Hipshaker, Hampshire, UK

An unlikely source of Northerness from Ernest Evans the twistmaster. Cut in 1965 and, one of his final recordings for Cameo Parkway.

In any event, we are privileged to discover his best work and amazingly the rarest. Coming 'atcha like a whore laced with rocket fuel, the big beat cuts the room up like the finest Harley Street surgeon.

Another 45 where the American issue is exceedingly scarce, suffice to say, the initial find was on the UK Pye distributed Cameo label. One final insult to CC, is that the song is the official 'B' side!

CONSTELLATION
RECORDS, INC.

Disc Jockey
Advance Sample

NOT FOR SALE

C-65-279
VOCAL
A Bill Sheppard
Production

Costoma
Music-BMI
Time: 2:25
Arr. By
Richard Evans

JUST LIKE THE WEATHER
(Richard Parker)
NOLAN CHANCE
C-161

Nolan Chance
Just Like The Weather

Top 500 Position: **53**
Original Label: **Constellation**
Current Value: **£150**

*'One of the very first
three figure records'*

Tony Banks, DJ, Leeds, UK

A massive injection to the scene complete with early tales of the even rarer second issue on Bunky fetching upwards of £200 in 1973!

Vastly underrated Soul act from Chicago works the lyrics a treat, which is just as well as competition in the same market came from Chess by the way of Denise Lasalle's 'A Love Reputation'. Both sides are almost identical, with probably Ms. L gaining most sales locally, as Chance's release is pretty scarce.

Made for the timeless golden era, the relaxed effortless delivery, cleverly builds climatic similies with a love pledge. Born one Charles Davies, he also recorded for Thomas and Scepter.

A vintage production line showing from 'Bunky' Bill Sheppard.

Bobby Paris

Night Owl

Top 500 Position:	**54**
Original Label:	**Cameo**
Current Value:	**£100**

'Wigan's ultimate anthem'

Dave 'Paris' Ibbetson,
Soul Fan, West Yorkshire, UK

Bobby Paris ended up with no less than three huge floor fillers, this being the last of the trio. Originally a B side to 'Tears On My Pillow', the track was released on Cameo in 1966.

The man, it appears, was on a mission from Wigan, with 'Owl' in '66, 'I Walked Away' on Capitol in '67 and 'Per-so-nally' for Tetragrammaton in '68!

A badge was created off the back of the song and no aspiring soulie could be without customary holdall with the 'symbol'

The song is a cover of the Tony Allen hit and Italian-American Paris rasps his way into the Station Road Hall of Fame. Visiting these shores in 1999, he sang his famous three in Blackburn of all places to an amazed but appreciative audience.

Doni Burdick
Bari Track

Top 500 Position:	**55**
Original Label:	**Sound Impression**
Current Value:	**£250**

'Big big Detroit'...

Greg Tormo, Collector, USA

A terrific double sider, but we'll focus on the constantly played one, as the sax lead 'Bari Track' rips into our hearts and minds.

We all knew the vocal version already via Rose Batiste which suffered a lack of turntable play due to it's flipside 'Hit and Run'. Burdick's local tribute is no more than a throw a way jam session, but in Britain it has swarmed consistently over the scene for over 20 years.

It has instant appeal on the floor, and appears to grow in stature year on year, an unusual disc, but white hot!

Dean Courtney

I'll Always Need You

Top 500 Position: **56**
Original Label: **RCA Victor**
Current Value: **£100 Issue**
£50 Demo

'Len Barry's original will always be second best to this incredible cover version'

Chris Toothill, Collector, Manchester, UK

Major labels have the budget to record well, plus manufacture and distribute their products to maximum effect.

Why oh why, did they not do the full monty on this slab of excitement from '67. Nipper looks as bemused on the RCA label as we do about the lack of success of this pure gem.

Rising above the wild and wacky echelons of crude aberrations such as 'My Hearts Symphony' or 'Hawaii 5-0', the side was Wigan all it's own, and while the classy Blackpool Mecca were championing their own cause, here's one that had the 01942 dialling code stamped all over it.

Dean is also a recent visitor to the UK. As per usual, totally gob-smacked at his notoriety 'up North'.

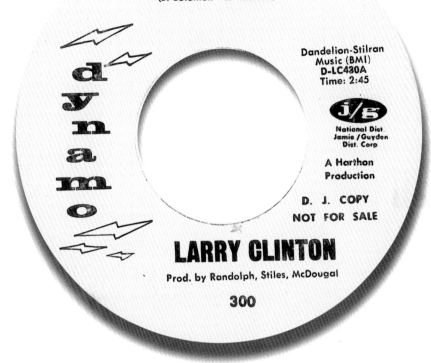

Larry Clinton
She's Wanted

Top 500 Position:	**57**
Original Label:	**Dynamo**
Current Value:	**£1,500 Issue**
	£1,000 Demo

'Larry's mesmerising performance is to die for'

John Poole, Collector, Nottingham, UK

From the great Harthon stable in Philadelphia comes one of the last all niter pioneers of the late 70's.

DJ Richard Searling made this song all his own, covering it over to conceal identity.

You can hardly blame a DJ when a track is as good as this, although he didn't have to worry, the record is so scarce that even today there must be less than 20 copies known.

The trademark, well that's simple, a crunching bass driven groove with strong vocals from one-time Lawn recording artist.

Philly cut a lot of stuff like this, but 'She's Wanted' just has that bit extra to satisfy dancers and collectors alike.

Lou Ragland
I Travel Alone

Top 500 Position:	**58**
Original Label:	**Amy**
Current Value:	**£300**

'Part of the new wave of Casino finds that rebuilt the venue's credibility'

Steve Phyllis,
Soul Fan, Nottingham, UK

Slipping neatly into the fold of '74, this super Soul plodder revived the fortunes at the main event, just as the pop influence was starting to infiltrate.

Cleveland based Ragland was no stranger to collectors and for a time his early 70's outing for Warner Bros was gathering pace amongst them. However this remains his ace card which got a release on Bell subsidiary Amy in 1967.

An inventive 45 with Lou and strong backing vox intertwining with each other to hit home a dark and moody song which will always be known as 'Travellin' Man'.

Freddie Chavez
They'll Never Know Why

Top 500 Position:	**59**
Original Label:	**Look**
Current Value:	**£400 Issue**
	£200 Demo

'But they'll never know why I love you'... AWESOME!'

Steve Taylor-Collis,
Soul Fan, Jersey, Channel Islands

A Tex-Mex Northern Soul single that is reaping the rewards of almost a play-a gig since '73!

Freddie also doubles as Dave Newman on the same label but it's the 1968 Motownesque kicker that works best for Chavez.

The strength lies in the song, and when even the most energetic are 'out there', they can't help singing along to the effortless solo, similar in range to Bobby Paris.

Tennessee was never a hot bed of uptempo Soul sounds, so it is refreshing to hear one that is original in concept at the very least even though as I said Detroit is in there hovering!

The Seven Souls

I Still Love You

Top 500 Position: **60**
Original Label: **Okeh**
Current Value: **£300 Issue**
£200 Demo

'It took 15 years to break, phew! It was worth the wait'

Roger Stewart,
Record Dealer, London, UK

Massive pop influence as Larry Williams takes charge of the unknown group from LA, who later recorded for Venture and gained a French EP release. The track is a classic... and thanks only to the collectors who continually reminded the scene of it's quality.

I returned from LA in March of '74 clutching Willie Hutch, Obrey Wilson, and a zillion other goodies including this. On the second Saturday of my return I aired it for the first time (unless you know otherwise), it promptly cleared the floor! I could not believe it, and even worse I sold the thing for £3. The notion being at the time that Okeh 45's were not rare.

Oh how gullible we all were, and certainly concerning the longevity of the tracks popularism

Dean Parrish

I'm On My Way

Top 500 Position:	**61**
Original Label:	**Laurie**
Current Value:	**£10 issue**
	£30 Demo

'The finest amongst the 'three before eight"

Carl Kingston,
Radio DJ, Leeds, UK

Parrish is apparently living in Sicily and remains unaware of the UK popularity of his sides for Boom and, more importantly of the special place held by 'I'm On My Way' as the last record played at Wigan at 7.57am.

Discovered at Rediffusion in Nottingham in 1971 it became a local cheapie amongst collectors before the Casino's Russ Winstanley made it his own, raising it to the anthem status it has retained ever since.

Together with Brenda Lee Jones' 'You're The Love Of My Life' it also gained a British release on Jonathon King's UK label in the mid 70's.

The Contours

Baby Hit And Run

Top 500 Position:	**62**
Original Label:	**Tamla Motown**
Current Value:	**£20**

'Dennis Edwards is simply magnificent'

Chris Conroy,
Journalist, Preston, UK

Discovered languishing on a budget label LP containing The Contours hits and one other previously unissued cut.

Quite irresistible is this final recording by the group before Edwards joined the Temptations. Many Motown tracks of course should enter our chart, but we'll reserve the right to placement on only the real floorshakers.

Originally recorded in 1966 it was released as a single in the UK in 1974.

The band enjoyed a brief revival via 'Do You Love Me', but the real deal is Dennis Edwards' performance who obviously had the Temps in his sights!

Possibly one of the best Tamla Motown non-hits ever.

Darrell Banks
Open The Door To Your Heart

Top 500 Position: **63**
Original Label: **Revilot**
Current Value: **£10 Issue**
£100 Demo

*'The first of the 'legends'
in the North of England'*

Jan Barker,
Collector, Todmorden, UK

Probably the most respected 45 ever. Discovered shortly after UK release, the sheer quality of the echoes through the corridors of the Northern museum like the golden treasures of Tutankamen.

Born Darrell Eubanks, he died in a shooting incident in 1970 but not without a whole a selection of recordings that are quite frankly - FANTASTIC!

Here's the US hit from 1966, and one often wonders whether the A&R team at Stateside or the preceding promo only London release were just unlucky in not gaining a hit for their respective employers. Back in vogue once again, the track is slightly above a beat ballad, and the whole aura of Darrell's vocal presence is sumptuous.

79

The Detroit Spinners

I'll Always Love You

Top 500 Position:	**64**
Original Label:	**Motown**
Current Value:	**£8 Issue**
	£25 Demo

'It's hard to discount Motown within the scene and this is my personal favourite'

Terry Finn,
Collector, Doncaster, UK

In terms of sheer quality we are staring at a no. 1 single.

Our chart though traces the history of each disc, and though we all love and cherish this 1965 outing from Bobby Smith and the boys, the position allocated is based on the overall success rate on the dance floor.

In the corridors of Hitsville, USA, this is the one that got away, the inch perfect melody being coupled with a killer hook. The 45 has possibly sold more post release than any other non-hit single, and here in Britain we certainly have played our part in it's continuing popularity.

Stunning in the approach, Smith controls the production rather similar to the Isleys - This Old Heart Of Mine, which does not figure in our chart, but symbolises precisely the sound that Northern Soul is based upon.

Earl Jackson
Soul Self Satisfaction

Top 500 Position: **65**
Original Label: **ABC**
Current Value: **£150 Demo**

'My kind of dancefloor satisfaction!'

John Atkinson,
Collector, Burnley

An express train dancer steeped in Torch folklore, Earl Jackson's 1967 demo only release for ABC is nonetheless shrouded in mystery.

Excellent production work by Chicago main man Johnny Pate starts with one of the truly great intros leading you into a stunning vocal performance by this total unknown telling of how he needs some 'Soul Self Satisfaction' because 'since you've been gone I ain't seen nothing but heartache'... supported by heavenly backing vocals and express train instrumentation featuring a bright guitar and powerhouse drums.

Scarce today it is a snip at £150 (even though it's on a major label) for a piece of utterly supreme Northern Soul!

Major Lance
You Don't Want Me No More

Top 500 Position: **66**
Original Label: **Okeh**
Current Value: **£75 Issue**
£100 Demo

'Powerhouse Soul from the Major'

Gary Neale,
Soul Fan, Lancashire, UK

The master of 60's Chicago Soul decided on a real mover with this one. A superlative racer from Okeh that saw Major Lance provide the label with a real 'bomb'. Easy to see the label were clutching at straws with their former 'ace' card, and the main man promptly moved on to Curtom.

The aggressive nature of the production is superb for the UK, and one interesting piece of trivia is the 'B' side 'Wait 'Til I Get You Into My Arms' was recorded by Kenny Carlton on Blue Rock. The Major sadly passed away in 1994.

A Northern treasure that first gained widespread popularity at the Blackpool Mecca.

Bobby Hebb

Love, Love, Love

Top 500 Position:	**67**
Original Label:	**Philips**
Current Value:	**£6 Issue**
	£15 Demo

'An exemplary sound'

Paddy Grady,
Merchandiser, Northampton, UK

A Country/Soul singer from Nashville, on whom Philips scored a No.2 in 1966 with 'Sunny'. Jerry Ross was Hebb's producer and well versed in turning black talent into pop stars. Although a 'B' side the flip charted in '66 in the US, while a re-issue of 'Love' scored here in 1972 peaking at No.32.

While Hebb was wrestling with those 'country' roots, Ross supplied him with 'You Want to Change Me' another Northern gem. The real winner though will always be this classic anthem.

Bob Relf

Blowing My Mind To Pieces

Top 500 Position: **68**
Original Label: **Trans-American**
Current Value: **£40**

'Original stuff... and one of the big guns of '73'

Ron Simpson,
Soul Fan, New Zealand

After reigning supreme as the top turntable terror of 1973, the song was re-recorded for the Black Magic label in 1974 and, unknown to them, didn't feature Relf at all, even though he got the vocal credit. All a little confusing, and part and parcel of the scene at that time. Suffice it to say Relf is amused at the cult status of the disc. Many collectors think of him as one half of , this is in fact part fiction - he was the second 'Bob'. He was a key player on the LA music scene, writing many a tune for the Mirwood group of labels, mostly with partner Earl Nelson (aka Jackie Lee), he also recorded as Bobby Angelle on Money, TKO and Imperial records.

His moment of triumph is this epic from 1968 for the independent Trans-American label. The strings make it, and the chorus is about as Northern Soul as you could get.

The Drifters
You Got To Pay Your Dues

Top 500 Position: **69**
Original Label: **Atlantic**
Current Value: **£40 Issue**
                      £30 Demo

'A rare uplifting Soul groove from, of all people, The Drifters!'

Richard Pack,
Historian, Toronto, Canada

Out of left field comes a contract disputed song from the ever popular Drifters. The word 'THE' was dropped for this 1970 recording, a 'difference of opinion' cited by former lead member-the late Johnny Moore.

The pop influence is there for all to see with Paul Vance and Rupert 'Pina Colada Song' Holmes at the controls.

While the band were in limbo, the UK benefits from a super 'feel good' sound that the label obviously had no intention of promoting. The peak period of it's popularity was the 70's, but it has reared it's head in more recent times. Great to sing-a-long to!

The Invitations

Skiing In The Snow

Top 500 Position: **70**
Original Label: **Dynovoice**
Current Value: **£150**

"The weather's getting cold and snow is piling up on the hill' - a true 60's treasure!'

Jonathon Askew,
Soul Fan, Essex, UK

One had to ponder long and hard about this one. Powered on by Herman Coefield's lead vocal 'Skiing' certainly has a roller coaster feel to it.

Firstly, it was a monster in the early 70's, then a cover by Wigan's Ovation reached No.12 in the UK charts in '75.

That alone should propel either version high into our chart. The group feature again later on with the Wheel classic 'What's Wrong With Me Baby?', but this is the most commercial of their two chart entries.

If you truly dislike the UK pop cover then check out the equally poor US version by the Beach Girls!

The Poets
She Blew A Good Thing

Top 500 Position: **71**
Original Label: **Symbol**
Current Value: **£10 Issue**
                     £25 Demo

*'A monumental
group sound'*

Nancy Yahiro,
Collector, Orange County, California, USA

Issued in the UK as the American Poets because of an existing British act signed to Decca. The single, featuring Ronnie Lewis on lead, became a US R&B hit.

The group have had a number of popular Northern sounds and recorded the mega-rare 'Wrapped Around Your Finger' for New York label J-V in 1965.

A totally fantastic single that became massive at the Whitworth Street Wheel in the late 60's, it oozes appeal as the group harmonise perfectly behind Lewis' brilliant lead.

Joy Lovejoy
In Orbit

Top 500 Position: **72**
Original Label: **Chess**
Current Value: **£15**

'One great gallop to find some dancefloor space'

R, Doncaster, UK

Sensational is just one word that springs to mind when hearing this old style 1967 pumper from the little known Joy Lovejoy.

Chess, like Motown, experimented with new upcoming talent periodically, and Lovejoy paraded her wares hopefully, but it wasn't to be. In terms of original Northern Soul roots, this is about as good as it gets with Lovejoy wailing and squealing her way through the extra large Chicago production.

US copies were around in abundance during it's heyday, but try finding it now. Absolutely rivetting and one of my all time personal favourites.

Remember this is the type of track that made us fall in love with Northern Soul.

Lynne Randell

Stranger In My Arms

Top 500 Position: **73**
Original Label: **Epic**
Current Value: **£75 Issue**
£60 Demo

'Wonderful blue eyed Soul effort from the Aussie'

Alan Kline,
New South Wales, Australia

The A side is a cover of a Toys track for Philips, but it's the B side that won the Northern hearts. Co-written by Bob Crewe, a specialist in girl group material, the Spectoresque production proved to be a real winner in the golden era.

Fully atmospheric, Lynne nullifies the old accent, and sounds like she had been part of the Brill Building for years and in fact this single was recorded in New York and NOT Australia as is usually believed.

The single also was released in the UK on CBS, which is incredibly rare.

The Velvet Satins

Nothing Can Compare To You

Top 500 Position:	**74**
Original Label:	**General American**
Current Value:	**£200 Issue**
	£100 Demo

'Furious in it's approach, but a totally class act'

Gaynor Coffey,
Soul Fan, Delaware, USA

Can you imagine standing inside a record shop in Jersey City, New Jersey only to be told you have to provide a list before the owner will look for your wants. Imagine a red stock copy of this single sitting on his record player, with the owner saying he liked it! To this day, I still wonder who got THAT record and what on earth was behind the counter!

Let's get back to a total and utterly magnificent rarity from early 1965 and New York's Velvet Satins. A rather moorish slice of slick male vocal, sensational arrangement with piano riffs, old fashioned sax break and just about everything else. I can understand why we all fell for the 45 hook, line and sinker, it's a real shame it came out during the Beatles/Vietnam period, when simple danceable Soul was 'nowhere man'.

Shane Martin

I Need You

Top 500 Position: **75**
Original Label: **Epic**
Current Value: **£50**

'More of that pop-turned-Northern working up a treat'

Belle and Sebastian,
Recording Artists, UK

Internationally, confusion often arises with respect to what is a Northern Soul 45.

Imagine say, a collector from Japan trying to understand us Brits, when on one turntable were playing Johnny Sayles or perhaps Maxine Brown. On player No.2 is this little ditty from Martin, written by Jim Webb. It hardly conjures up the ghetto does it!

The scene has many emotional twists and turns and sometimes the whole aura of the groove is the winning factor in the disc's destiny. A smart mover from '68, this is pure dance floor, with 'yer punter dictating to Mr. Rare DJ, that in his or her eyes, this is really where it's at. At least for 2 minutes 5 seconds anyway! 'I Need You' was also released on UK CBS, but is incredibly scarce.

The Tams

Hey Girl Don't Bother Me

Top 500 Position: **76**
Original Label: **ABC Paramount**
Current Value: **£6 Issue**
£10 Demo

'A No.1 single? Now that's Northern Soul POWER!'

Tania Crossley,
Soul Fan, London, UK

The first No.1 for a single connected to the all nighter scene.

Who could ever forget the legendary group from Georgia led by the Pope brothers forgetting their dance steps on Top Of The Pops in '71! But hardly surprising with the fact that the song was a complete failure in the US on it's inaugural release in '64.

Musically, it is pure 'Sharon and Tracy', but who can argue with a group as legendary as these guys.

Collector wise it's common place, but the roots of its early turntable plays keep it firmly in the minds of even the staunchest of Northern bods!

Lou Pride

I'm Comun' Home In The Morn'un

Top 500 Position: **77**
Original Label: **Suemi**
Current Value: **£1,000**

'Psychedelic Soul - meets Rock - meets Northern'

Mark Sargeant,
Scootering Magazine, Oxford, UK

I feel this particular 45 only received as much play as it did (still does!) because of a similar rhythm to the Case Of Tyme's 'Manifesto'.

A sort of progressive Northern sound, with Pride soulfully riding the groove as if he's Isaac Hayes auditioning for Blood Sweat and Tears.

In and out of fashion for nigh on 20 years, the result being it's new found popularity and current value!

Originally around £20, say hello to £1,000 plus these days, such is the demand.

An out of left fielder, the side has stood the test of time and thoroughly warrants it's chart position.

Paul Anka

I Can't Help Lovin' You

Top 500 Position: **78**
Original Label: **RCA Victor**
Current Value: **£40**

'Paul Anka said the DJ, I remarked 'you're kidding''

Mike Atherton,
Journalist, Sussex, UK

When a seasoned pro like acclaimed pop singer Anka delves into the All Niter arena, one could be forgiven that we have lost the plot completely!

To anyone else who has heard, danced, and owned the masterpiece, you of course know different.

The track is absolutely magnificent, starting with bass n drums followed by melodic vibes and a crunching 1966 dance beat, all topped off with Anka doing it 'his way'!

During the Casino/Mecca race for supremacy, Wigan needed records like this desperately. They were a sort of warning shot to The Highland Room that Station Road meant business, and with 45's like this, it kept the momentum rolling at the newest venue on the manor.

Clairlyn Pub. Co.
BMI
Engr. by
Joe Tarsia

Time: 2:25
Arr. & Cond. by
Joe Thomas
Produced by
Kip Gainsboro

I'M NOT STRONG ENOUGH
(Steals-Thomas-Steals)
THE FOUR PERFECTIONS
PT-1001

The Four Perfections
I'm Not Strong Enough

Top 500 Position: **79**
Original Label: **Party Time**
Current Value: **£150 Issue**
£200 Demo

'Simply enormous'

Phil Kingswood,
Soul Fan, Mansfield, UK

The single looks and feels Northern, without even playing it!

A typical scenario emerges with a wonderfully obscure label from Philadelphia, percussive heavy production and the usual killer hook line that slays you.

One point that many Brits will find interesting is that certain radio DJ's in Philly at the time remember the track well.

Former New Jersey radio DJ Ron Diamond actually played it on his show back in '68!

The City of Brotherly Love had a massive influence on the North of England with both provinces creating their own destiny without the need to follow others.

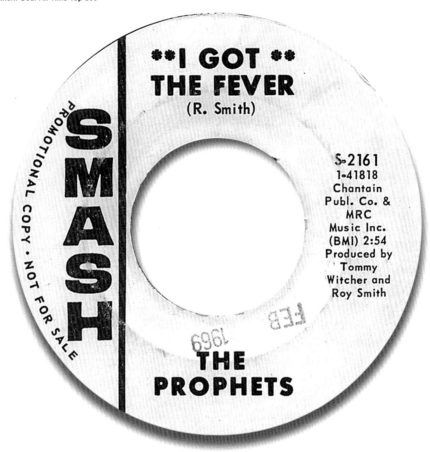

The Prophets/The Creation

I Got The Fever

Top 500 Position: **80**
Original Label: **Smash/Eric**
Current Value: **£20/£5**

'White psychedelia produces a killer Soul sound'

Rob Matthews,
Soul Fan, Midlands, UK

A long story this, so here is the shortened version. Originally released on Smash in the US, a specialist shop in the UK got Mercury to release it here two years after the initial US release. Apart from a small number of Northern fans who latched on to it in '71, it did in fact peter out fairly quick. Selectadisc, the main importer at the time, were suddenly besieged by collectors wanting to purchase it (Mercury deleting it too soon). The upshot was that they had a contact in the US (Eric records) who obtained the master, and engaged producer Bobby Martin to remix it.

The track was slightly more upbeat and sounded a lot fresher. A UK release on Stateside and subsequent reissues throughout the 70's, have made 'Fever' one of the most spirited and energetic sides ever to hit the North.

The Coasters

Crazy Baby

Top 500 Position: **81**
Original Label: **Atco**
Current Value: **£80**

*'The Coasters - dispensing
with Rock n Roll
for Northern Soul'*

Bob Fisher,
Connoisseur Collector, London, UK

Another unlikely rare 45 to infiltrate the scene.

Collector Dave Burton must have been bowled over to discover one of the last recordings for their label Atco.

Cut in '65 with Billy Guy on lead, the song is memorable throughout, as per the hook 'My Heart's Wide Open' (the original cover-up title). Many tracks in the 70's were covered up so as to conceal identity. The thinking behind it was that nobody would be able to find a copy. Such was the intensity of the 'exclusive', the artist was also changed to 'Freddie Jones'.

Back to reality and a truly superb dance anthem as far as the UK is concerned, however it is possibly the group's least successful recording.

Christine Cooper
Heartaches Away My Boy

Top 500 Position: **82**
Original Label: **Parkway**
Current Value: **£150 Issue**
£250 Demo

*'That wonderful
Parkway label again'*

Gary Macklish,
Soul Fan, Leeds, UK

Coming off like a cross between 'Back In My Arms Again' and 'A Lover's Concerto', Christine Cooper was a change of direction for the bubblegum producers 'Super K Productions'.

Years earlier, Cooper had another floor filler by the way of 'S.O.S' also on Parkway, but it's the more Motownesque 'Heartaches' that captures the floor, both were however US sales failures, and her third single for the label promptly flopped stateside too.

Co-written by Richie Cordell of Tommy James fame, the pop influence is there for all to witness, sadly Ms. Cooper fell from grace, the producers though went on to record such inane pop as 'Simon Says' and 'Quick Joey Small' amongst many others!

The Impressions

You've Been Cheatin'

Top 500 Position: **83**
Original Label: **ABC Paramount**
Current Value: **£10 Issue £20 Demo**

'One of the truly wonderful sounds from the late, great' Curtis Mayfield

Rob Messer,
Record Dealer, Essex, UK

Originally a non hit, gaining late 60's play but dying a death in the 70's, it received a spin or two in the following decade, before returning triumphantly to the past and current years in full working order. Perfect in every way, this is the complete 'dancer' from the 60's with Curtis controlling the whole epic. Mayfield, bless him, was undoubtedly the Steven Spielberg of the Soul business.

The group had a range of members at various times, but included Northern names Jerry Butler, Leroy Hutson and Nate Evans. After his well publicised stage accident of the early 90's Mayfield made a recovery and started recording and performing again, however this genius of melodic Soul with so many hits passed away in 1999.

As for the record itself, well everybody owns a copy don't they?

Harold Melvin and the Blue Notes

Get Out

Top 500 Position:	**84**
Original Label:	**Landa**
Current Value:	**£30 Issue**
	£40 Demo

'That 'just hung up the telephone' introduction just kills me!'

Ian Dewhurst,
Simply Vinyl, London, UK

Even without Teddy Pendergrass the group were pretty tasty, relying on more of a collective approach vocally.

The surprise with this dated workout from 1964 is the slow beginning, which just about puts the dancer to sleep except at the last moment the lead leaps out of the trap like the longshot on a hiding to nothing.

The song is produced by 3 Degrees former manager Richard Barrett, and while the group became enormous in the 70's, they can be comforted in the fact that their first serious attempt in the business did nothing but enhance their reputation.

The Dells
Run For Cover

Top 500 Position: **85**
Original Label: **Chess**
Current Value: **£15 Issue**
£25 Demo

'One of our best, but relatively poor sellers'

Chuck Barkesdale,
Dells member, USA

Oh the mighty, mighty Dells! Run For Cover was a poor seller by Dells' standards, selling a paltry 30,000! Played on and off for 30 years or more, it's a mid paced groover which Marvin Junior sails through.

You get the feeling that the lead was begging to do more on the vocal side, being limited as Phil Wright's arrangement created pleasurable but suppressive background vocals.

Either way Junior never fails and we are left with another 24 karat golden nugget from the world's longest surviving vocal group.

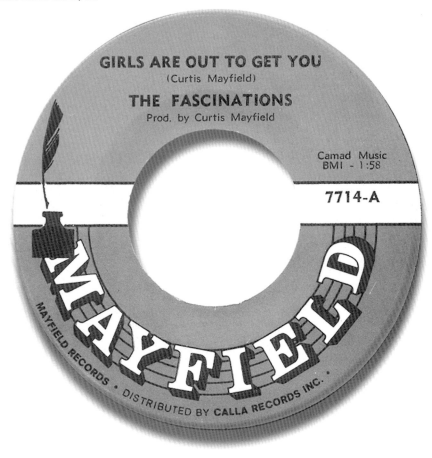

The Fascinations

Girls Are Out To Get You

Top 500 Position: **86**
Original Label: **Mayfield**
Current Value: **£15 Issue**
 £25 Demo

'One for the ladies'

Billy Swain, Soul Fan, Nottingham, UK

Originally recording for ABC, the girls signed to Curtis Mayfield's label, released here on Stateside and then Sue, before finally charting at No.32 in 1971 on Mojo.

To Mayfield it was all so simple. Create a melody, write a pop song with a hurricane hook all backed by his ingenious players, and wait for the sales.

Although it did not fair to well stateside, the song is an anthem here, with just about every girl imaginable bopping to the enchanting voices of Bernadine Smith, Shirley Walter, Fern Bledsie and Joann Leavell.

Eddie Foster

I Never Knew

Top 500 Position: **87**
Original Label: **In**
Current Value: **£150**

*'One of the great
all nighter songs'*

Benjamin Rassat, Soul Fan, Lyon, France

On the classier side of dance circa 1974, and one which got the initial play at the Mecca, but found fame at the Casino.

A slick production for this 1967 single from Berkeley, California which became so popular it could have been the first 'musical' tattoo!

A real stunner that you sing a long to, groove to, make love to!

There's little to say except please listen out for it if you like 'em sweet and sassy. Foster incidentally is still knocking around the Bay area and recorded another in demander 'Closer Together', although this one ranks much higher in popularity.

A proven winner, without any real hype.

The Van Dykes

Save My Love For A Rainy Day

Top 500 Position: **88**
Original Label: **Mala**
Current Value: **£100**

*'Pure, unadulterated
Northern Soul'*

Magnus,
Nitty Gritty, Stockholm, Sweden

Texas reigns supreme once again with the much loved Van Dykes who recorded this gem in Dallas, 1966.

Originally a Motown demo and written by Norman Whitfield, you somehow can't help thinking the song was created for Eddie Kendricks and indeed it was recorded by the Temptations and Undisputed Truth. The Van Dykes lead is so reminiscent of Kendricks, I'm quite sure the demo was similar.

In terms of popularity, it qualifies as a real monster in the golden era and, as time has evolved it always commands a full floor whenever it receives an airing.

The Pointer Sisters

Send Him Back

Top 500 Position: **89**
Original Label: **Atlantic**
Current Value: **£60**

*'Cleethorpes really made
its mark with this one'*

Mary Chapman, Promoter, Lincoln, UK

An unlikely spin from Oakland's Pointer Sisters, who recorded this 'hard to find' item in 1972.

Co-written by Richard Caiton, who is no stranger to rare Soul, and produced by Wardell Quezergue in New Orleans.

Preliminaries aside, the new venue of 1975 Winter Gardens, Cleethorpes, broke this full on after being serviced by record dealer John Anderson (Soul Bowl).

A quirky but seriously effective 45, the value and popularity are soaring again. Best get in the queue.

The Yum Yums

Gonna Be A Big Thing

Top 500 Position:	**90**
Original Label:	**ABC Paramount**
Current Value:	**£500**

'A smooth girl group with that little extra'

John Hulme,
Soul Fan, Greater Manchester, UK

Ironically the other version by the Sapphires was the initial playmaker. Largely due to the raucous tempo which suited most back in '74.

As the slowing down process took a toe hold, the Yum Yum's version also discovered around the same time was revisited, and has since become one of the most played 45's of the last 10 years.

A Philadelphia sound, with girl group specialists Ross/ Renzetti at the controls, this is a totally superior side that was long overdue a comeback.

Nolan Porter

If I Could Only Be Sure

Top 500 Position: **91**
Original Label: **ABC**
Current Value: **£40**

'The changing face of Rare Soul and much better for it'

Craig Caukhill,
Vital Distribution, London, UK

Here's the scoop, firstly the track is fairly motionless, moody and non-traditional it even gained a UK release well and truly in the middle of the golden era.

Porter had already tasted underground success with another oddity 'Keep On Keeping On' during the Torch era. At the time, I likened it to Norman Greenbaum's 'Spirit In The Sky', with it's weird sound effects. On this selection, he excels his first UK discovery, and I now find myself waiting for a cover version by a major rock act.

This track could form the basis of a massive worldwide hit - attention all major A&R executives!

Hoagy Lands
The Next Line

Top 500 Position:	**92**
Original Label:	**Laurie**
Current Value:	**£20 Issue**
	£50 Demo

'A gifted performer'

Jeff Hunter,
Soul Fan, Loughborough, UK

A fantastic record that has remained popular since its first plays in 1971 and perhaps the most sought after of all British collectors' items, worth in excess of £150 on Stateside.

Lands recorded for both MGM and Atlantic before teaming up with New York's Laurie label.

A truly sparkling 7" featuring a fabulous girlie chorus backing up Land's vastly underrated lead. The superb 'Next In Line' was monumentally popular in 71/72 and pure demand from the scene eventually resulted in another UK release.

Lainie Hill
Time Marches On

Top 500 Position: **93**
Original Label: **New Voice**
Current Value: **£300**

'A quaint, subtle song, that you just can't help singing along to'

Laura Jennings,
Soul Fan, Inverness, Scotland

Emotively, the track has it all. A simplistic orchestral arrangement with young female lead capturing the innocent side of the 60's.

An old hand at hitmaking, Bob Crewe saw no reason why this should not attain another chart success for the New Voice label. This one however took a dive - that is until the 1976 when it was discovered by our beloved Northern scene, who embraced it whole-heartedly.

Filed in the DJ box alongside Dena Barnes, Lynne Randell and Nancy Ames, the dancefloor era to which they belong remains a poignant one to many of the scene's female members, who often identify strongly with this type of record.

Bobby Paris

I Walked Away

Top 500 Position: **94**
Original Label: **Capitol**
Current Value: **£100 Issue**
£50 Demo

'Bobby Paris is a legend'

Bobby Paris,
recording artist, Los Angeles, USA

The middle part of Paris' trio of Northern classics involves the Capitol label, which was tucked neatly in between his Cameo and Tetragrammaton sides.

While the other two are out and out stompers, 'Walked' reveals itself as an emotive blue eyed rumbler with those ever-so-tearful lyrics.

During the frantic years the disc often got a end of night spin, today it is about as upfront as you can get.

His visit to the UK is well documented, and while we may have questioned his ability as a Soul artist, 'the boy done good' at a recent Soul festival.

Spyder Turner
I Can't Make It Anymore

Top 500 Position: **95**
Original Label: **MGM**
Current Value: **£8 Issue**
£35 Demo

'In and out of fashion for 30 years, the track thrills to this day'

Richard Moore, Soul Fan, Kent

Dwight D. Turner will be remembered for the amazing rendition of 'Stand by me' in the US, peaking the charts at no. 12 in 1967. As a vocalist from Beckley, West Virginia he had a remarkable range and would probably have been the best warm up man in the business for Otis or Jackie.

His recordings from twelve months earlier at the Terra Shirma studio in Detroit provided us with the masterpiece herein. Played almost constantly since 1970, it reigned supreme at Wigan Casino where DJ Dave Evison reactivated it into a classic revived 45 breaking much of the unwritten 'rarity' rule in the process.

Frankie Valli

You're Ready Now

Top 500 Position: **96**
Original Label: **Smash**
Current Value: **£6 Issue**
£10 Demo

'A monumental pop tune reserved strictly for the scene'

Mick Fitzpatrick,
Soul Fan, County Durham, UK

Arguably the first Northern 45 to chart due to regional demand.

Valli who departed briefly from the Four Seasons, cut two sides for Mercury subsidiary Smash. One upshot being the catchy 'You're Ready Now', which reached No.11 in 1970 in the UK charts. Although recorded in '66, it failed on both sides of the pond, that is until the great North West took it to heart and played it religiously every Saturday.

Valli, born Francis Castellucio, also encountered the scene once again with 'The Night' a veritable Wigan monster in '74/75, which appears later in the chart. In terms of real commercial Northern, this possibly is the forerunner of a generation, and although scorned by purists, if it were not for such sides the scene might never have flourished.

Earl Wright

Thumb A Ride

Top 500 Position: **97**
Original Label: **Capitol**
Current Value: **£25**

'There's a myth among collectors that a vocal exists. Pure fiction, although not a bad idea'

Wayne Smith,
Soul Fan, Greater Manchester, UK

Walking into the Golden Torch in 1972 was a real eye opener. The array of tuneful dancers was unrivalled, and Earl Wright's oddity on Capitol was just another A listed turntable favourite.

The track was a throwaway 'B' side (Wright covering Dylan's 'Rolling Stone' on the 'a' side) and has all the attributes of being a big single for the major. Unfortunately Capitol deemed it an 'easy' single, while North of Watford we took to it like Fred Astaire and Ginger Rogers. This big beat instrumental was produced by Dave Axelrod possibly at their own studios on Vine Street in LA.

The Sapphires

Gotta Have Your Love

Top 500 Position:	**98**
Original Label:	**ABC Paramount**
Current Value:	**£15 Issue**
	£25 Demo

'The ultimate one for the girls'

Dave Pointon, Soul Fan, London, UK

The UK HMV label must have been inundated with fantastic Soul cuts such as this, due to their licensing agreement with ABC in the US.

The track flopped but became a minor hit stateside almost surpassing their only hit 'Who Do You Love'.

Carol Jackson had a terrific voice and, complete with George Garner and Joe Livingston on background, they became the darlings of Philadelphia in '64 while returning to glory here in '71. The mid tempo piano lead with Jackson's first line followed by the group yelling 'hold on baby' is pure magic.

With 'Evil One', 'Slow Fizz' etc under their belts, it is difficult to decide on the most prominent side. The judges decision reveals 'Love' to be the most popular, and who's arguing!

Michael and Raymond
Man Without A Woman

Top 500 Position: **99**
Original Label: **RCA Victor**
Current Value: **£300 Issue**
£50 Demo

*'An exquisite
Detroit monster'*

Gary Givens, Soul Fan, Detroit, USA

Pied Piper productions were a key link to RCA's US black music output. Mike Campbell and Raymond Monette are an unusual combination, sounding a lot like another Detroit duo, Bob and Fred.

Dennis Coffey arranged the track which the label released in 1967 only to relegate it to the 'b' side in favour of the old standard 'Walking the Dog'. MWAW is atmospheric to say the least, with an orchestral overture to savour. Not a work of art but close, and pretty darn popular too.

Furthering the Pied Piper connection, Michael and Raymond had a rare single on Giant which, though not as good, is much sought-after by collectors.

Millie Jackson
My Man Is A Sweet Man

Top 500 Position: **100**
Original Label: **Spring**
Current Value: **£6 Issue**
£10 Demo

'Fortunately this is one to dance, not fornicate to!'

Millie Jackson, Artist, USA

A baaaadddd gal from Thompson, Georgia kicks up her heels and goes 'pop' on this minor 1972 hit.

Taken from her first album, it's not hard to understand the appeal of such a track. Gospel delivery over a sort of Philly arrangement complimented with a title hook that is sung more times than almost any song I know (pre-75).

When the calibre of songs such as this are confronting the scene the term 'rare' is relegated to the wastebin, even by the most hardened collectors.

A well seasoned performance by a veritable newcomer (at the time), having previously only released a minor effort for MGM in 1969.

Top 500 Position: **101**
Original Label: **Autumn**
Current Value: **£15 Issue**
£30 Demo

'Humungous Soul'

Chloe Smith,
Soul Fan, Liverpool, UK

Bobby Freeman

I'll Never Fall In Love Again

Written by Sly Stewart, and a side that went even further than the former Northern giant 'C'mon and Swim'.

Absolutely top notch stomping Soul from San Francisco from former lead of the Vocaleers and Romancers.

When in penetrative discussion about the real McCoy this must be almost at the pinnacle. A forceful guitar lead (Larry Graham?) complimented by drums a'plenty and Freeman's wailing climax make a mockery of chart success. Freeman himself realises this as the single is considerably livelier and more upbeat than his original album version. Sly Stone also recorded it, so too did John Lee's Groundhogs.

One of the first big imports after the Wheel's closure in 1970.

Top 500 Position: **102**
Original Label: **Epic**
Current Value: **£50 Issue**
£30 Demo

'One of the sweetest 45's of its generation'

Gail Thompson,
Soul Fan, Stafford, UK

The Poppies

There's A Pain In My Heart

Along with Fern Kinney (Malaco), Rosemary Taylor (ABC) and Patsy McEwan, Dorothy Moore lead this girl group from '66 to minor success with Epic records.

'Pain in my heart' was such an anthem during the 70's largely again to the female crossover appeal.

Dorothy belts out the song with conviction and although producer Billy Sherrill's production is full of Spector'isms, the Jackson, Mississippi born gal reaches beyond the monstrous reverb instigated by Sherrill.

Pop Soul at it's finest!

Top 500 Position: **103**
Original Label: **Island**
Current Value: **£100**

'Jamaican Soul rules'

Lester Sands, Soul Fan, Croydon, UK

Jackie Edwards

I Feel So Bad

One of the original clutch of British-only releases to kick start the scene in the late 60's.

The red and white Island label is synonymous with Ska collectors and Edwards himself was no stranger to the cool Rock Steady scene of that time.

We are focusing though on a song recorded in England with producer Syd Dale in 1966. Basically it's a love song with a beat, but the melody drives it to fulfilment as far as the dance floor goes.

There is a rare duet version too, and I can't help wondering if someone like Brenton Wood was to have recorded it in the US it could have realised more sales for Edwards here.

Top 500 Position: **104**
Original Label: **Ric-Tic/Gordy**
Current Value: **£10 Issue**
£20 Demo

'A fierce instrumental that sounds like Mantovani on acid!'

Gordon Wilton, Soul Fan, Mansfield, UK

The San Remo Golden Strings

Festival Time

Taking the name from the Italian city and titling the song of the annual festival. The end result being Detroit meets Europe and climaxes in rainy Manchester.

The vocal of course is superbly done by Laura Lee, but on this occasion I fancy the instrumental.

With a string arrangement that even Andre Previn would be proud of, the groove is remarkable. I can't help wondering what the angle was. Did Mr. Gordy intend to parade the single as some sort of theme tune at Midem '67?

Either way it's a blockbuster that all and sundry have at one time 'done their back in' to.

Originally on local Detroit label Ric-Tic, Gordy acquired the master from label owner Ed Wingate.

Top 500 Position: **105**
Original Label: **Columbia**
Current Value: **£15 Issue**
£30 Demo

'Discovering a single by the Spellbinders is the highlight for any record collector'

Simon Richards, Soul Fan, Hull, UK

The Spellbinders

Help Me
(Get Myself Back Together Again)

Big time production from Van McCoy, song written by Ken Williams and with Columbia records behind it, the scene is set for the group led by Robert Shives.

From the 'git go' the vibes sweetly announce the melody, followed by a massive beat and slick vocal, all topped off with a orchestral crescendo that marries the backing vocals and lead perfectly.

Yep, it's an old timer, but if like me you found yourself recording the ultimate in car tape play, 'Help Me (Get myself back together again) would feature on side 1.

Recorded in 1966, the golden year for 'our' music.

Top 500 Position: **106**
Original Label: **Uptown**
Current Value: **£30 Issue**
£60 Demo

'A rip-roaring corker for this multi-talented lady!'

John Anson,
Soul Fan, Greater Manchester, UK

Gloria Jones

Come Go With Me

The Del-Vikings' Rock'n'Roll classic given a 60's Motown style makeover. Taken from her Uptown album which contains a clutch of Northern anthems 'Come Go With Me' with its massive Lincoln Mayorga and Ed Cobb production is undoubtedly the best floorfiller.

Later her career flourished with the late Marc Bolan and her own creative songwriting and performing talents for the likes of Motown in partnership with Pam Sawyer.

'Come Go With Me' first gained exposure at Hanley's Top Rank allnighter in mid-1973.

Top 500 Position: **107**
Original Label: **Congress /Philtown**
Current Value: **£200 C £400 P**

'Instant romp-appeal'

Terry Lowe, Soul Fan, Norfolk, UK

The 7th Avenue Aviators/Frankie Karl and the Chevrons

You Should 'O Held On

'Held On' has risen to cult status during the recent years, despite being originally discovered in the 70's, it falls into the category of 'oddities waiting to be re-found', and boy is it sought after!

The way to gauge a 45 in the popularity stakes is when the official value is, say, £150 but you can still easily get 200+.

I remember Barbara McNair's 'You're Gonna...' for Motown some years ago, reaching astronomic proportions for a single that ain't rare. I digress, the 'Aviators' fly up into the top 200 with their one shot wonder.

Frankie Karl, formerly of the Chevrons and the Dreams is the vocal behind both the Kapp release as the 7th Avenue Aviators as well as the Philtown release with the Chevrons.

Top 500 Position: **108**
Original Label: **Musicor**
Current Value: **£150 Issue £100 Demo**

'Revel in that gospel - and dance sister dance'

Karen Harvey, Soul Fan, Oldham, UK

Marie Knight

That's No Way To Treat A Girl

Gospel singer Knight released a couple of pearlers for Musicor, along with the original version of 'Come Tomorrow' which Manfred Mann scored with and a sublime version of 'Cry Me A River'.

The big city production is pure New York, and Knight attacks the Tony Bruno co-written song full on.

From the first four bars she establishes exactly where the performance is going and spends the balance of the 2.23 yelling and hollering much to the delight of the backing singers who suddenly realise who they are dealing with.

A real butt kicker of anthemic magnitude.

Top 500 Position: **109**
Original Label: **Ric-Tic**
Current Value: **£5 Issue**
£25 Demo

'A dark, enduring Don Davis production classic'

Edwin Starr, Artist, Nottingham, UK

Edwin Starr

Agent Double-O Soul

Charles Hatcher travelled from Cleveland, Ohio to sign a deal with Don Davis's Solid Hitbound productions in 1965.

Before embarking on a breathtaking career(mainly in the UK), he was recording as far back as 1957 with the Futuretones. After a stint with Bill Doggett's combo he secured his first US hit with this super smooth 60's anthem.

It sort of typifies the authenticity of the scene with the bubbling bass line and dramatic intro all pulled together by one of the best live performers ever.

He of course is Edwin Starr, who probably has more influence on the Northern scene, artist wise, than anyone else.

Top 500 Position: **110**
Original Label: **Chess**
Current Value: **£50**

'Ouch! this is really great'

Mitch Reed, Soul Fan, Chicago, USA

The Valentinos

Sweeter Than The Day Before

The intro as so often makes this particular 45.

Co-written by Mary Wells and Cecil Womack, who with his brother Bobby, recorded for Sam Cooke's SAR label before instigating an even more successful career as solo performers.

The track hardly needs an introduction suffice to say, if discovered today it would instantly raise four figures.

Due to the amount of copies floating around in the 70's the turntable play was somewhat muted early on. Two decades on and it's back to the real fighting weight for this Chicago recorded icon of Northern soul.

Interestingly enough the single is possibly bigger now than at its point of discovery.

Top 500 Position: **111**
Original Label: **Tangerine**
Current Value: **£10 Issue**
£25 Demo

'Annie Mae tearing up the dance floor'

Larry Hall, USA

Ike and Tina Turner

Dust My Broom

Anywhere, everywhere this argumentative couple went, the end result was recorded heaven.

Married from 1958-76 (how did it last so long?) the duo recorded for Sue, Tangerine, Pompeii, Loma, A&M, Phil Spector, United Artists, Kent and Modern.

Two outstanding recordings in 1966 bore the brilliant 'Beauty Is Just Skin Deep' and 'Dust My Broom', the latter winning hands down.

Tina, as with all her performances gives an eleven out of ten, and complete with Ray Charles produced thunderous rhythm, the result is an AWESOME update of Elmore James' blues standard!

Top 500 Position: **112**
Original Label: **Ric-Tic**
Current Value: **£10 Issue**
£20 Demo

'Pure genius'

Brain Philips, DJ, Manchester, UK

JJ Barnes

Real Humdinger

This production which developed out of a demo entitled 'Sweet Honey Baby' became one of the first major rarities (at the time) at the Twisted Wheel.

Yet another classic on which Dennis Coffey played bass, he recently commented on how 'up' everyone was on the very first take!

Few would argue that JJ is one of the best loved of Northern Soul heroes with this just one of many many classic sounds from the great man.

Top 500 Position:	**113**
Original Label:	**RCA Victor**
Current Value:	**£100 Issue**
	£50 Demo

'Reminds me how my first wife left 'cause I was paying more attention to gear at Wigan than I was to her!'

Big Mick, Soul Writer, Bolton, UK

Beverly Ann

You've Got Your Mind On Other Things

Country singer turned Northern star. I agree it's somewhat bizzare. Songs, for no apparent reason spring out of left field and become 'classics'. Personally, I could never understand why it has remained popular alongside the Joanie Sommers, Holly St. James of this world. I think the emotional side of us takes a bit of a toe hold. The chorus is certainly catchy, the rest belongs where it originated - Nashville.

To top it all, BA scored again on RCA with 'He's Coming Home'.

In a copy of the Togetherness magazine, a photo appeared of Beverly Ann, all kitted out and ready to take on Petula Clark in a 'battle of the sexties'. Well it was in fact Station Road, Wigan where Ms Ann's won her skirmish!

Top 500 Position:	**114**
Original Label:	**MGM**
Current Value:	**£200 Issue**
	£100 Demo

'Everything a Northern record should be'

Tony Dent, Soul Fan, Merseyside, UK

The Charades

Key To My Happiness

Discovered around 1973 and surprisingly never reached it's peak until the 90's. There are many reasons for this, the main one being that the first Verve/MGMs turned up on issue (rather than the ones which are principally demos and are harder to find).

Basking in bass, hi-hats, killer vocals and group harmony, this is the business!

Maybe the timing of it was all wrong, it certainly was for the 50's group who planned a comeback but refused to sign for MGM who promptly formed this group - their very own 'Charades' for this '66 release.

If this were your first lesson in Northern Soul, I would insist we start with the letter C for Charades.

Top 500 Position: **115**
Original Label: **Sussex**
Current Value: **£2,000**

'The ultimate rarity that has lived to tell the tale'

Bill Robinson, Soul Fan, Cheshire, UK

Billy Woods

Let Me Make You Happy

A classy outing from former Verve recording artist Billy Woods for Van McCoy productions.

Can a 70's 45 really be worth the amount quoted?

Well, hear it once and you will be hooked regardless of price.

The single has reached a junction of credibility both in price and stature. All that's left to say is, that a dozen copies or so were found in 1974, with a further promo being unearthed in 1981. There are no others known, leaving the label's swan song a delight for anoraks plus the McCoy legacy attaching itself neatly to this wonderful offering.

When a dance beat and lead vocal combine to deliver the line 'wipe those teardrops from your eyes' it's liable to be special, and it is.

Top 500 Position: **116**
Original Label: **Mirwood**
Current Value: **£25 Issue**
£50 Demo

'Travelling to the Catacombs we heard about a great new discovery by Richard Temple'

Les Hare, King Bee Records, Manchester, UK

Richard Temple

That Beatin' Rhythm

Temple is also known as Jimmy Conwell, who was part of the Mirwood/Mira/Keymen set up. Basically the names of Jackie Lee, Bob and Earl etc were a talented bunch of studio guys churning out their own brand of uptempo soul music.

From the piano intro and the spoken words of 'dancin' is a part of life, it's one of the thrills of young America' you know what's coming! The instrumental version 'Cigarette Ashes' had a firm following also, but lyrically it all but sums up Northern soul and the dance floor.

Conwell is still around after being tracked down to appear in the video 'The Northern Soul Story'

Top 500 Position: **117**
Original Label: **Perception**
Current Value: **£50 Issue**
£125 Demo

*'One of the coolest
tracks ever'*

Arthur Chisholm, Soul Fan, New York, USA

Otis Smith

Let Her Go

When the Golden Torch in Stoke on Trent closed it's doors in March 1973, it took all of six months for the scene to re-group and witness the opening of one Wigan Casino. During this time a few add-ons to the successful Torch playlist emerged outside of Rubin's 'You've Been Away'. I believe this New York recording from 1970 to be the best discovery during that time. The original label was almost a Jazz outlet and quite why the 60's sounding effort from Smith even got out is a mystery. The fact is, it was released in June 1970 and sold positively zilch!

One even stranger twist is the level of promotion it got. I can reveal whilst being a young record hound in New York in 1975, I just about found copies in every store I visited, leading me to the conclusion that 'somebody, somewhere liked it'.

Top 500 Position: **118**
Original Label: **Tie**
Current Value: **£1,000**

*'Extremely rare,
and oh so good'*

Jeff Milton, Soul Fan, Yorkshire, UK

Jon and the Wierdest

Can't Get Over These Memories

On many occasions I have studied the growth of 'really rare' 45's, and concluded that many are undesirable on the dance floor. How refreshing then to see this wonderfully obscure single from Los Angeles.

As for the group name I wonder how many copies are lying in a box of psychedelic collectables?

Front man John is John Hendley who is no stranger to the scene after his mini monster 'My Baby Came From Out Of Nowhere' created a stir.

Emotive and timeless, this four figure treasure which was first spun by Richard Searling as 'Spyder Turner' is pure class.

Top 500 Position: **119**
Original Label: **Hi EP**
Current Value: **£50**

'That driving Hi beat is just Champion!'

Chas Alcock, Soul Fan, Greater Manchester, UK

Willie Mitchell

The Champion

Legendary musician/producer Mitchell hardly needs an introduction especially with Al Green in tow during the 70's.

His own brand of instrumental R&B culminated from his big band days in Ashland, Mississippi.

The Champion is taken from the 'Driving Beat' album which is full of essential 60's tracks. The word 'stomper' is synonymous with the scene and, if anyone has heard the term but struggling to fully understand it, simply play this dynamic Memphis boss waxing and you too will be 'stomping'!

DJ John Vincent well and truly 'championed' this epic.

Top 500 Position: **120**
Original Label: **Uptite**
Current Value: **£25 Blue**
£40 Yellow

'A pulsating group sound from the Kyser stable'

Mick Love, Soul Fan, Dublin, Eire

The Superlatives

I Still Love You

In the vein of other stormin' group sounds such as the Tempos, comes a real boss waxing from New Jersey.

Paul Kyser was the local guy who recorded a fair amount of Jersey talent. Along with Robert Banks, Joe Evans, George Blackwell, Kyser was in and out of the studios of Newark and East Orange working with a series of undiscovered groups.

The Superlatives from Newark are not to be confused with the Detroit group of the same name. Lead by Julian Bonaparte with Robby 'Burning Sensation' Lawson on backing vocals. Why is this one-off release on on Uptite so good? Well, the tempo is ferocious, string arrangement tuneful, and as for the lead and background harmony...just awesome. A perfect dancer and quality old school.

Top 500 Position:	**121**
Original Label:	**20th Century**
Current Value:	**£5**

*"Reaching For The Best'?
What are you taking about?'*

Bob Relf, Singer, Los Angeles, USA

The Exciters

Reaching For The Best

How intriguing, the player being played. Key record dealer Simon Soussan invented the fictitious title by artist Bob Relf. Maybe Soussan had it in mind to record, but a creative DJ from Blackpool beat him to it.

Levine, intrigued himself by the title, used the platform to realise his venture into the music industry by utilising the services of the Exciters, who at the time were looking for a record deal.

The upshot of Ian's entrepreneurialism was a fantastic, fresh sounding Northern mover, which to this day remains totally original.

Eventually making the UK charts, the song paved the way for Levine to utilise his knowledge of the scene to great effect in the studio.

Top 500 Position:	**122**
Original Label:	**UK MGM**
Current Value:	**£150**

'We used to hum it at football matches'

John Mahoney,
Soul Fan, Nottingham, UK

Father's Angels

Bok To Bach

Jerry Ross decided to record a church band from Pennsylvania to record a cover of Wilson Pickett's 'Don't Knock It' and release it on his own Heritage label.

Requiring a B side, the band put together a throwaway titled 'Bok To Bach', the result being not a US release, but a UK one, with his licensee MGM.

Four years later the disc was discovered and taken to the Golden Torch, the top allnighter of 1972... every Nighter goer knows the rest.

One final note on the confusion of the influx of 'Heritage label imports' which are common place within the scene. They are in fact reissues, the original 1968 record was only released in Britain.

Top 500 Position: **123**
Original Label: **Musette**
Current Value: **£150**

'Totally storming Northern'

Jackie Lovell, Soul Fan, Preston, UK

Mickie Champion

What Good Am I?

From the outset Mickie Champion is out to kick some ass with a full blooded appeal for her man to stay home.

The futility of the recording session is felt 6,000 miles away as the little label from California had about as much chance for a hit as Sheffield Wednesday have of winning the European Cup!

An absolute Wigan MONSTER, listening in the light of today's all-nighter sounds I am struck by just how much of and R&B sound it is for a period of stomp-driven cuts. Recorded originally with the Nic-Nacs on RPM, Mickie had two and a half minutes to convince us that the record is good, I can reveal it is GREAT!

Top 500 Position: **124**
Original Label: **Hickory**
Current Value: **£10 Issue**
　　　　　　　　£25 Demo

'I thought it sounded like a Top Ten hit'

Barbara Mills, Artist, Nashville, USA

Barbara Mills

Queen Of Fools

Very strange indeed that a country singer signed to Hickory records, Nashville should find herself in the Northern Hall of Fame.

The track recorded in 1965 actually got a release here, and with a mock Motown beat one obviously imagines a sort of change of direction for the label.

It is authentic and typical of the time of playing (1971/2), plus it has the advantage of a soaring chorus with the background vocalists all chanting 'she's the queen of foooollls', which becomes the 45's focal point.

Although out of step today and somewhat 'cheesy' in comparison to more soulful offerings, that should not detract from the awesome popularity it once had.

Top 500 Position: **125**
Original Label: **Modern**
Current Value: **£50 Issue**
£80 Demo

'Cute, slick with the most soulful finesse'

Linda Lewis, Artist, London, UK

Mary Love

You Turned My Bitter Into Sweet

Mary Love Comer recorded the evergreen in 1965 for Modern in Los Angeles and surprisingly enough it got a UK release courtesy of King.

Published by Jobete and with that in mind we conjure up ideas of that elusive publisher's acetate (Kim Weston, Brenda Holloway?) being used as a door stop at Hitsville in Detroit.

In the UK it was covered twice by Linda Lewis, once on Polydor in 1967 then later on Electricity in 1984.

Perfectly executed by Love who warbles smartly around the Chester Pipkin production, the sugar coated hook is irresistible and works a treat even today, some 32 years since the inaugural play.

Top 500 Position: **126**
Original Label: **Groove City**
Current Value: **£1,000**

'The cream of Detroit rarities'

Tom Hickman, Soul Fan, Grand Rapids, USA

The Professionals

That's Why I Love You

Superb group harmony, an excellent lead and a brilliant song in the Detroit groove... what more could anyone ask for?

This is a sumptuous piece of vinyl that even got a limited gold vinyl release - now there's confidence in a true piece of SOUL perfection! Indeed there were several takes of 'That's Why I Love You'- Goldmine were lucky enough to track them down and compile them all on various CDs... I for one never tire of any of them!

This Groove City release was a brilliant one-shot wonder for the boys, they must have been shattered to see it fail - especially as they clearly felt so confident of well deserved chart success.

Top 500 Position: **127**
Original Label: **Linda**
Current Value: **£150 Issue**
£200 Demo

'Soul Mexican style'

Huggy Boy, KRLA, Los Angeles, USA

The Majestics

I Love Her So Much (It Hurts Me)

A spin off from the Rampart group of labels comes this Doo Wop flavoured effort from East Los Angeles.

The Mexican influence is apparent with soft latino guitar riffs, a neat string arrangement and a raft of 'Tijuana' brass.

Playing in the major league towards the late 70's, the group are one of a series of acts using the same group name.

The song was also released on Warner Bros by David and Reuben.

In terms of danceability, its the trumpets and violins that make it, as the arranger gets 'up and at 'em' and creates a terrific hum along tune right from the off.

Top 500 Position: **128**
Original Label: **Dynamo**
Current Value: **£400 Issue**
£300 Demo

'Real meat and potatoes Detroit Soul'

Martin Koppel, Record Dealer, Canada

Stanley Mitchell

Get It Baby

The most invigorating thing about Richard 'Popcorn' Wylie and Tony Hester is their knack for testing out 'other' versions of newly written material. A classic case being this rampant dancer from Mitchell, who in fact 'raps' his way through (yes it was 1967!) a rippling Detroit groove.

Hester himself cut the demo as 'Down in the Dumps' which also proved itself in the late 70's, after being unearthed on acetate.

Longevity wise we plump for Stanley's raw screecher which is reminiscent of Rex Garvin, Jerry-O etc, and one even Puff Daddy might enjoy!

Top 500 Position:	**129**
Original Label:	**Amy**
Current Value:	**£300 Issue**
	£200 Demo

'I used to think he sang 'Too Much Sulphate' but then, of course, that's what I'd had!'

Dave Carne, Soul Fan, Penrith, UK

Morris Chestnut

Too Darn Soulful

Former lead singer of the Bell group, the Attractions and the Soundmasters on Juliet, Morris also recorded with Street Corner Symphony in the 70's.

Sources inform me of a budding TV career, with an appearance in an American hospital drama.

The multi-talented Chestnut really wows us with one of the best nighter sounds EVER. Produced in Los Angeles by Anthony Renfro, this 1967 rarity originally discovered by Ian Levine is today a very sought after piece of vinyl.

Top 500 Position:	**130**
Original Label:	**Dynamo**
Current Value:	**£10 Issue**
	£25 Demo

'The Mockingbird duo in fine fettle'

Billy Foster, Soul Fan, Lancashire

Inez and Charlie Foxx

Tightrope

Brother and sister duo from Greensboro', North Carolina who hit paydirt with 'Mockingbird'. The track recorded with Luther Dixon for Dynamo/Musicor is a wonderful piano laden, all horns blazing gutsy workout by Inez.

You can hear the 'performance' as she shrills through the song in a desperate attempt to revive fortunes. The single was released in the UK on Stateside, hence the very early discovery and subsequent all nighter plays.

Every classic Northern in demander needs something to fire off dance floor imagination, and apart from the duo begging to 'walk that tightrope' it's the opening sixteen bars that do it.

Top 500 Position: **131**
Original Label: **Elbejay**
Current Value: **£30**

'Jailer... Bring me Bragg'

Dave Lee, Soul Fan, London, UK

Johnny Bragg

They're Talking About me

Originally a member of the Prisonaires who were famous for recording the original of Johnny Ray's 'Just Walking In The Rain' while serving life sentences.

Bragg apparently recorded this track in Nashville while in the slammer in 1967, modelling it on Jackie Wilson's upbeat style.

Joyously buoyant, the clinky intro sets the scene as to the next 2 minutes. Bragg sings up a storm, and the UK (Especially Wigan Casino where it became an anthem) loves it enough to have demanded his parole, sadly in the US they seem unaware of his real talent.

Top 500 Position: **132**
Original Label: **Calla**
Current Value: **£20 (Short)**
                      £60 (Long)

'Is it the long or short version?'

Ron Diamond, Los Angeles, USA

Frankie and the Classicals

What Shall I Do?

Almost a national hit when released on Calla in 1967. The origins of the recording derive from Teddy Vann who created a backing track that no less than six other versions(some with different lyrics and song title), with F/C edging the contest.

A former Philadelphia DJ Ron Diamond played it to death upon release and that is where the promotion ended.

The disc received a UK release on Philips which is really scarce, then the subsequent re-issue on Pye's Casino Classics. A rarer long version with spoken intro. exists on another Calla number with a different flip.

Top 500 Position: **133**
Original Label: **Columbia**
Current Value: **£100 Issue**
£150 Demo

'British Gospel?'

Mick Yeats, Soul Fan, Leicester, UK

Solomon King / Levi Jackson

This Beautiful Day

Very strange indeed, as the serious British collectors item attacked under two guises. Firstly as a 'b' side released in 1969. Then as if EMI 'knew something' they re-released it in 1970 under the name of Levi Jackson.

Either way both releases flopped, and during the Torch all nighter heyday it became a part of the furniture. King of course is the hit balladeer on 'She wears my ring', but on this flopped 45 you would think he was auditioning for Stax.

A single that is a credit not only to the scene but to the UK recording industry since Solomon was in fact a Jewish guy from Prestwich, Manchester!

Top 500 Position: **134**
Original Label: **Fusion**
Current Value: **£5**

'In terms of strangeness, this ranks in the Top Ten'

Tilly Rutherford, Soul Fan, London, UK

Mistura, featuring Lloyd Michels

The Flasher

To be associated with a 'great' Northern Soul single is of course satisfying - unless it is a unique single like the Flasher!

Never in my wildest dreams did I envisage this throwaway instrumental being anything more than another 'new release'.

A friend of mine who was mailing 45's to me from the New York disco pool had sent this along with many previous goodies such as Oscar Perry and further oddities like Barnaby Bye. On first hearing I was unimpressed and following a trip to Blackpool Mecca I watched in amazement as DJ Ian Levine aired it for the first time. The rest of course is history as I cut my first record deal in the UK leasing it to Route in 1976, who promoted it well to secure a No.23 hit.

Now that's the strange world of Northern soul!

Top 500 Position:	**135**
Original Label:	**ABC Paramount**
Current Value:	**£100 Issue**
	£60 Demo

The Reflections

Like Adam And Eve

'A hard-hitting, big label monster'

Pauline Lovell, Soul Fan, West Midlands, UK

Major label signing the Reflections had hoped to re-capture the form that gave them a US hit in 1964 with 'Just Like Romeo And Juliet'. Timing was all off so it was left to the UK to unearth the non seller and put it to the test.

The upshot was an even bigger 'hit' north of Watford.

Tony Michaels who is no stranger to the scene via his wonderful 'Love The Life I Live' for Golden World sang with conviction but you rarely score twice two years apart with the same theme.

Apart from a further single for ABC the group disbanded, the north of England revelled with 'Adam And Eve' and possibly was the biggest sound of '75.

Top 500 Position:	**136**
Original Label:	**Revilot**
Current Value:	**£15 Issue**
	£80 Demo

Darrell Banks

Somebody (Somewhere) Needs You

'Mister Banks singing on a Frank Wilson/Marc Gordon song - it doesn't get better'

Thierry Moulange, Soul Fan, Brussels, Belgium

Co-written by Frank Wilson and Marc Gordon for Motown's publishing arm Jobete.a variety of artists recorded this 1965 classic and its alternate vocals with Banks just edging out the great Ike and Tina Turner version on Loma.

Never a monster on the scene, it sort of just appeared as everyone took it to heart as if 'it had always been around'.

A delectable Don Davis production at his United Sound studio, Banks excels himself over an enduring melody and typical Detroit backing track.

Wilson himself acknowledges the song as 'almost' a hit and with a hook so generous as this, I totally agree.

Along with Spyder Turner's chart entry this remains one of the most affordable and cherished scene 45's... every home should own it!

Top 500 Position: **137**
Original Label: **Music Merchant**
Current Value: **£30**

'Could easily have been the new Supremes single'

Melanie Sawyer, Soul Fan, Detroit, USA

Eloise Laws

Love Factory

With an array of super talented brothers and sisters including Ronnie, Hubert and Debra, Eloise almost had a smash with this in the States. A massive radio hit, but for some reason it failed at the last hurdle.

Conjuring up another vocal find, Holland Dozier Holland released this commercial attempt in 1973, and on the face of it, looks like they should have scored again.

Fair play then to Ian Levine who created 'the hit' albeit super regionally (somewhere north of Wolverhampton) and gave this tremendous Honey Cone style groover a place in our own piece of history making.

Top 500 Position: **138**
Original Label: **ABC**
Current Value: **£10 Issue**
£15 Demo

'An irresistible floor shaker'

John 'Hector' Heathcote,
Soul Fan, Derby, UK

The Shakers

One Wonderful Moment

I often wonder why soft rock writers/producers such as Cashman and Pistilli, would record a mock soul single such as this. Maybe rock stalwarts attempted the soul thing in an attempt to crossover, rather like Sly Stone doing the progressive line. Either way the record is superb, with a stunning intro and on the fours back beat, all topped off with falsetto harmonies and OTT reverb.

The original was lying in wait, searching for a big name to play it, due to a few copies surfacing in the old 'sales and exchange' junk shops of the early 70's.

Old style stomper with mucho dance appeal that ranks alongside the best of 'em for sheer exuberance.

Top 500 Position: **139**
Original Label: **Revilot**
Current Value: **£800**

'A two sider that remains one of the very best from Detroit'

Don Davis, Groovesville, Detroit, USA

Jackie Beavers

I Need My Baby

Manchester proved an unlikely source to hear and learn all about this marvellous discovery. Richard Searling had played it at the Casino, I remember hearing it in Manchester around 1979. Shortly after, the flip side 'A Love That Never Runs Cold' started to get action.

Ten years later hosting a radio programme in the very same city, I'm interviewing Johnny Bristol, who notices I am playing the Beavers disc. The next few minutes are spent listening to JB's account of his friend. Firstly as Johnny and Jacky the pair wrote and sang on the original 'Someday We'll Be Together' (for Harvey Fuqua's Tri-Phi label), which became the departing anthem for Diana Ross and The Supremes. Bristol knew him well and proceeded to reveal all about this character who recorded for Revilot, Sound Stage 7 and Dade amongst others.

Top 500 Position: **140**
Original Label: **Bell**
Current Value: **£1,500**

'A top tune oozing credibility'

Dave Brown,
Philly Archives, Philadelphia, USA

Bernie Williams

Ever Again

The current asking price for the original is quite breathtaking. Before we take a reality check, let's examine the facts...1. The track is excellent. 2. Even though 'Ever Again' is on a major label, it's mega rare.

The situation regarding the discs history is one of turmoil. Firstly Del Val the indie label from Philadelphia produced the track but used Gene Woodbury as the chosen vocalist. The subsequent release flopped. Label owner Joe Stevenson then leased a second version by Bernie Williams, not to be confused with former Blue Notes lead, Bernard Williams well (known for his Harthon recording 'It's Needless To Say') to Bell, that also failed.

UK wise the single has grown and grown reaching a pinnacle rather late in the day.

Top 500 Position: **141**
Original Label: **Cuppy**
Current Value: **£700**

*'A superb doo-wop
influenced soul shaker'*

Ian Thomas, Soul Fan, Swindon, UK

The De-Lites

Lover

Bill Haley decided on a new record label in 1965, naming it Cuppy after his wife.

Resisting the temptation to travel down the rockabilly road, he astutely (or as he thought) followed 'what the kids wanted'.He was half right. The track kicks, great vocals, and lovely hook. Unfortunately the song felt dated even then.

Many years later, cue old Blighty to turntable it to death, and create a showcase for the catchy little number.

Hailing from Chester, PA, the label, band and single disappeared quickly. In terms of collectors, this is a prime contender for the 'most wanted' list.

Top 500 Position: **142**
Original Label: **Warner Brothers**
Current Value: **£75 Issue
£100 Demo**

*'One of a host of supreme
stormers from the girls'*

Lawrence Toulan, Soul Fan, Essex, UK

The Apollas

Mr. Creator

Loma and Warner Brothers stalwarts the Apollas, made up of Leola Giles, Ella Jamerson and Dorothy Ramsey recorded many singles and made several US TV appearances. Sadly they didn't quite crack it.

After a wealth of turntable exposure the UK finally succumbed to the charms of 'Mr Creator'. The song which was written by Ashford (Nick not Jack) and Simpson also saw a demo cut by Candy and the Kisses which was scheduled for release on Scepter. With an accomplished production by Dick Glasser this is undoubtedly one of the scene's best girl group sounds.

Top 500 Position: **143**
Original Label: **Audio Arts**
Current Value: **£15 Issue**
£30 Demo

'The strings could have been from a Hitchcock movie'

Graham Coulter,
Soul Fan, Inverness, Scotland

The Incredibles

There Is Nothing Else To Say

A 'bubbling under' hit from 1966 on Madelon Baker's Audio Arts label. The group fronted by Cal Waymon gained a release here on Stateside.

The string ensemble make it and coupled with the 'galloping hoof' effect, Waymon controls the vocal like a seasoned pro.

Unlike the syrupy Wheel sides of the time like 'I'm Gonna Miss You', 'Apple, Peaches Pumpkin Pie' and the like, this was as hotter than fire and became the song you would sing for the rest of the week!

Top 500 Position: **144**
Original Label: **End**
Current Value: **£450**

'A perfect dancefloor anthem'

Richard Searling, DJ, Bolton, UK

Lenny Curtis

Nothing Can Help You Now

Recorded for the New York based End label in 1965, this single has certainly been slow in reaching its full potential having regularly changed hands for £50 for over ten years.

Merely a bit-part player in the Wigan Casino make-up, this track that represents the finale for the legendary Doo-Wop label is now one of the top DJ spins on the scene. Suddenly every collector wants a copy and it is today one of the most sought after 45s in the UK!

Top 500 Position: **145**
Original Label: **Brunswick**
Current Value: **£10 Issue**
                      £20 Demo

'Regarded as THE version, surpassing Soul Brother No.1'

Bridget Jones, Soul Fan, Newport, Wales, UK

Gene Chandler

There Was A Time

Highly regarded as the definitive version, Gene delivers his own rendition of James Brown's classic, showing the grit and determination side to his game.

Popularised at the Casino via the Mr. M's oldies sessions, the man from Chicago (born Eugene Dixon) has for many a year added the song to his repertoire when touring Europe.

Regarded as a Soul icon, his fan base is high and together with Major Lance and Curtis Mayfield is one of the legendary Windy City soul stars.

Top 500 Position: **146**
Original Label: **Pameline**
Current Value: **£250 green**
                      £40 orange

'Producer Wylie smiles yet again as another 'B' side is the UK winner!'

Frank Elson, Blues & Soul, 1975

The Detroit Executives

Cool Off

Richard Wylie and Tony Hestor were the eternal optimists, recording at least one other version of each of their creations.

No change here then, as The Ideals (from the same stable) recorded a similar track titled 'mighty lover'.

Cool Off, became one of the first alternate 60's singles to reach a slightly different audience, mainly at Blackpool Mecca, where a more stylish club goer was beginning to emerge. On saying that, the record 'broke out', and to this day is an essential spin for most DJ's.

Top 500 Position: **147**
Original Label: **Stateside**
Current Value: **£5 Issue**
£25 Demo

'Now this is a hit'

Biddu, Songwriter, London, UK

Jimmy James

A Man Like Me

Suddenly from out of nowhere comes a new release (at the time) that revolutionised the scene and put paid to the myth that 'it has to be rare'.

A 45 one could say was 'made for the scene', but it wasn't according to songwriter and producer Biddu.

Apparently he had produced a demo that just felt right, which his client Lenita productions then leased to EMI, promptly releasing the song in November, 1972.

Famous all-night venue the Torch, Tunstall, Stoke-on-Trent latched on to it around 4 weeks prior to release, you can imagine the demand!

According to Jimmy, the song sold in excess of 50,000 copies, but as the sales were all regional (ie THE NORTH) it failed to chart.

Top 500 Position: **148**
Original Label: **Boom**
Current Value: **£30 Issue**
£50 Demo

'Big, gruff Italian New York soul'

Barry Aswith, Soul Fan, Hertfordshire, UK

Dean Parrish

Determination

Parrish remains one of soul's great mysteries. We know so little and have yet to see a photo, but it's still as if we have known him for so long.

Utterly distinctive, the 'northern' hits are legendary with sides for Boom, Musicor and Laurie, eventually ending up on Polydor with a rock band.

Determination is the first of his classics and easily the best dancer. The song is fairly simple with Deano's unmistakable voice rasping through the big NY production.

Released here on Stateside, the man has to be the finest white soul singer of his generation. A duet with Janis Joplin would have changed the course of his career methinks.

Top 500 Position: **149**
Original Label: **Wand**
Current Value: **£40**

'An awesome, ferocious rip-roarer

Carol Poole, Soul Fan, Derby, UK

Al Wilson

Help Me

A crazy, wild dancer from Wilson who fought tooth and nail to get his vocal heard, while DJ's initially plumped for the instrumental.

This is northern soul with a rip roaring intro followed by cooking guitar licks and heavyweight brass riffs.

The Casino rose to the challenge when first exposed, and for a few months this could easily have been the No. 1 single in the country.

Tempos have changed, but 'Help me' is fondly remembered and danced to at many a revival.

Top 500 Position: **150**
Original Label: **Hi**
Current Value: **£8 Issue**
£15 Demo

'A wicked instrumental version of Chuck Berry'

Derek Allen, Soul Fan, Leicester, UK

Bill Black's Combo

Little Queenie

Absolutely massive in the early 70's and one real left field dancer.

The Memphian famous for his work with Elvis, had one of the most formidable bands in the US, and this stone soul workout of Berry's original was worthy of a hit. The plays though came from the north of England and while Black never experienced it's popularity here (passing away in 1965), the track remains one of the really big oldies.As a 'current spin' it was big for quite a while from the late Torch to the early days of Wigan.

Recorded in 1964, the single was released here on London.

Top 500 Position: **151**
Original Label: **Crazy Horse**
Current Value: **£30**

'Obviously in contention for the pop and soul chart'

Rod Law, Soul Fan, Australia

David and the Giants

Superlove

On the crest of a wave in 1974, this pop ditty from David Huff had all the right ingredients from master chef Rick Hall at Muscle Shoals, Alabama using his Soul roots to break into the Top 40. Ironically, three years later Hall did score with the Osmonds' 'One Bad Apple', a similar effort to Superlove.

While Huff, fluffed his chance, those cover-merchants Wigan's Ovation worked their 'magic' over a cute song with masses of dance floor appeal.

The group meanwhile had 'Ten Miles High', another scene fave, unfortunately petering out some 12 months later.

Top 500 Position: **152**
Original Label: **Decca**
Current Value: **£200 Issue**
£100 Demo

'Carribean Soul?'

Keith Walsham, Soul Fan, Merseyside, UK

Johnny Caswell

You Don't Love Me Anymore

Caswell had earlier been discovered by former Danny and the Junior - Johnny Madara. A source recently informed me that Madara is in fact Caswell, who in turn was trying to capitalise on Madara's other new hitmaker Len Barry. They sound remarkably similar. Anyway, the track written by Leon Huff was released by Decca in 1966 and flopped.

Caswell's vocal career was blunted, though he later recorded for Colossus it was left to the music hungry Brits to unearth this gem and then play it to death!

Wonderful major label release, great song, accomplished performance.

Top 500 Position:	**153**
Original Label:	**ABC Paramount**
Current Value:	**£300**

'Bigger than ever in 2000'

Karen Singer, Soul Fan, Scotland

Holly St. James

That's Not love

A common theme runs through the veins of the scene with songs such as this pop outing from Holly, who no doubt is a failed actress or something.

Straight out of the Beverly Ann, Joanie Sommers, Paula Durante charm school, the girl wallows in 60's naïvety, as the Spectorish backdrop suits the little miss perfectly.

Hey, I am not mocking the disc, it is one which I honestly don't like, but boy is it big.

Our loyalties to these little chicky love grooves is legendary, one can't help thinking though that if the track was by Jackie Trent or Tammy Wynette, we would use it as the customary ashtray.

Top 500 Position:	**154**
Original Label:	**Canterbury**
Current Value:	**£40 Issue**
	£50 Demo

'One of my own perennial favourites'

Keith Minshull, DJ, Stoke-on-Trent, UK

The Tempos

Countdown (Here I Come)

The Tempos, have nothing to do with the Detroit group of the same name, they were in fact the Younghearts, who's 'A Little Togetherness' is also a Northern classic.

I myself recorded a dance version of the song by Kofi and the Lovetones - which became a monster in Asia!

Back to the original, the falsetto lead is delectable as is the ecstatic intro which sets the scene for what is one heck of a 60's classic that became one of the first Blackpool Mecca spins following its reopening in 1973.

Top 500 Position: **155**
Original Label: **Chess**
Current Value: **£10 Issue**
£15 Demo

'The first major instrumental'

Chrissie Jones, Soul Fan, Nantwich, UK

Ramsey Lewis

Wade In The Water

Chicago keyboard legend Lewis has a long association with the scene.

That apart, his instrumental contribution would easily make a top 5 if we were only concentrating on '67-72.

Just about as effortless as you can get, with the man simply laying down the track as he plays.

A superb rhythm with Young/Holt in attendance creating the atmosphere for a legendary jam session.

Top 500 Position: **156**
Original Label: **Brunswick**
Current Value: **£200 Issue**
£125 Demo

'The group's name is off-putting, the track certainly isn't'

Paul Leka, Songwriter, USA

Adam's Apples

Don't Take It Out On This World

The New York connection of Paul Leka and Brunswick records, saw psyche-soul band Adams Apples turn in a gutsy performance from '67. Later that year they recorded 'You are the one I love', which got it's fair share of play.

The chorus on this stomper makes it, with the backing vocals sounding black while the lead certainly has visions of being the next Felix Cavaliere (Young Rascals).

Sometimes the unusual gets to you, and this is certainly in that category.

Top 500 Position: **157**
Original Label: **Bell**
Current Value: **£6 Issue**
£10 Demo

'A song with distinctly crude overtones!'

Mark Wales, Soul Fan, Sheffield, UK

James and Bobby Purify

Shake A Tail Feather

The Duo who hail from Pensacola, Florida have a long association with the scene starting with Wheel classics 'Let Love Come Between Us', 'Do Unto Me' and 'Wish You Didn't Have To Go'.

Originally a hit for Chicago group the Five Dutones the Purify's version surfaced at the Casino's Mr M's and more recently got a boost courtesy of the Blues Brothers - but either way a good time was had by all!

Top 500 Position: **158**
Original Label: **Back Beat**
Current Value: **£15 Issue**
£25 Demo

'The Boy Wonder of Soul?'

Carl Carlton, Artist, USA

Little Carl Carlton

Competition Ain't Nothin'

No stranger to the scene is the ever-youthful Mr. Carlton, a Detroit vocalist who recorded for Lando in 1964, then Golden World and on to Don Robey's Back Beat label and a real career lift-off on the latter in the 70's before moving to 20th Century.

The youthfulness of Carlton is uncanny as he sounds the same on 'Bad Mama Jama' as he did on his earliest performances.

A totally uplifting commercial slab of 60's soul that one never tires of. Due to a lack of rarity it probably doesn't get enough attention today, but it should, this is a total killer.

Top 500 Position: **159**
Original Label: **Top Ten**
Current Value: **£100 Issue**
£150 Demo

'Harmonies to die for!'

Mark Rosenbourg, Soul Fan, Ohio, USA

The Dynamics

Yes I Love You Baby

With voices flying here, there and everywhere, this is a Wigan anthem that has really stood the test of time... Even its weird 'B' side, 'Soul Sloopy' got plays a few years ago!

With an irresistible tempo and a superb falsetto lead riding high on the Ernstat production this stunning dancer was ripe for national release and was picked up by New York's Laurie records from the Detroit based Top Ten label, it is a real shame that it just didn't make it for the boys.

Lovers of the track will be interested to know that there is an unusual out take and instrumental version that were released on a Goldmine/Soul Supply CD.

Top 500 Position: **160**
Original Label: **Mary Jane**
Current Value: **£75**

'A top-notch discovery and perfect for the scene

Donald Moore, Soul Fan, Michigan, USA

Edward Hamilton and the Arabians

Baby Don't You Weep

Back to credibility with collectors' champion Edward Hamilton and the Arabians. Recording as early as 1960 with the group, Edward waxed lyrical on some great sides for Le Mans, Carrie and Mary Jane, as well as working solo - as did the Arabians who featured other lead singers.

Although I personally plum for 'I'm gonna love for you' for danceability factor, I can understand the popularity of 'Weep' as the song is far stronger.

There is a whole heap of Detroit male vocalists who would have made a fantastic 'revue', guys like Gino Washington, Joe Matthews, etc, and Hamilton would probably have topped the bill in this second tier fantasy of mine.

Top 500 Position:	**161**
Original Label:	**Okeh**
Current Value:	**£125 Issue**
	£200 Demo

'Cool as you like... The Major does the business'

Bri Mosely, Soul Fan, Lancashire, UK

Major Harris

Call Me Tomorrow

When the first copy arrived in 1974 the label, artist and title looked 'bob on' for a smasheroo. The reality is collectors loved it, but dancers denounced it as "too slow".

After hanging around for 15 or so years and refusing to lie down, it sort of got its second wind.

Harris of course has a totally credible career, he was one one of the Impacts along with Herb Johnson, cut 'Call Me Tomorrow' during his contract with Okeh before joining the Delfonics, topped off nicely with a worldwide smash on Atlantic with 'Love Won't Let Me Wait' and 'After Loving You'.

Top 500 Position:	**162**
Original Label:	**Impact**
Current Value:	**£150 Issue**
	£200 Demo

'The intro alone makes it a winner'

Carol Harvey, Soul Fan, Stafford, UK

Duke Browner

Crying Over You

First played at Tunstall's Torch, the instrumental and vocal sides gained equal exposure.

Barney 'Duke' Browner was responsible for many productions whilst working for Impact owner Harry Balk but this is by far the strongest. The first 4 bars are really infectious and state clearly the disc's intentions - this is a mean Detroit groove that typifies the scene.

Extensively played by DJ Tony Jebb.

Top 500 Position: **163**
Original Label: **Soul Clock**
Current Value: **£15 Issue**
£50 Demo

'A super niter goodie from '72'

John Thomas, Soul Fan, Nottingham, UK

The Fuller Brothers

Time's A Wasting

Deliciously self satisfying romper from the early 70's featuring Los Angeles based Fuller Brothers.

We often forget the validity of such discs in today's big money scene, but ask yourself this question, what price would you put on this if discovered today?

Quite simply this is the type of record that made Northern Soul what it is... a stunning opening few bars, a feel good song, a terrific hook and a dancers delight!

YES I am biased, not to the cache of oldies I seem to be raving over, but simply towards records bathed in pure magic!

Sure the act had visions of going head to head with Sam and Dave. Fellas don't shatter my ellusions, you'll do for me!

Top 500 Position: **164**
Original Label: **Modern**
Current Value: **£30**

'Long forgotten but an inspiration to many'

Keith Alexander, Soul Fan, Fife, Scotland

Mel Williams

Can It Be Me

Originally played at the Mecca, 'Can It Be Me' found major status at the Casino's Mr M's before going on to be a 6T's classic at the 100 Club.

Fast and furious, this is the business as far as all nighters are concerned. Also recording a demo of Wally Cox's 'This Man', Mel's other giant 'Burn Baby Burn' commands some serious money these days.

One of the best intros ever!

Top 500 Position: **165**
Original Label: **MGM**
Current Value: **£25 Issue**
£35 Demo

'Sending girlie dance sounds soaring to new heights!'

Paula Rose, Soul Fan, Stoke-on-Trent, UK

April Stevens

Wanting You

A stunning dance favourite that actually got a UK release circa 1967. Yep that's right - it's that old standard reworked into a Motown style groove.

Born Carol Lo Tempio at Niagra Falls, April had already achieved chart success working with her brother Nino Tempo - but, in terms of Northern popularity, this one is one of THE all-time greats!

Initially exposed at the Torch in 1972 the track was important in putting MGM on the map amongst Northern collectors.

Top 500 Position: **166**
Original Label: **Capitol**
Current Value: **£20**

'Straight out of the top drawer'

Keith Fielding, Soul Fan, Warwick, UK

Jodi Mathis

Don't You Care Anymore

Difficult to understand the thinking behind record executives at a major label such as Capitol.

Firstly, Mathis is a fine vocalist. The song too is great, and bang on the money during that period of time - but who the hell let her use a name like that? Imagine the ensuing confusion on radio shows of the time - therefore it just got lost in the rush.

The creativity of Ian Levine brought the 45 to the fore far earlier than other more traditional dancers. In terms of floor appeal, it simply has an all round coolness about it, building quickly out of a teasing intro and following the great string arrangement is young Jodi giving the performance of her life.

Top 500 Position: **167**
Original Label: **RCA Victor**
Current Value: **£30**

*'Light the blue touch paper
and stand well back!'*

Jeremy Wright, Soul Fan, London, UK

The Exciters

Blowing Up My Mind

Dynamite and nitro glycerine wails Brenda Reid, as the Exciters make their second entrance into our chart.

Taken from the 'Caviar and Chitlins' album, the subsequent 45 release became a massive club hit.

The group were excellent and had it not been for a volatile relationship between Brenda and the late Herb, the act may have gone even further than the mini revival under Ian Levine.

As a quartet in the early 60's they had a million seller with 'Tell Him', covered in the UK by Billie Davies, and in the US by Dean Parrish slightly changing the lyrics to answer 'Tell Her'.

Top 500 Position: **168**
Original Label: **Calla**
 Issue
 £40 Demo
Current Value: **£30**

'INSTANT'

Tina Royce, Soul Fan, London, UK

Doris Troy

I'll Do Anything

Doris Payne together with Gamble and Huff... It just had to be sensational and IT IS!

First hitting paydirt in 1963 with the original version of 'Just One Look' which was covered by the Hollies, plus of course 'Whatcha Gonna Do About It' this time done over by the Small Faces. A perennial artist she went on to record for the Beatles ill-fated Apple records as well performing backing vocals on Pink Floyd's 'Dark Side Of The Moon' album.

The lady who's life story was documented in the hit West End musical 'Mama I Want To Sing' has here produced a true Northern classic, a record so good in fact that even DJ Tony Blackburn covered it!

Top 500 Position: **169**
Original Label: **HIB**
Current Value: **£150 Issue**
£200 Demo

'Both sides are monumental

Mick Chesterton, Soul Fan, The Wirral, UK

Luther Ingram

Exus Trek / If It's All The Same To You

Both sides of this Wylie/Hestor gem have fulfiled their potential on the Northern scene.

Ingram from Jackson, Mississippi, made his mark with Stax prior to a short lived association with the legendary writers. Strangely enough he also recorded the song 'I Spy For The FBI' which Wylie and Hestor also penned, but hit for Jamo Thomas.

Rare these days to see a vocal and instrumental getting the same amount of plays, but the backing track is one of the greatest instrumentals ever.

Top 500 Position: **170**
Original Label: **Dynovoice**
Current Value: **£40**

'This is the real deal'

Gaynor Forrest, Soul Fan, Hampshire, UK

The Invitations

What's Wrong With Me Baby?

Although running second to 'Ski-ing in the snow', the maturity of 'baby' has the scene buzzing again.

Released here on Stateside, it has the typical Curtis Mayfield links and though it may be a New York recording it does have the Windy City feel to it.

The clip-clop backbone, faultless harmony and solid hook helps it to cross the finish line in record time.

The band hail from NYC, and recorded for Diamond, MGM, Dyno Voice, Big Tree, Red Greg and Silver Blue. They toured the UK in the 60's masquerading as the 'original' Drifters with Herman Colefield as the front man. Lew Kirton who is no stranger to the scene took over as lead in 1972.

Top 500 Position: **171**
Original Label: **Capitol**
Current Value: **£20 Demo**
£10 Issue

Nancy Wilson

The End Of Our Love

'As someone remarked at the time 'they're playing a record by Shirley Bassey''

Noel Barrington, Soul Fan, Wales, UK

An unusually brilliant offering from the legendary Nancy Wilson. It is the type of 45 you would never look for, until exposure of course.

The 'this is the end' chorus makes it, accompanied by the slick Vine Street production.

'Ms. Jazz' from Columbus, Ohio was recording as early as 1956 and surprisingly had only two hits, the flip 'Face It Girl It's Over' being one of them.

The lady herself was the 'all hidden treasure' that the majors were unfocused on, however the great director Don Siegel used two of her tracks in the 'B' movies The Killers and Charley Varrick, which raised her profile.

Top 500 Position: **172**
Original Label: **Ric-Tic**
Current Value: **£8 Issue**
£50 Demo

JJ Barnes

Please Let Me In

'JJ's finest Soul sound'

Dennis Coffey,
Guitar Legend, Artist and Producer, USA

'Please Let Me In' has the distinction of being one of the first Solid Hitbound productions supervised by Don Davis, Pat Lewis and George Clinton.

Discovered by a young Ian Levine in a New Orleans junk shop in 1968 it was loaned to Les Cokell, resident DJ at the Twisted Wheel. It caused a real stir and this fantastic 1965 recording was quickly picked up by other DJs around the UK. Thousands of over stocks quickly arrived from the States somewhat stunting its financial growth.

This really is a fantastic record!

Top 500 Position:	**173**
Original Label:	**RCA Victor**
Current Value:	**£300 Issue**
	£150 Demo

'That unique Detroit sound again'

Alan Mahoney, Soul Fan, North Wales, UK

Willie Kendrick

Change Your Ways

The GWP/Pied Piper production team settled in at RCA in 1966 and made for the major a series of fantastic sides. The list of artists they handled looks like a who's who of northern, including, The Hesitations, Freddie Butler, The Metros, Lorraine Chandler, etc. Not all were on the 'nipper' logo, but the best certainly were.

Kendrick has two other excellent 45's - but this is the best of 'em with triple tracked backing vocals, tip-top lead and that big Motor City groove.

Top 500 Position:	**174**
Original Label:	**Coral**
Current Value:	**£125 Issue**
	£100 Demo

'A gem of an artist even in the 60's at 15 years old'

Sidney Barnes, Writer, Chicago, USA

Patti Austin

Take Away The Pain Stain

Thank heavens for the French CD retrospective released in 1999. The recordings for Coral are some of the best non-sellers the scene has ever witnessed.

We all have our favourites, but it is this raucous dancer from '66 has been a consistent turntable hit since '73.

Is it any wonder the lady went on to better things being the Goddaughter of Quincy Jones and making her first recordings for adverts at just 4 years old?

She also has a US No. 1 to her credit in 1982 in duet with James Ingram as well a providing vocals for Quincy's legendary 'The Dude' album.

A 'better' offer in 1998 saw Ms. Austin plum for a Carribean jazz festival as opposed to rainy Fleetwood, and though she made the right decision financially, I doubt it emotionally!

Top 500 Position: **175**
Original Label: **Fat Fish**
Current Value: **£75 Issue**
£100 Demo

'One of the first BIG money sounds'

Nick Regan, Soul Fan, Essex, UK

Leon Heywood

Baby Reconsider

Houston born Heywood has had an indifferent career musically. Recording with Arthur Wright and Cliff Goldsmith in the 60's he went on to have a big US hit in '75 with 'I want to do something freaky to you', moving on to a European hit in 1980 with 'Don't Push It Don't Force It'.Certainly lots of innuendo in Leon's songs.

But we concentrate on the Mirwood-esque 'Baby Reconsider.

At the Twisted Wheel this was almost impossible to get and for a time was the UK's rarest in-demander. A forceful performance with all the regular LA instrumentation in place, (which borrows heavily from the Contours' 'Just A Little Misunderstanding') Haywood must be well proud of this US failure as judging by his video performance recently, he positively revels in it.

Top 500 Position: **176**
Original Label: **Karen**
Current Value: **£70 Issue**
£100 Demo

'Sublime D-town soul'

Sharon Colley, Soul Fan, London, UK

The Soul Twins

Quick Change Artist

Many Sam and Dave types came and went during '66-69, sadly Detroit's Soul Twins were another casualty.

They did however leave us this fantastic memory as well as a three other minor releases for Karen records.

As a live act their potential was spotted by label boss and Ann Arbor radio DJ - Ollie Mclaughlin, who quickly signed them to cash in on the 'soul duet' boom, sadly by '68 they were on their way.

Totally 'golden era' and a definite Top 20 song at the Torch, which spawned many a 'cartwheel'. Now, how DO you do that once again!

Top 500 Position: **177**
Original Label: **Lizard**
Current Value: **£10 Issue**
£30 Demo

NF Porter

Keep On Keeping On

'No matter how hard it gets - keep on - keep strong!'

Bob Evans, Soul Fan, Leicester, UK

Featuring strange keyboards that sound like leftovers from Three Dog Night's 'Mama Told Me Not To Come', this odd 45 had all the makings of the monster floorfiller it became.

Released in 1971 and played to death within months of its initial release, it was until just a few years ago the man's most popular waxing of his two tracks on the scene... That is until the equally enigmatic 'If I Could Only Be Sure' surfaced only a few years ago, rising to massive popularity and a No. 91 placing for NF (Nolan) Porter in this chart.

Top 500 Position: **178**
Original Label: **Columbia**
Current Value: **£100 Issue**
£80 Demo

Lee David

Temptation Is Calling My Name

'A 'tempting' offering from Columbia records'

Jon Lomas, Soul Fan, Greater Manchester, UK

It's hard to find records with the pure magic of Lee David today amongst the easy to find 'average' soul records played in clubs.

This is a top-notch one shot wonder from the little known Columbia artist, who also recorded for Bell and Janus.

The girlie chorus chanting over the first few bars gets the engine warmed up for David to do 0-60 in 3 seconds.

Tracks like this used to keep dance floors full for the DJs - and they continue to do so today. Whilst I remain the proverbial fan of the discoveries of the late 60's/early 70's, I cannot see justification in anyone sneering at true 'Northern' records like Lee David's classic.

Top 500 Position:	**179**
Original Label:	**Arctic**
Current Value:	**£25 Issue**
	£50 Demo

'A mighty Philadelphia Soul classic'

Tom Marlond, Soul Fan, Philadelphia, USA

The Volcanos

(It's Against) The Laws Of Love

The Arctic label produced so many excellent singles that it's hard to believe they did not achieve chart success barring Barbara Mason.

The group, featuring Gene Faith on lead, of course evolved into The Trammps and the 70's proved fruitful for the band.

For label owner Jimmy Bishop and distributors Jamie/Guyden this could have been their worst seller. True, 'Help Wanted' and 'Storm Warning' were minor hits but 'Laws' bombed big time!... until a youngster from Bolton acquired a copy while on a buying trip (for former Swan label owner Ed Balbia and his Manchester based Global records) in Philadelphia.

Richard brought it back and played it at Wigan Casino... the rest, as they proverbially say, is history!

Top 500 Position:	**180**
Original Label:	**Curtom**
Current Value:	**£15**

'Superfly power Soul!'

Robert Bentley,
Soul Fan, Bedfordshire, UK

Curtis Mayfield

Move On Up

Surprisingly enough this is not an easy 45 to find on Curtom largely due to the poor sales in the US. In the UK though it was a different story with the constant radio play turning in a high chart position in 1971.

The Northern Soul involvement comes via DJ Dave Evison who played it one night as 'filler' - this became the birth of the oldies and the rest is history.

The artist, well what can you say apart from probably being the finest songwriter of a generation - he is sorely missed. The legacy of Northern hits such as the Five Stairsteps, the Impressions, Leroy Hutson, Marvin Smith, the Fascinations and many more lives with us forever.

Top 500 Position: **181**
Original Label: **UK Mowest**
Current Value: **£10**

'Darkly compelling'

Cliff Moore, Soul Fan, London, UK

Frankie Valli and the Four Seasons

The Night

Switching to Motown after a long and successful period with Philips, Francis Castellucio and the boys returned with two Mowest singles that caused a real stir on the scene.

Wigan perennial 'The Night', a darkly haunting early 70's cut re-invented the group as far as the Northern scene was concerned... for a bunch of white guys they certainly had a 'Soul' following!

The Motown period was generally disappointing for the band, but like Frankie's 'Your Ready Now' this oddity propelled him into the Northern Hall of Fame one more time!

Top 500 Position: **182**
Original Label: **Salsoul**
Current Value: **£40**

'Modernistic happening on the dance floor'

Chris Holmes, Collector, York, UK

Skip Mahoney

Janice (Don't Be So Blind To Love)

Big shortly after it's initial release and huge one more time.

Skip Mahoney and the boys debuted for DC International in 1974, however their best work was for A-Bet a little later.

Salsoul is the unlikeliest label for Northern deemed as 'too disco', but the label scored on the scene with this one, even though it became one of their poorest sellers - though did get UK release on Underworld.

His band were actively touring in the 80's.

Top 500 Position: **183**
Original Label: **Groove City**
Current Value: **£350**

'An awesome Wigan spin'

John Baggaley, Soul Fan, Luton, UK

Sam Ward

Sister Lee

Singing Sammy Ward, who also recorded as Little Sammy Ward, was very much one of the old school R&B singers, with his first recordings in the late fifties. Initially kicked off by the fame of his brother, Billy Ward of the Dominoes fame, he went on to become one of Motown's earliest recording artists, cutting both solos and duets (with Mabel John) as well as working as a staff writer.

From the Groovesville stable this great cut has remained a major player on the golden playlist up North.

Top 500 Position: **184**
Original Label: **Fame**
Current Value: **£200 Issue**
              £75 Demo

'A classic Penn/Oldham song'

Bobby Simpson, Soul Fan, Glasgow, Scotland

Art Freeman

Slippin' Around With You

One of two releases on Fame for Art who also worked for 'Jumbo', 'Slippin'' is very much an old school romper from '66 that gained a UK release on Atlantic.

If it does sound a little 'too sweet' for the Fame sound, the Northern scene see that as an advantage.

Girls weaving in and out of Freeman's tale of cheat and lie, the production as you would expect is spot on. I particularly like the synthesiser sound at the beginning, now that <u>was</u> ahead of its time in 1966!

Top 500 Position: **185**
Original Label: **Deto**
Current Value: **£250**

'O Level Maths at school on a Monday - after a two all-nighters? I just know I'm not going to pass!'

Bob Lowe, Soul Fan, Glasgow, Scotland

Ronnie McNeir

Sitting In My Class/
Isn't She A Pretty Girl

The superb 1968 double-sider is Ronnie's first record - and he is of course no stranger to the UK having worked with Ian Levine and Expansion records.

Whilst these Northern Soul gems are held dear by our scene he has risen to become truly legendary on the Modern scene with recordings for RCA, Prodigal, Motown (Berry Gordy had previously wooed him in the sixties hoping to sign him for the short lived Workshop Jazz label) and many others.

This, his inaugural recording, got a reissue in 1978 itself, complete with a remix!

Top 500 Position: **186**
Original Label: **Atlantic**
Current Value: **£40**

'The telephone ring is just about the best gimmick to be aired on the scene'

Terry Hamilton,
Soul Fan, Greater Manchester, UK

Tony and Tyrone

Please Operator

From the creative intro, the duet roar through this strange phone routine to great effect.

The duo recorded two fine sides for Columbia as well as working for Ston-Roc and G.M., but it's the commerciality of this Atlantic master that really does the business.

The infectious lyric and rhythm turn the ordinary melody into something else. The single first brought to our attention by DJ Ian Levine is also unique in the fact that the last few seconds are spoken, that in itself is a rarity.

Top 500 Position: **187**
Original Label: **Pandora/ Mohawk**
Current Value: **£400/£40**

'A great 100mph stormer!'

Rachel Twiss, Soul Fan, Manchester, UK

Rita Dacosta

Don't Bring Me Down

Many years ago the late Irv Spice, owner of the Mohawk label told me of his great desire to chart this good but unauthodox effort from 1968.

The timing of the discovery could not have been better as it's tailor made for a 'Casino' type venue the eventual home of its popularity.

A piano and bass intro coupled with Dacosta and wailing gals pleading 'Don't Bring Me Down' was as inspiring as many other 45's with enhanced reputations.

Still immensely popular today at most revivals you can pick up the Mohawk copy (which is still the original) quite inexpensively-the rarer Pandora copy is extremely hard to find.

Top 500 Position: **188**
Original Label: **Neptune**
Current Value: **£20 Issue £35 Demo**

'Just who the hell is 'Ponch' and what IS he going to show her?'

Dave Lee, Soul Fan, South Wales, UK

The Vibrating Vibrations

Surprise Party For Baby

Already featured with the classic 'Cause You're Mine', this later single was practically a new release when exploding onto the scene at the Mecca in 1971.

The intro and subsequent 'Hey, Hey, Hey, Hey'... harmony work a treat in dragging you onto the dancefloor. A further hook, 'Hope She's Going To Show Up' is typical Gamble and Huff, being highly reminiscent of Intruders cuts of a couple of years later.

Absolutely IRRESISTIBLE.

Top 500 Position:	**189**
Original Label:	**Erica**
Current Value:	**£1,000**

'A galloping Chicago mega-rarity'

Keith Murphy, Soul Fan, Lancashire, UK

Jimmy Burns

I Really Love You

A sensational side that gets everybody groovin', if only there were more copies to go around!

Even though it's so obscure many DJ's are only too happy to play the later UK release on Grapevine.

Written by Bobby James, he himself doing a version, the track is a worthy Top 500 entrant.

Burns, a native of the Windy City also recorded for Tip Top, Expo and Minit, but it is this glorious release on Erica that got the all important 'North of Watford' totally soul shakin'.

Top 500 Position:	**190**
Original Label:	**Ric-Tic**
Current Value:	**£15 Issue**
	£25 Demo

'Just unbeatable'

Terry West, Soul Fan, Cornwall, UK

Laura Lee

To Win Your Heart

Born Laura Rundless, daughter of a Gospel Choir leader, I must agree with Ian Levine's summation of her roots being buried deep in the Gospel style.

Vocal to 'Festival Time' (chart position 104) 'To Win Your Heart' features male backing vocals by JJ Barnes and Edwin Starr (WOW!).

Laura really is a superb singer who went on to record some great material with for Chess, Cotillion, Hot Wax and Invictus, but it is this great Ric-Tic outing that became a Mecca anthem in 1971.

Top 500 Position: **191**
Original Label: **Gateway**
Current Value: **£10**

*'The biggest single of
the first wave'*

Jim Ryan, Soul Fan, London, UK

Donnie Elbert

A Little Piece Of Leather

New Orleans born vocalist with a killer falsetto, and although he had established himself as an accomplished R&B virtuoso in the 50's, it was this 1965 recording for Gateway and subsequent re-recording for All Platinum that gave him Euro success.

In fact he moved to the UK in 1964 to get married.

Business wise he was pretty shrewd too becoming A&R director for Polygram in Canada during the 80's.

The track is legendary amongst Mod/Soul boys and along with the driving 90mph beat Elbert wails that highly pitched falsetto onto the half inch master.

He sadly passed away in January 1989, and is sorely missed.

Top 500 Position: **192**
Original Label: **Soul**
Current Value: **£8 Issue**
£30 Demo

*'Six by Six' captured
everyone at the Wheel'*

Gary Sweeger, Soul Fan, Scotland, UK

Earl Van Dyke and the Motown Brass

Six By Six

Apart from being one of the great Motown session guys, Earl scored with several of his own tracks between 1964-67.

The unusual title has a lot to answer for as it became a myth in as much as several people claimed to have 'heard the vocal' by Tony Turner on Musicor.

Kidology aside, I'll stick with this delightful brass bombing instrumental. The groove is sort of Herb Alpert meets Berry Gordy, as the vibrant percussion makes way for the trumpet solos which are so tuneful my Bert Kaempfert loving mother would probably demand the side on her shopping list of easy favourites.

Top 500 Position: **193**
Original Label: **Thomas**
Current Value: **£80**

'Hear the screaming whistle of the Psychedelic Express'

Beth Keating, Soul Fan, London, UK

Saxie Russell

Psychedelic Soul

Born Vernon Taylor, Saxie has made a superb one-off for Eddie Thomas' stable, blowing his horn as if his life depended on it.

There's total dancefloor mania every time this is played and it features excellent vocals to boot! Why this was a one-off recording I will never know!

'Psychedelic Soul' was the ultimate Northern floorshaker at just about every Soul Night in 1974.

Top 500 Position: **194**
Original Label: **Pye**
Current Value: **£60**

'A brilliant British Soul effort'

Gavin Potter,
Soul Fan, Greater Manchester, UK

Kenny Bernard

What Love Brings

Bernard hails from Sydenham in Kent, but is based in Norfolk.

He found himself at the forefront of the scene in 1974 when DJ Richard Searling gave the sound its initial airing, subsequent discoveries such as 'Ain't No Soul', 'The Tracker' and 'Isn't It A Good Idea' failed to make it.

His 'Pity My Feet' recorded for CBS was also popular but it was 'What Love Brings' that was his Northern swan song, massive at Wigan it is today largely forgotten.

As an interesting aside, David Bowie played Sax in his band at one time!

Top 500 Position: **195**
Original Label: **White Label**
Current Value: **£20**

'It's a real surprise that Motown failed to release it at the time'

Robin Chivers, Soul Fan, Suffolk, UK

Brenda Holloway

Reconsider

Brenda Holloway's popularity in the UK has always been a key component for her during the revival years.

When the amazing 'Reconsider' was unearthed Brenda sort of re-invented herself... one more time.

Hailing from Atascadero, California, the history of the lady is one of 'almost, but not quite', with her co-authorship on the standard 'You Made Me So Very Happy'. The brilliance of 'When I'm Gone' and 'Just Look What You've Done' and the real glamour of her live performances show us that Motown lost a real gem.

Top 500 Position: **196**
Original Label: **Parlophone**
Current Value: **£400 Issue**
£150 Demo

'TB Super Soul'

Jimmy Thomas, Artist, London, UK

Jimmy Thomas

The Beautiful Night

Thomas was one of the Ike and Tina Turner Revue who settled in England in the late 60's after a brief recording spell with Mirwood records.

Just when you thought he could never top his immaculate 'Where There's A Will' , JT debuts on our side of the Atlantic with a masterpiece.

The song is sexy, and with the amphetamines rolling at the Torch, DJ Tony Jebb with his afghan coat and groupies in tow, this was the disc to 'get off' on!

Jimmy and I made a record with Shirley Lewis in 1983 and my passion for this work of art allowed me to slip out to Highbury to see my beloved SWFC. Jimmy I owe you!

Top 500 Position: **197**
Original Label: **Columbia**
Current Value: **£40**

'Wigan - of course!'

Carol Smith, Soul Fan, London

Wayne Gibson

Under My Thumb

Written by Mick Jagger and Keith Richard this Stones album track found it's way on to the UK Columbia label via Wayne Gibson.

He had several cracks at playing 'superstar' with a career starting in 1963 on Decca, before moving to Pye, Parlophone, Columbia and finally back to Pye.

The latter actually licensed the in-demand 'Thumb' from producer Terry King.

In theory it is a fairly good record, soulfully executed by Gibson before petering out when chart success removed the scene's blinkers. For a time though this was massive.

Top 500 Position: **198**
Original Label: **GSF**
Current Value: **£80**

'Smooth as silk for this nifty New York mover'

Keith Wilson, Soul Fan, Cheshire UK

The Anderson Brothers

I Can See Him Loving You

Written by Ray Dahrouge who recorded the track himself a couple of years later.

Absolute killer new recording in 1974, although never issued. The perfect accompaniment to the changeover from mono to stereo.

DJ Ian Levine who was the master at diversity within the scene, played this floating oddity with real conviction.

Strangely enough I met Lloyd Price then owner of GSF, who vaguely remembered the 'nice bunch of white guys'. Never released commercially, the single got no airplay but has become a firm favourite over the years.

Top 500 Position: **199**
Original Label: **A&M**
Current Value: **£100 Issue**
£40 Demo

'A major adrenaline rush'

Mike Stevenson, Soul Fan, Derbyshire, UK

Towanda Barnes

You Don't Mean It

Recorded in 1968, this New York scorcher is a full on gospel tinged romp over an erstwhile lyric with Barnes and backing vox, yelling 'you don't mean it'. The percussion is immaculate and straight out of the King Errison drum school.

Discovered by DJ Ian Levine at the famed Blackpool Mecca, from the same year you may also remember the Ohio Players' .excellent version for Compass.

Top 500 Position: **200**
Original Label: **MGM**
Current Value: **£40**

'Powerful, rhythmic and destined for the scene'

Brian Moore,
Soul Fan, Greater Manchester, UK

Dottie Cambridge

Cry Your Eyes Out

Typical of the time, Cambridge with amplified vocals races through the 60's song with ease.

Though she is none other than Dorothy Moore of Dollettes, Poppies and 'Misty Blue' fame she only had one other attempt as Dottie Cambridge by way of a cover version of 'She's About A Mover'.

One of a clutch of discoveries from Bradford market whereby stall owners Bostocks had acquired thousands of MGM, Verve and other odd American 45's.

1973 was to be the golden year for a good all round Northern Soul single with an anthemic hookline to savour.

Top 500 Position: **201**
Original Label: **Legend**
Current Value: **£25**

'Could have easily been covered by Chicago'

Lester Shaw, Soul Fan, London, UK

A Case Of Tyme

Manifesto

The weirdness on Northern knows no bounds as this rock single from 1970 shook the scene back in '74.

This band who were oblivious to the scene here, must have thought they were on to a real winner, capitalising on the 'rock with horns' sound the US was championing at the time.

Lead singer James Lewis is no David Clayton Thomas or Robert Lamm but he sure delivered excitement to their one and only offering.

In terms of the dancefloor it ranks in the Top 40, although short lived on the scene.

Top 500 Position: **202**
Original Label: **Columbia**
Current Value: **£150 Issue**
£30 Demo

'A wonderful Motown cover'

Mark Gregson, Soul Fan, Dublin, Eire

George Carrow

Angel Baby (Don't You Ever Leave Me)

I suspect Carrow is a white singer signed by a major label to break more soulful recordings a little more easily.

Still, he serves up a treat, with Stevie Wonder's original put well and truly in the shade.

In fact Darrell Banks' version also emulates the wonderman too. The Columbia man, who later moved to United Artists, though pips it with just a tad more energy and aggression to totally wow all dancers.

The track hurtles at speed (no pun intended!) and has the typical big city feel about it. When playlisted at the Torch alongside the many songs in the book, you can understand why this type of track was so popular. Another cover by the

Another version by the '3 1/2' on Parkway featured none other than Jeff Conaway (Kenicke in Grease!).

Top 500 Position: **203**
Original Label: **Decca**
Current Value: **£150**

*'Frighteningly popular
for AT LEAST a decade'*

Chris Luckett,Soul Fan, Middlesborough, UK

Frankie and Johnny

I'll Hold You

Marvin and Tammi they were not, but as far as the scene goes they outdid the Motowners for a while.

Sounding more like R and J Stone, the duet worked a treat on a European song and licensed to Hickory in the US.

It is basically a boy/girl song with Q and A as it's main content. Recorded in 1966, it has remained very popular, and while I am pleased the commercial sounding 45 that was a real Wigan giant is still being played, it is somewhat looked down upon by serious collectors.

Top 500 Position: **204**
Original Label: **Minit**
Current Value: **£150 Issue**
£100 Demo

'A gorgeous soulful melody'

Steve Smith, Soul Fan, Nottinghamshire, UK

Shawn Robinson

My Dear Heart

A top tune of 1974, 'My Dear Heart' is full of vitality with a cute melody and the customary vibes tinkling about.

More recently a version ostensibly by Diana Ross (it isn't listed in the Jobete publishing catalogue) surfaced courtesy of collector/DJ Gilly. Many will also remember dealer and producer Simon Soussan's US smash hit with the Patti Brooks cut 'After Dark', featured in 'Thank God It's Friday'... Following on from Shalamar's 'Simon's Theme' he did yet another piece of major Northern Soul 'homage' - ie he pinched the tune good and proper!

Top 500 Position: **205**
Original Label: **Wingate**
Current Value: **£10**

'Try saying the title when under the influence'

Gary Chalmers, Soul Fan, Essex, UK

The Dramatics

Inky Dinky Wang Dang Do

The group lead by Ron Banks scored in the early 70's on Volt with some superb singles. We concentrate though on the oddly titled 45 cut in 1966. The appeal is all there to see with an explosive intro followed by bass lead and excitable harmony , topped off with a 'whoooo' at the end of each title line.

That's the cue for the relevant gymnastics, and while this all sounds a little odd, it has to be placed in the context of one of the most credible Soul groups.

Top 500 Position: **206**
Original Label: **Warner Brothers**
Current Value: **£150 Issue**
£100 Demo

'Sounding much better than even Kim Weston's version'

Graham Toothill, Soul Fan, Worcester, UK

Alice Clark

You Hit Me (Right Where It Hurt Me)

George Kerr wrote this song while under contract to Jobete publishing. Kim Weston recorded the original but it was never released due to the abundance of great hits that were 'ready to go' at Grand Ave.

The publishing arm were quick to spot any opportunity and when Kerr suggested to Warner Brothers he had found an excellent new singer in Alice Clark the song was born again.

It did not fair too well until the cravings of the north of England discovered the sound in 1973, where it has remained a classic ever since.

Top 500 Position: **207**
Original Label: **Soul Hawk**
Current Value: **£20 Issue**
£50 Demo

'That smouldering intro suddenly erupts into a magnificent dancer'

Gary Marshall, Soul Fan, London, UK

Jimmey 'Soul' Clark

(Come On And Be My) Sweet Darlin'

Clark, who originally recorded as plain Jimmy Clark became a protegé of Detroit producers Richard 'Popcorn' Wylie and Tony Hestor and recorded several undiscovered gems during 66-69. The UK not only found Clark's work, they uncovered a plethora of unreleased material from Wylie.

A long association with the UK has flourished with the Detroit Executives, Tommy Neal, Theresa Lindsay etc.

One-time boyfriend of the great Betty Lavette, Clark's dance anthem is superb with the almost ad-libbed intro leading into the big motortown backbeat of this immensely catchy record.

Top 500 Position: **208**
Original Label: **Decca**
Current Value: **£100**

'Wigan meets a TV ad'

Gary Cole, Soul Fan, Essex, UK

John E Paul

I Wanna Know

A record I had in my collection in 1971 before I had chance to expose it!

Still, DJ Russ Winstanley had the nouse to play it to death in the mid-70's to the rapturous applause of the Casino faithful.

Interestingly enough this British only release has now reached a new audience via the exposure of a 'cat food' commercial. Bizarre or what!

The single is a full-on romp aimed at giving the UK some credibility against the influx of star quality soul that was being played on Radio Caroline, Luxembourg and the discotheques. It sort of works!

Top 500 Position: **209**
Original Label: **Strata East**
Current Value: **£20**
                      (French 45)

'Changing the course of Northern Soul'

Paula Cole, Soul Fan, Essex, UK

Gil Scott Heron

The Bottle

Played shortly after release on the 'Winter in America' album, Heron, the ever creative poet, eventually caused a worldwide stir with this sensational creation. Initially the preserve of the Northern scene this unique track eventually 'crossed-over' to disco-funk popularity

The value of the 45 is due to the French release, all other copies being the album version which featured a longer mix.

Incredibly successful although it still attracts critics for it's non-Northerness.

Top 500 Position: **210**
Original Label: **Super Sound**
Current Value: **£200**

'Southern Soul at it's very best'

Mike Rogers, Soul Fan, Lancashire, UK

Eula Cooper

Let Our Love Grow Higher

An early 70's single that became an instant smash and, for a time at least, an ultra-rare soaring gospel groove from Georgia that was exclusive to Blackpool's Mecca.

Originally signed to Clintone, Ms. Cooper had other 45s hanging around titled 'Beggars Can't Be Choosey' and 'Standing In For Love' about the same time, but the real winner is 'Higher'. It has a lot of ingredients that many 80's divas used to full effect, with wails and yells throughout.

A real shame there was no accapella flip, then we would see some sampling action.

Top 500 Position: **211**
Original Label: **Gordy**
Current Value: **£6 Issue**
£15 Demo

'Undoubtedly one of the best records ever'

Guy Stevens (deceased),
DJ, London, UK

The Contours

Just A Little Misunderstanding

Possibly one of the first big 'imports' at the time. Unbelievably a non-hit in the US it recovered to secure a UK chart placing in 1970 as a result of its Northern popularity.

Yep, British radio eventually loved it and once again we would have a Top 10 Northern favourite had it not been 'commercialised' so soon. Billy Gordon, Billy Hoggs, Joe Billingsea, Sylvester Potts, Huey Davies and the late Hubert Johnson. The legendary Dennis Edwards joined in late '66 and became the lead prior to his move to the Tempts.

This is the kind of record that paved the way for Northern Soul.

Top 500 Position: **212**
Original Label: **RCA Victor**
Current Value: **£50 Issue**
£30 Demo

'The Liberaces of Soul'

Yvonne Parker, Soul Fan, Lancashire, UK

Derek and Ray

Interplay

For some, this is about as ghastly as it gets, to others the single represents the time of their lives.

Either way, soul is cast out as this harpsichord led instrumental sounds more at home with curiosity collectors.

To be positive though, this really wowed the dancers and still has a fan base to this day despite the critics.

RCA in 1967 released an updated version of Dragnet to support the TV series, on the flip side they used the throwaway 'Interplay'. As is often the case the other side becomes in-demand, but as quite a few artists have been traced in recent times this pairing can forget that exclusive appearance in Blackburn!

Top 500 Position: **213**
Original Label: **Blue Star**
Current Value: **£700**

'Oh-so sought-after'

Dave Flynn, DJ and Soul Fan, London, UK

Arin Demain

Silent Treatment

Writing a book and charting the most popular northern sides should be easy. I can reveal after six painstaking months I am still rejigging positions due to obscure singles like this coming out of the sub-conscious and staking their claim in the popularity stakes.

Very few own the original, and you could (if on the sidelines) be forgiven for thinking it therefore can't be that popular.

Demain's attempt has worked, people do love it, despite it happening in the wrong country for the guy who also hit the Northern scene with his recordings under the aliases 'Karl Evans' for Skyway (see Louise Lewis) and 'Ernie Lucas' on Okeh.

Top 500 Position: **214**
Original Label: **Philips**
Current Value: **£10 Issue**
£15 Demo

'Raw and dirty 60's Soul'

Brenden Mac, Soul Fan, Merseyside, UK

The Flamingos

Boogaloo Party

Released on Philips in '66, played at the Mojo in Sheffield, Pete Stringfellow's fave rave in '67, and re-released in '69 climbing to No. 26. We could be staring at the first Northern single to ever make the British charts!

Fairly easy to see the popularity, with the party like atmosphere running through at wild animal pace.

The group had been around since '52, launched by Zeke and Jake Carey. Tommy Hunt joined for a while too though despite stories to the contrary, it was Doug McClure and not Tommy who sang lead on 'Party'.

Collectively they will be known for the 50's hits, but this 1966 New York romp put the words 'all nighter' firmly on the map.

Top 500 Position: **215**
Original Label: **Tollie**
Current Value: **£200 Issue**
£150 Demo

'Big Beat ballads and Fletcher go arm in arm'

Tim Garstang, Soul Fan, Sheffield, UK

Sam Fletcher

I'd Think It Over

Acknowledged as the first 'big beat ballad' that was to gain entry level to the scene in the early 80's.

The record is excellent and with timing being everything it helped bring about a change in the persona of many soul nights.

Recording for Vee-Jay subsidiary, Tollie, in 1964 Fletcher was an uncrowned Prince of middle of the road balladeers.

No one at the time could have realised the impact of this marvellous side, and this one will go down in history as the song that changed the mood of the scene.

Surprisingly the UK was not in fact the first European nation to appreciate Sam's talents, this record was very popular on Belgium's 'popcorn' scene of the seventies and spawned a 'lookalike' bootleg that has become the bain of UK collectors.

Top 500 Position: **216**
Original Label: **Chess**
Current Value: **£25 Issue**
£40 Demo

'The instant floor filler to get the groove going

Stuart McKenzie, Soul Fan, Scotland

Marlena Shaw

Let's Wade In The Water

The vocal prowess of Ms. Shaw just shades the classic instrumental from Ramsey Lewis, although intertwined at various junctions of exposure, the vocal wins hands down by almost incessant play in the 80's.

The trend has continued via the scooter enthusiasts with both versions securing major airtime.

Originally recording for Cadet in the US, Marlena has received many accolades, none more so than her version of 'Go away little boy', but in terms of forceful dancefloor action this Richard Evans arrangement could be one of the first ever 'rarities' to attach itself to the scene.

'Let's Wade In The Water' is actually an adaption of an old negro spiritual, listen to the lyrics you'll find them interesting!

Top 500 Position:	**217**
Original Label:	**SPQR/ LeGrand**
Current Value:	**£40 SPQR**
	£80 Le Grand

'Soaring Soul from Virginia'

Mark Thompson, Soul Fan, London, UK

Lenis Guess

Just Ask Me

One of the scenes favourite oldies, the oddly named front man evolved out of the SPQR stable which spawned pop artists Jimmy Soul and Gary US Bonds.

Unusually the record hails from Norfolk, Virginia instead of the usual NY, LA or Detroit.

There is a Elsie Strong version, released some years later, and a release on Route in the UK in '75 inspired a cover by Etta Thomas. A good trading name if nothing else.

Incidentally SPQR is, strangely, an abbreviation for the motto of ancient Rome - meaning 'For the senate and the people of Rome' - not perhaps the most obvious source for a record company name!

Top 500 Position:	**218**
Original Label:	**Decca**
Current Value:	**£100 Issue**
	£75 Demo

'Delightfully obscure and truly exquisite'

Mick Rogers, Soul Fan, Derby, UK

Lee Roye

Tears (Nothing But Tears)

A track that typifies the scene. Cute vocal and song, unknown singer, and smart dancer to boot!

Lee Roye hails from Burlington, New Jersey and got picked ahead of JR Bailey to record the song. Bailey's version being a one off acetate only.

Rather moorish, if not only for the 'ah tears nothing but tears' hook. It brought together both sexes together on the large maple wooden sprung dance floor.

Definitively Wigan, the 45 is one of a clutch of great obscure soul sides for Decca.

Top 500 Position: **219**
Original Label: **Kent Anniversary Single**
Current Value: **£10**

'THE 80's anthem'

Sean Chapman,
Soul Fan, Buckinghamshire, UK

Melba Moore

The Magic Touch

An unreleased master from 1967, that should have been released by Musicor.

The scene had already sampled Ms. Moore on 'Don't Cry, Sing A Long With The Music', but this, the original version of The Bobby Fuller Four track played at Wigan is far better.

Recorded in New York, Moore was known as an accomplished backing singer working with Aretha, Jerry Butler etc. One of her 'back up' friends was Valerie Simpson who encouraged her to go solo, unfortunately the Musicor deal was unproductive, but try telling that to the Northern faithful who positively adore it!

Top 500 Position: **220**
Original Label: **Sound Stage 7**
Current Value: **£300**

'Richie sounds brilliant for an unknown'

Malc Warman,
Soul Fan, Birmingham, UK

Little Richie

Just Another Heartache

Bass drum intro followed by horns a'plenty and rasping vocal over the John Richbourg production.

John R was a DJ and label owner who nurtured local talent in the hope of gaining lucrative deals.

There seemed to be a couple of 'littles' on SS7 (Hank and Richie) and ironically they both found fame not in Nashville but England.

Despite the authentic Soul sound, Richie turns out to be a white artist... I mean what self respecting black singer would have a name like that - well apart from Little Richard!...

Top 500 Position: **221**
Original Label: **Holton**
Current Value: **£75**

"S-T-O-M-P-E-R"

Bob Harris,
Soul Fan, London, UK

Rufus Lumley

I'm Standing

Discovered on UK Stateside, later followed by the US copies on Holton. The track is simply full on excitement with Rufus wreaking havoc over the unbelievable brass arrangement.

This white boy, who looked suspiciously like Billy Idol, later weighed in with a cut called 'Stronger Than Me' for his RCA album, which became briefly popular and a version of Fats Domino's 'I'm In Love Again' on Skyscraper - mis-credited as Rufus Lunley.

Discovered by 60s collector Bob Stevens.

Top 500 Position: **222**
Original Label: **Bonnie**
Current Value: **£1,500**

'The group display all the characteristics of the 50's'

Rod Keene,
Soul Fan, Belfast, Northern Ireland, UK

The Magnetics

Lady In Green

Both sides of this ultra rare 45 for Bonnie of Detroit are exquisite. The top side has been around the scene now for over 20 years and although the single is almost impossible to get, it has connected well with the dancers and probably has benefited from the real scarcity.

The group recorded in the 60's as The Volumes for Twirl, American Arts, Inferno and Impact, sometimes featuring Duke Browner and are definitely not to be confused with the groups who recorded for Ra-Sel, Sable, JV and Sound Trip.

Top 500 Position: **223**
Original Label: **Hem**
Current Value: **£1,000**

*'Vocally this track
is truly exceptional'*

Eddie Singleton, Label Owner, USA

The Cashmeres

Show Stopper

Recording for Hubba Hubba, Hem and Ninandy, the group from Washington lead by Eddie Jefferson recorded this delightful single in 1967, produced by Shrine supremo Eddie Singleton.

Breaking big at the Casino in 1979 for Richard, I'm not sure if I actually discovered it, but when I came across it in a basement in Baltimore I absolutely flipped.

This wonderful sound's popularity, together with it's flip, 'Don't Let The Door Hit Your Back' (though this has been more popular in its unissued alternate version), has seen unbroken dancefloor and collector popularity ever since its first spins even though few DJs own a copy.

Top 500 Position: **224**
Original Label: **Andre**
Current Value: **£100**

*'An annoyingly exciting
production'*

Miles Grayson,
Producer, Los Angeles, USA

The Mylestones

The Joker

During the last 30 years any underground scene needs a little quirkiness to draw attention to itself. LA producer Miles Grayson drew upon the soul rhythms of '66 with the fascination of TV hit 'Batman'. The result being a wild 'freak out' dancer that was lying in the warehouse gagging to be heard.

Timing is everything in business and cue record dealer Simon Soussan who discovered the single in '74, sent dubs over under the guise of 'Butch Baker' and ka-pow an instant Northern Soul hit.

Cover versions were instantaneous with UK labels Creole and Casino Classics racing for the novelty hit.

I, together with fellow Casino DJ Richard Searling played it 'til the grooves wore out (you had to!), but it was our 'team leader' Russ Winstanley who really hammered it. Club goers cheekily still call him 'the Wigan Joker', that in itself compliments the size of this 45!

Top 500 Position: **225**
Original Label: **Atlantic**
Current Value: **£50**

*'Replacing his other giant
is a feat in itself'*

Robert Harrison, Soul Fan, Chester, UK

Prince Phillip Mitchell

I'm So Happy

Leapfrogging over his mammoth 'Free For All' is the 1979 single 'I'm So Happy'. The reason for the overtaking is that 'Happy' has quite simply fast tracked on two fronts. Firstly it has been constantly played since the early 80's while his original biggie for Shout has dipped over the years.

Secondly, the scooterist crowds totally dig it, and many a rally will have witnessed the ditching of the Lambretta to race to raid the dancefloor!

Mitchell started out in the 60's with Smash recording 'Keep On Talking' which is featured in the top 500 by James Barnett.

Top notch recordings for Event and Ichiban have made the 'Prince' a sought after commodity in collector circles with 'I'm So Happy' being particular sought after, it seems that because collectors opted for the album rather than the single in '79 that it is pretty scarce.

Top 500 Position: **226**
Original Label: **Amy**
Current Value: **£150**

*'The odd sounding title is
enough to turn anyone off,
the fact is, it is excellent'*

Nick Turner, Soul Fan, London, UK

Tony Middleton

Paris Blues

The first of two entrants for The Willows' lead singer, Tony Middleton.

Following a brief hit on Melba in 1956, Middleton remained one of the great unsung heroes of rhythm and blues.

The 45 hit the scene at a strange but opportunist stage, as pop dancers were infiltrating big style. Paris Blues and its somewhat 'middle-of-the-road' big-voiced vocal made an almost idiosyncratic impact on the scene which lit the touch paper for the man's other recordings.

Top 500 Position: **227**
Original Label: **La-Cindy**
Current Value: **£500 Issue**
£1,500 Demo

'Massive first play'

John Atkinson, Soul Fan, Burnley, UK

Ernest Mosley

Stubborn Heart

Producer Eddie La Shea from Chicago cut two versions of the song, the commoner Sheppards was leased to Mirwood in LA, and then the ridiculously hard to find cut on La-Cindy (his wife?).

If any 45's have made giant strides in both play and value look no further than Moseley's one shot wonder.

Major backing vocals wail 'ohhhhh ohhhhhhh I love you' throughout the song with the unknown lead doing a sterling job, unfortunately to no avail commercially.

An Ian Levine discovery.

Top 500 Position: **228**
Original Label: **GM**
Current Value: **£20**

'The rock edge gave the Northern Scene a new twist'

Gary Griffin, Soul Fan, Shropshire, UK

Mr. Flood's Party

Compared To What

Ray Charles, Les McCann and others have put their own mark on this underground Jazz classic. The unusual version by Mr. Floods Party saw a UK release in 1971 and within a year of the Ember issue it became a cult at the Torch all nighter.

Possibly the youthfulness of the recording and a touch of soul realised a winner for the Northern scene. Excellent brass throughout, the song has the stop and start routine which dancers love. Still, a strange sound at the side of a Frank Beverly or Frank Wilson, but immensely popular.

Top 500 Position: **229**
Original Label: **Genuine**
Current Value: **£1,500**

'One of the last major cover-ups'

Derek Whiting, Soul Fan, Lincolnshire, UK

Mr. Soul / Al Scott

What Happened To Yesterday?

Amazingly credited to two different artists this late 60's monster was covered as 'Maurice McAllister' by DJ Richard Searling. Truly speaking, had it not been for discoveries of this magnitude, the scene may have petered out after the closure of Wigan Casino in 1981. Smooth Garland Green type vocals, nice big city sounding back beat, and a hook that repeats the line 'your love is slipping away',which of course is not the title. You can understand the mystery concerning the single, firstly two credited acts, then the title/hook dilemma, all adding up to a real rarity of some repute.

Top 500 Position: **230**
Original Label: **Kapp**
Current Value: **£50 Issue**
£50 Demo

'These boys were definitely 'Soul Supermen''

Tony Hunt, Soul Fan, London, UK

The Hesitations

I'm Not Built That Way

This was first single on the great Kapp label for the Hesitations, their are unconfirmed reports of a preceding 1965 release for the legendary D-Town label entitled 'Remember'.

'I'm Not Built That Way' was taken from the sought-after 'Soul Superman' album (which also spawned a scarce French EP featuring another classic 'She Won't Come Back') and indeed features that title track on the reverse. The group was led by George 'King' Scott (deceased) and remained together until 1969 when their final release for GWP featured Debbie Taylor on lead.

Top 500 Position:	**231**
Original Label:	**Sue**
Current Value:	**£200**

'One of my favourites, it's pleasing to see the UK enjoying it too'

Sidney Barnes, Songwriter, New York

Billy Prophet

What Can I Do?

Prophet's attempt on Sue quickly petered out, as had his previous release on Barry in '65. The track suitably placed for the artist by Sidney Barnes and JJ Jackson (who met while working as writers for Motown's publisher Jobete) and had a taste for the Motor City coupled with the singers New York vocal styling.

Sadly it flopped for Billy (sometimes credited on other 45s as Billy Profit and also an ex-member of the Jive Five) but some nine years later Midlands DJ Pep took his latest find and cultivated another 'top sound'.

Top 500 Position:	**232**
Original Label:	**Tuff**
Current Value:	**£400**

'The catchiness of the record does not detract from the Soul quality'

Ron MacKenzie, Soul Fan, London, UK

Little Joe Roman

When You're Lonesome (Come On Home)

Arguably the same vocalist as Billy Joe Young on Paula with 'I've Got You On My Mind Again' - leastways all the production credits are the same on this unashamed piece of Little Anthony plagiarism.

The Chicago based Tuff Label released some absolute pearlers including Bobby Treetop, E. Rodney Jones etc. With Romans' outing certainly the rarest on the label and most different in production style.

Reminiscent of the California Soul indies such as Danny Monday on Modern, the track has all kinds of 'hooks' rippling through the track without anyone really identifying the title. Maybe that was the problem in the US, making for an instant rarity for us to walk into over in the UK.

Top 500 Position: **233**
Original Label: **Compass**
Current Value: **£100**

'You could offer me your drugs on a silver platter - but I won't take them baby!'

John Gooding, Soul Fan, London, UK

James Bounty

Prove Yourself A Lady

Philadelphia based Bounty was written and produced for by Bobby Eli. Collectors may have come across the dreadful mutant cover version under the name Bryson Bay Brass entitled 'Permanent Injury' - a side swipe at producer Simon Soussan!

With a strong intro that rips straight into an ultra-danceable powerhouse sound, James Bounty's opus was guaranteed to go massive at the Torch.

Other great sides on the label include Helena Ferguson and the Adventurers.

Top 500 Position: **234**
Original Label: **St. Lawrence**
Current Value: **£25 Issue**
 £50 Demo

'Simply the best Northern record ever!'

Tim Brown,
The World's Leading Northern Soul Collector

Johnny Sayles

I Can't Get Enough

As a business colleague of mine Tim Brown said 'It's hard to beat this - I can't believe that such a tremendous record failed to sell at the time', and he's right. A superstar on the underground with efforts for Chi-Town, Mar-V-Lus, Minit and the sensational St. Lawrence.

The production is fantastic, starting with a smouldering intro before erupting into a cymbal crashing, horn blasting frenzy, completed with Sayles sending out a clear message to messrs. Pickett and Womack that a new star has emerged.

As a short footnote, the now-deceased Sayles went on to become quite a smash live act in Alaska!

Top 500 Position: **235**
Original Label: **Four Brothers**
Current Value: **£50**

'To achieve legendary status a 45 has to have atmosphere similar to Sam and Kitty'

Gail Macy, Soul Fan, Stoke-on-Trent, UK

Sam and Kitty

I've Got Something Good

A short lived duet from Chicago, although Singin Sam had a solo 45. Without doubt one of the finest all-nighter records ever. Storming brass intro, bubbling bass line and the duo wail 'I've Got Something Good' with the entire dance floor at the Torch in '72 chanting a replacement for Got with Dropped.

Ah youth! but seriously this is the type of single that raised awareness and to this day keeps us very much young at heart.

Top 500 Position: **236**
Original Label: **Warner Brothers**
Current Value: **£35**

'A Northern legend, Sheen delivers something new to savour...'

Mark Smith, Soul Fan, County Durham, UK

Bobby Sheen

Something New To Do

The Dr. Love man is in fine fettle as his short Warner's career debuts with a fabulous beaty smoocher. A song recorded in Alabama in 1972, it caved in under the weight of the sweet ballads and James Brown influence happening at the time.

The artist has been the lead voice of one of the revived Coasters groups, and is currently living in Los Angeles.

Smooth as you like, this sought after 45 brings most Soul Nights to a classy ending.

Top 500 Position: **237**
Original Label: **Columbia**
Current Value: **£8**

'Pop kitsch - lovely!'

Martin Raynor, Soul Fan, Bretton, UK

Spiral Starecase

More Today Than Yesterday

A sprightly chart outing from a Sacramento outfit which was lead by Pat Upton.

DJ Ian Levine had the nerve to play it and why not - it's superb in its own right.

Rare 45 collectors would ask-why? The fact is this song is about dancing and having a good old sing a long.

Further singles such as 'She's Ready', 'No One For Me To Turn To' and 'Baby What I Mean' stirred up some interest too, but the female sounding male lead coupled with the delightful song makes you feel glad to be part of the 60's and 70's.

Top 500 Position: **238**
Original Label: **Atlantic**
Current Value: **£40**

'The emergence of this B side in the last few years has been something else'

Philip Lee, Soul Fan, Cornwall, UK

The Soul Brothers Six

I'll Be Loving You

The A side 'Some Kind of Wonderful' during the 60's was a regular play at most discos (not all nighters), however the truly remarkable flip 'I'll Be Loving You' has turned into a veritable monster during the past decade even surpassing the popularity of the top side.

The group hailed from Philadelphia and were led by John Ellison recording for Fine, Lyndell, Atlantic and Phil-LA of Soul before disbanding in the 70's, Ellison himself taking the name to his new Canadian base.

Top 500 Position: **243**
Original Label: **Keymen**
Current Value: **£40**

'Sensational mid 60's 45 that has everything'

Tim Ashibende, Collector, Stoke-on-Trent, UK

The Fi-Dels

Try A Little Harder

A group formed by Fred Smith, who had previously recorded on Dore and later signed to Maverick. A record that has been played in just about every Northern club at some stage since it's discovery in 1971.

From a collectability point of view, I rank this among many £2/300 singles, unfortunately the demand is fairly non-existent (why?), and therefore represents the given value.

Coming from the Mirwood stable, the single looks fantastic, never mind the sound. Produced by the great Bob Relf.

Top 500 Position: **244**
Original Label: **Dial**
Current Value: **£15 Issue**
£25 Demo

'Tex scores again with another amusing and original tale'

Mick Allen, Soul Fan, London, UK

Joe Tex

Under Your Powerful Love

Apart from his other book entry 'Show Me',there was a time when another classic might have replaced this 70's racer. 'You Better Believe It' was on everyone's lips for a short time, that is until the 70's collectable started to gather momentum.

'Powerful Love' is now known to be the man's definitive Northern hit, although 'Show Me' slightly edges it in mass appeal. Strictly downhome 'Southern Soul', you can't help but check out the spoken intro, as Tex cheekily listens at the adjoining motel room door to a argument between man and woman, hoping she becomes the damsel in distress. Fellas, we would never do such a thing!

Suddenly as Joe has set the scene for us, he, together with a string arrangement frenzy, tears down the motel room door and... A totally original dance floor smash.

Top 500 Position: **245**
Original Label: **GSF**
Current Value: **£75 (Album)**
£10 Reissue 45

'The week the Northern Scene got real funky'

Bernie Golding, Soul Fan, Lancashire, UK

The Skullsnaps

I'm Your Pimp

You may own a 45 on this 1973 cult classic, which is in fact a late 70's reissue, the original remains the album. The group had minor success on the scene with 'My Hang Up Is You' a UK released single which was a 'Back Stabbers' type effort from this talented NY outfit.

When the oddly sounding 'Pimp' received the inaugural play at Blackpool Mecca in 1975, the usual raised eyebrows were evident as the fresh new groove mingled with the Salvadors etc. Boy, were we creative and brave!

A group formed out of the 60's act the Diplomats.

Top 500 Position: **246**
Original Label: **Roulette**
Current Value: **£40 Issue**
£30 Demo

'The boopity boop intro sent pulses racing'

Geoff Laidlaw,
Soul Fan, Renfrewshire, Scotland

Ila Vann

Can't Help Lovin' That Man Of Mine

DJ Ian Levine gets more than his fair share of adulation in this book, and not surprisingly so, when from the creativity of the last chart entry he skillfully slipped in another 60's recording that is more in line with the roots of the scene.

So, what do we have here, well, the song is the old Rogers and Hammerstein standard, given the full mid 60's soul treatment. Ila Vann was a competent young thing who later went on to release a killer for P.I.P in '73.

Shortly after she found herself with a UK release on Pye Disco Demand, DJ Richard Searling hammered a new 60's version by 'Navy Blue' hitmaker Diane Renay, which at the time was covered up as 'Laura Greene' and even issued as such on UK Grapevine.

Top 500 Position:	**247**
Original Label:	**United Artists**
Current Value:	**£200 Issue**
	£100 Demo

'One of my least successful but certainly a more pleasurable one!'

Carl Douglas, Artist, London, UK

Carl Douglas

Serving A Sentence Of Life

Jamaican born, raised in California, and became an engineer before meeting Pierre Tubbs who produced his first single for UA. A UK only release, Douglas later found fame recording with producer Biddu with the worldwide smash 'Kung Fu Fighting' preceded by another drift into the Northern scene with the UK-recorded 'Marble and Iron' which originally only saw light in the US on Buddah.

Discovered with the centre bashed out at Shudehill Market in 1971 by a long-haired and youthful Richard Searling, as a young 'un I found my own in Tottenham Court Road, London in Jan '73 - along with the Cherry People in Bethnal Green! Both songs had not been played before, and one I am certainly glad did, the other, well...

Top 500 Position:	**248**
Original Label:	**RCA**
Current Value:	**£100 Issue**
	£80 Demo

'Ward is another nearly man with a cache of tracks he can be proud of'

Gary Lester, Soul Fan, Lincoln, UK

Herb Ward

Honest To Goodness

Ward, from Philadelphia made various attempts as a soul star with three Northern great tracks for Argo, Buddy and RCA.

'Honest to Goodness' was first played at the Mecca.

It's all Philadelphia, with Tommy Bell doing the business as usual with a heavy but lethargic intro before the beat really kicks in and the girlies back up Herbie a treat.

Originally released in the UK on a compilation LP.

Top 500 Position: **249**
Original Label: **Bronco**
Current Value: **£40**

'About as entertaining as it gets on the dancefloor'

Barry Stone, Soul Fan, Sussex, UK

Johnny Wyatt

This Thing Called Love

Call this favouritism, but if confronted by someone who asked the question 'What is Northern Soul?',I would instantly think of this Barry White penned masterpiece from 1966.

Stomping beat, girls, vibes, sax break, and awesome lead vocal who gave us a couple of great Soul sides for Challenge. During my part in the revival of the scene, I have come to the conclusion that the majority of punters want what I want, to enjoy top notch records without any interference from any sort of 'politics of Soul'.

Wyatt, who died in 1983, provides the perfect answer to any critic who refuse to judge a record by the music alone.

Top 500 Position: **250**
Original Label: **Argo**
Current Value: **£80 Issue**
£100 Demo

'A wonderful change of direction for the Northern Scene'

Rob Perry, Soul Fan, West Midlands, UK

Doug Banks

I Just Kept On Dancing

One of the new Soul discoveries of the 80's was Philadelphia's Doug Banks. The artist was in the doo-wop group The Dreamlovers, and recorded for Guyden in 1963.

Simply speaking, the R&B groove has been pretty much the 'norm' over the past few years and due to an influx of copies in recent years this Chess group 45 (which was one of the first really big sounds to emerge in the 80's when the scene was at its least successful) has rocketed in popularity.

Top 500 Position: **251**
Original Label: **ABC**
Current Value: **£60 Issue**
£40 Demo

'I don't know about a Slow Fizz - at this pace you just go off pop!'

Derek Foster, Soul Fan, North Wales, UK

The Sapphires

Slow Fizz

Carol Jackson leads the Philly group to yet another triumphant storming Northern classic. A cornerstone of the Torch sound, there is an alternative version played by Chris 'I Got It From The Vaults' King which has found subsequent release on the Sapphires CD compiled by producer Jerry Ross, and limited edition 7" vinyl.

Another group tracked down recently by ace act detective Ian Levine.

Top 500 Position: **252**
Original Label: **Cadet**
Current Value: **£200**

'A smooth sultry recording by a new legend'

Brian Astle, Soul Fan, Nottinghamshire, UK

Terry Callier

Look At Me Now

Recording for Chess, Elektra, Prestige among new Acid Jazz workouts, Callier's folk roots have lead the man down a completely different avenue to the northern scene. That is until the focus turned to this former £1 - 70's find.

Suddenly both Northern and Modern scenes embraced the man and we find several of his sides getting played including 'Ordinary Joe' which just missed the big chart.

I well remember coming across at least 100 copies of the single in 1978 in a Baltimore warehouse - languishing simply because no one wanted them!

Top 500 Position: **253**
Original Label: **20th Century**
Current Value: **£60**

'A once highly fashionable item... rather like the tank top - never to be seen again!'

Karen Riding,
Soul Fan, Wrexham, Wales, UK

Jeanette Harper

Put Me In Your Pocket

Without wishing to be too unkind in reminding you this claimed victory at many a gig north of Watford during the 70's. Today, it barely gets a spin, due to the change of direction the scene has took.

A super fashionable item in '75 with the cutesy vocal dribbling over a mock Motown beat. Personally, for me it is everything that relegates Northern Soul to the back woods, but that is part of the magic and mystery of the scene.

Top 500 Position: **254**
Original Label: **Pye**
Current Value: **£40**

'Cultivated by the youth clubs and Mod discos'

Chris Collins, Soul Fan, Mansfield, UK

Jason Knight

Our Love Is Getting Stronger

In 1969 I ventured to my first 'official' club, where among the pop hits of the day were the customary Motown spins topped off with a few regional tracks. This 1967 single from Pye was still available and to hear it alongside The Marmalade- 'Lovin' Things' seemed fairly natural (hey I was 13!).

Imagine my surprise, when at the Torch a crowd of regular gymnasts were getting off to this UK - only romp. Obviously a stage name conjuring up visions of a Peter Wyngarde type character all donned out with matching cravat and moustache!

Seriously, the 45 is pretty good, and one of the top British discoveries of all time.

Top 500 Position: **255**
Original Label: **Goldmine**
Current Value: **£10**

Tony Hestor

Down In The Dumps

Originally an alternate studio demo to Stanley Mitchell's 'Get It Baby'. John Anderson of Soul Bowl tracked down Richard 'Popcorn' Wylie in Detroit in the late 70's and unearthed a treasure trove of Wylie/Hestor unreleased goodies. From Betty Boo to Willie Harvey to work by the two producers themselves, there is a huge diversity of Wylie and Hestor material.

Even though you can sense the rawness of the rehearsal, Hestor had the knack of positioning a song right where the public wanted it to be. DJ Richard Searling got behind it and Wigan Casino claimed another exclusive.

Top 500 Position: **256**
Original Label: **Mercury**
Current Value: **£150 Issue**
£100 Demo

Alfie Davison

Love Is A Serious Business

A release from '79 which in some quarters is unthinkable.

The great mystery of Northern soul is the 'yes and no' trials and tribulations of clubbers.

Sure, the DJ himself has influence and can often nurture a track along, this modernistic dancer, sailed through the cloud of nostalgic fog with ease, and allowed newcomers to experience a fresh sound during a period when Northern was at its nadir.

The 45 itself percolated on the New York disco scene too, but the longevity will always remain 'up North'.

Top 500 Position: **257**
Original Label: **Back Beat**
Current Value: **£60**

'It says exactly what I was thinking back in 1974'

Mike Wilson, Warrington, UK

Jeanette Williams

All Of A Sudden

A fantastic gritty performance from Texan Williams. We know her for 'Something Good Gotten' A Hold Of Me' and prior to that dance favourite, dabbled with 'Stuff' a meaty soul cut from 1968. I played the heck out of this acquiring the single from Simon Soussan, who at the time went British label collecting crazy. OK so I swapped a copy of the Carrolls on Polydor for it, let ME at least get the edge sometimes!

The gal is quite superb, and from a group of labels headed by Don Robey, she ought to have had better promotion, as Back Beat could have been onto something.

Top 500 Position: **258**
Original Label: **Giant**
Current Value: **£30 Issue**
£75 Demo

'The first Northern 45 I bought and still my all time favourite'

Rod Moore, Perth, Western Australia

Jo Armstead

I Feel An Urge Coming On

Josephine Armstead has many classic soul singles to her credit, including the Motown period as a writer alongside Ashford and Simpson.

Her Northern output includes 45's on Giant and Gospel Truth and productions for Wise World, most notably the Salvadors.

Born in Yazoo City, Mississippi and a former member of the Ikettes, 'Joshie' as she is known took the Northern scene by storm in '71 when it was first aired at the legendary Blackpool Mecca.

Top 500 Position: **259**
Original Label: **Twirl**
Current Value: **£500**

'My favourite dancer of all time'

Cynthia Morgan, Soul Fan, Wales, UK

JoAnn Courcy

I Got The Power

I had the good fortune of discovering this powerhouse of a dancer in, of all places, a newsagents. Just prior to my selection as a Wigan Casino DJ (August, 1973), I strolled into my father's newsagents to collect the local rag when a large box of 45's had been placed on the counter with the sign attachment 'ex-juke box' only 25p each.

Supplied by a greeting card firm from Derby, they obviously thought having no centres meant the above. How wrong they could be, as I perused over around 80 discs, nearly all were soul and cutting to the chase, I found 'You're Not My Kind' - Paula Durante and this absolute dynamite dancer from Detroit.

Sadly, I never managed to play it at the Casino, as I traded it for around £40 worth of essentials I needed to play!...

DUMB MOVE KIDDO!

Top 500 Position: **260**
Original Label: **Eastern**
Current Value: **£10**

'A stomping time was had by all!'

Jeff Lincoln, Soul Fan, Hertfordshire, UK

Eddie and Ernie

I Can't Do It (I Just can't Leave You)

Eddie Campbell and Ernie Johnson were very much cast in the Sam and Dave mould. As a live act they regularly opened for the Ike & Tina Turner Review, whilst their Mod classic 'Outcast' was covered by the Animals and was mutated into Jesse Johnson's 'Left Out' for Old Town.

Back to this chart entry - well it's a stomper time as the duo work up Richard Tee's arrangement a treat. Interestingly enough the pair's manager is none other than Hadley Murrell one-time producer of Northern Soul hitmakers the Servicemen.

Top 500 Position: **261**
Original Label: **Grapevine**
Current Value: **£15**

'We could have sworn the 45 was just another cover up!'

Gail Marchant,
Soul Fan, Greater Manchester, UK

Betty Boo

Say It Isn't So

When a DJ exposes a new 'rarity' and reveals the artist as Betty Boo, you get the feeling you are being had, even if the side is an excellent dancer. The fact is producer Richard 'Popcorn' Wylie can't remember the lady's real name, but does admit to the pseudonym simply to add a little sexiness to the track.

History out of the way as Wylie supplied a tape to Soul Bowl, who wisely dubbed an acetate for long serving Wigan Casino DJ Richard Searling and the rest IS history. The usual suspects are evident –Wylie, Hestor etc, complete with new female talent looking 'for a break'.

Top 500 Position: **262**
Original Label: **Sound Stage 7**
Current Value: **£20 Issue**
£30 Demo

'To hear this and see the man live, was a dream come true'

Rick Foster, Anglo American, Todmorden, UK

Roscoe Shelton

Running For My Life

A Soul and Blues artist of great repute from Lynchburg, Tennesssee. The Nashville label had minor successes with the man in '65/66, and he proved to be key act in the South performing live on many occasions. It must be said that 'Running' is somewhat at odds with most of the man's R&B tinged southern material. Eventually the well ran dry material wise Shelton found a new audience via the lucrative blues scene.

A fantastic singer, which you don't have to be a rocket scientist to ascertain after hearing this Golden Torch anthem from 1972.

Top 500 Position: **263**
Original Label: **Deesu**
Current Value: **£60**

*'The stomp stomp intro
is totally irresistible'*

Jeff Williams, Soul Fan, Humberside, UK

Maurice Williams

Being Without You

Leader of early 60's hitmakers the Zodiacs and preceded by a launch into the music industry as the Gladiolas. Williams, from Lancaster, South Carolina, re-invented himself twice during his career, firstly signing to the New Orleans label Deesu and recording the Motownesque 'Being Without You' which was first brought to the scene's attention by Martin 'Soul Sam' Barnfather.

During the 80's, the hit movie Dirty Dancing popularised his one and only hit 'Stay',where that and other material keeps him working, mainly in Georgia and the Carolinas.

Top 500 Position: **264**
Original Label: **Soul Series**
Current Value: **£10**

*'If this ain't the finest
Northern discovery ever,
I'll quit my 60 a day habit'*

Glen Malrose, Collector, California, USA

Spencer Wiggins

Let's Talk It Over

Discovered by true Northern Soul original Brian Rae on an obscure US CD, this 1967 unreleased cut is of absolute stunning quality. Made for the scene - well not quite - but it's as if producer Quinton M Claunch 'knew something'.

Quite how this was unreleased is an intriguing mystery, with Writers Penn/Oldham protegee Wiggins tearing the roof off with a corking piano riff which weaves in and out of a New York type back track.

Spencer does his usual 'Southern style' and delivers a 'creature from the deep', ready and waiting to suck you in. After hearing it, I would not mind in the slightest!

Top 500 Position: **265**
Original Label: **Mo-Groov**
Current Value: **£800**

'You guys in England still looking for that Nomads record?'

John Hook, DJ, North Carolina, USA

The Nomads

Somethings Bad

A North Carolina 45 that even the locals are searching for, so tear up the plane tickets to Charlotte!

Sunny Threatt and Phyllis (Brown?) recorded the 1967 side for the ridiculously obscure Mo-Groov label. The duo also made music with Major Bill Smith for his Texas based Charay label.

Very much Richard Searling's baby, the price tag has slightly diluted the potential of the side, but the minute you do hear it, you are up and dancin'... they certainly were at Wigan!

Top 500 Position: **266**
Original Label: **Maverick**
Current Value: **£100 Issue**
£60 demo

'Terrible Tom for me represents the true meaning of Northern Soul'

Ginger Taylor, DJ, Todmorden, UK

Terrible Tom

We Were Made For Each Other

Terrible Tom, real name Tom Bowden, recorded for Mickey Stevenson and Ernie Shelby's Maverick label in early '68. The unknown Tom is by know means Terrible as the lead vocalist rips through the 100 mph track like a buzz saw. In the heady days of '74 the scene thrived on such discs and captured the very essence of soul that only a dance enthusiast could describe.

Owning a copy back then would have set you back £20, and if you are lucky enough to own the 'B' side (most are double sided promos), you could name your price. Discovered by DJ Ian Levine, and played initially at Blackpool Mecca, the 45 was made for Wigan Casino!

Top 500 Position: **267**
Original Label: **Goldwax**
Current Value: **£15 Issue**
£25 Demo

James Carr

That's What I Want To Know

'Its raunchiness, coupled with Carr's fantastic delivery, make it one of THE top sounds ever'

Brian Mottram, Soul Fan, Greater Manchester, UK

The man with the unique sound from Memphis started out as a gospel singer with O. V. Wright. Carr, being spotted by Goldwax supremo Quinton Claunch was signed to the company in 1964.

During the four years the company operated, he recorded a wealth of Chips Moman, Dan Penn, Spooner Oldham material. In later years he recorded for River City before re-appearing to record two albums in the early 90's.

Totally underrated, this B side, found it's way onto UK Stateside, before its discovery a couple of years later whereupon it became a Twisted Wheel anthem.

Top 500 Position: **268**
Original Label: **Smash**
Current Value: **£125 Issue**
£100 Demo

Kelly Garrett

Love's The Only Answer

'Country-meets-Soul-meets-Northern'

Keith Alton, Soul Fan, London, UK

One of those typical pop dancers predictably massive for at the Casino, Kelly Garrett therefore caught the imagination of the ever faithful,.

Released in 1968, the song didn't sell a bean in the US, which is surprising, as the feel of it suggests it ought to be some kind of TV sitcom theme.

There is also a version by pop artist, Margaret Whiting, even more akin to Tammy Wynette, it came out on Canadian London.

Top 500 Position: **269**
Original Label: **Revilot**
Current Value: **£10**

'Sweet soul without a hint of P-Funk'

Will Davis,
Groovesville, Detroit, USA

The Parliaments

Don't Be Sore At Me

Due to the thousands of imported copies in the early 70's, you are staring at a ten pound record, the fact is, the quality of such a single ought to be commanding 100 times that!

Superb from the outset, George Clinton and company ride the Detroit groove perfectly and deliver the right hook, amazingly not connecting with the chart in 1965. Clinton from Kannapolis, North Carolina formed the group as far back as 1955, releasing their first single on ABC 12 months later. Moving to an independent in '63, New records, they auditioned for Motown and after recording several demos, Clinton stayed in Detroit and hooked up with Don Davis at Solid Hitbound productions.

His status over the past 25 years is legendary by way of the P-Funk interest. In Northern Soul terms he is one name that appears on many rare soul discs.

Top 500 Position: **270**
Original Label: **Unity**
Current Value: **£350**

'One seriously hard record to find!'

Barry Hollingsworth,
Soul Fan, Bedfordshire, UK

Candi Staton

Now You've Got The Upper Hand

The darling of all eras, with this her first 45. In 1968 right through to her one liners being sampled to create a variety of dance hits in the 80's and 90's. In between, why she was recording the best material of her life with producer Dave Crawford in Alabama, with hits such as 'Young Hearts Run Free'.

Just prior to her first recording contract with Fame in the summer of '68, the lady from Hanceville, Alabama recorded a great single for Unity that failed to get any interest even in her home state.

Married for a time to Clarence Carter who's kinky 45 'Strokin' certainly reaffirmed the divorce courts as Staton moved into the gospel field. A super groove that never quite hit the ultimate heights, largely due to it's scarcity.

Top 500 Position: **271**
Original Label: **Decca**
Current Value: **£250 Issue**
£100 Demo

'Pure danceability'

Lisa Holliman, Soul Fan, San Francisco, USA

Lada Edmund Jnr

The Larue

When DJ Ian Levine first played this at Blackpool Mecca it raced to the top of my wants list, I knew that if I could track it down that it would become the new No. 1 sound at the Casino...

Lada was in actual fact an all-round talent. A singer and dancer, she recorded for Coral and Roulette as well as producing two 45's for Decca. Shrine supremo Eddie Singleton was the man behind 'The Larue' a cash-in dance tune which nonetheless has fiery appeal!

Amazingly Lada Edmund also appeared on the big screen in the 70's blaxploitation movie 'Savage' (1973) before fading into obscurity. The promotional picture of her was one fronted by a white model!

Top 500 Position: **272**
Original Label: **Kyser**
Current Value: **£1,000**

'The story of Robby Lawson is legendary and we still know nothing about him'

Stan Krause, Store Owner, Jersey City, USA

Robbie Lawson

Burning Sensation

One of the scenes great discoveries. The story is as follows, a collector from San Francisco Bob Cattaneo discovered it in 1974, and being aware of the Northern scene sold it to a collector. DJ Soul Sam was the first to play it who then promptly sold it to DJ Colin Curtis who then moved it on to me!

The total exchange deals constituted a mere £100, with each of us finding the sound a little unresponsive with the dance floor. Moving on, the 45 well and truly matured and has the distinction of being the first northern 45 to sell for £1, 000.

A busy production by Paul Kyser who released this as his first single on his own label. Trivia wise, here's an absolute peach. An old friend of mine Stan Krause, owner of the Catamount label in Jersey City, distinctly remembers putting the labels on the wax as the record was being made at his fathers pressing plant in Little Ferry, New Jersey in 1967!

The flip side is 'I Have Searched', if only Lawson knew !

Top 500 Position: **273**
Original Label: **A&M**
Current Value: **£100**

'If this is disco then I'm John Travolta!'

Rick Foster, Manager, Anglo-American, UK

Collins and Collins

Top Of The Stairs

A 1980 release in a Northern Soul book?... Well in recent times this disc has moved from the Modern Rooms into the cavernous All-nighter halls as a result of massive popularity. Nor is the original quite the obscurity often demanded - hitting number 68 on the US Black Music Top 100 chart. You may then gauge from a price into three figures that this is a hot ticket item.

Collins and Collins were a brother and sister outfit (Bill and Tonee) whose recorded career would appear to be brief. 'Top Of The Stairs' is an Ashford and Simpson song (they did in fact also record it) and with Philly Disco-General John Davis behind the production it is perhaps no surprise that a small amount of commercial success ensued. It *is* a surprise that it should become such a big record on an essentially 60's based music scene though!

Top 500 Position: **274**
Original Label: **Mala**
Current Value: **£25**

'The whiplash effect distinguished this single from others and proved to be its trump card'

Steve Davies, Soul Fan, Merseyside, UK

Reparata and the Delrons

Panic

So easy to score at Wigan Casino in '74 with such a large and eager audience. Panic represents the 60's well, without a hint of soul. Mary 'Reparata' Aiese from New York had minor US success with 'When A Teenager Cries' in '65.

The UK became the group's next port of call with 'Captain Of Your Ship' in '68. She also recorded for Polydor in the 70's, but it is this lightweight but effective racer from '68 that most folk on the scene remember.

You definitely needed stimulants to be able to dance to this!

Top 500 Position: **275**
Original Label: **De-Lite**
Current Value: **£30**

'Disco dross in some quarters - considered a Northern classic in others'

Liz Crowley, Soul Fan, Oxford, UK

Benny Troy

I Wanna Give You Tomorrow

Every so often a 45 appears that has little to do with Northern soul. However that very statement adds mystique to the unique movement we are investigating. Troy is a East Coast 'lounge' type singer. A sort of Tony Christie type full of frilly shirts and platforms. Joking apart, the label De-Lite released many soul 45's and was the home for Kool and the Gang.

Checking out the single further, it slips in well to 'North of Watford' playlists, with the sing-a-long chorus and soft disco beat.

The unfortunate thing I remember about the single is, that I traded a now £600 single for it 20 years ago!

Top 500 Position: **276**
Original Label: **Capitol**
Current Value: **£75 Issue**
£50 Demo

'Even though the song is her first attempt the performance is still there'

Carolyn Hart, Soul Fan, Yorkshire, UK

Thelma Houston

Baby Mine

Many years later in her career she recorded a song titled 'Saturday Night, Sunday Morning' which could somehow be a cryptic message to the northern scene. OK so I'm imagining things, the brilliant female singer from Leland, Mississippi is probably oblivious to the fact that her first single ever is really popular here. Please, someone show her this book!

Accomplished singer with a US No. 1 to her credit with 'Don't Leave Me This Way', the Capitol single from 1966 is perfect Motownesque. Appearing in movies too, the lady is now legendary, and if there was anyone I would like to see live (currently) it's Thelma. If you have never heard it before, try and do so, it's a 'play it on CD and remember the good times' type of single.

Top 500 Position: **277**
Original Label: **New Voice**
Current Value: **£8 Issue**
£20 Demo

'You can feel the excitement in the recording'

Peter Harrison,

Soul Fan, Northamptonshire, UK

Mitch Ryder and the Detroit Wheels

Breakout

Ryder, born William Levise Jnr. had a knack of treating the studio session as a live one. His other Northern winners including ' You Get Your Kicks','Devil With The Blue Dress' and 'Sock It To Me Baby' had that very same feel. His poorest US seller has turned out to be his most fondly remembered UK dancer.

'Breakout', produced by Bob Crewe in 1966, was released on Stateside here and did not take long to become a nighter favourite, gaining regular turntable action as early as 1968. Known originally as Billy and the Rivieras, Ryder is still a cult figure among many celebs, most notably Bruce Springsteen.

Top 500 Position: **278**
Original Label: **Scepter**
Current Value: **£25**

'Another vintage career 45 for THE girl group of the 60's'

Steve Ellis,

Soul Fan, Northamptonshire, UK

The Shirelles

Last Minute Miracle

In the US the group from Passaic, New Jersey had bottomed out as early as 1963. After a string of hits, it was a case 'where to next'. Label boss Florence Greenburg held faith with the quartet and matched them with a variety of happening producers such as George Kerr.

The track was originally written for Linda Jones on Loma, but who could doubt the sheer brilliance of lead singer Shirley Alston. Sure, Jones was a magnificent vocalist too, but Alston knew how to add a little extra gloss. Put that down to chart experience and without diversifying too much the girls output during this period (1965-68) was exemplary.

Originally discovered by DJ Ian Levine it fought for plays in 1973 and, if discovered today, collectors would be talking about it for years.

Top 500 Position: **279**
Original Label: **Musicor**
Current Value: **£80 Issue**
£60 Demo

'A plodding intro - and then WALLOP!'

Jeff Martin, Soul Fan, Australia

Porgy and the Monarchs

My Heart Cries For You

Lead by Porgy Williams. Recorded originally for Mala, Sylves onto Musicor then Verve, the act from Chicago. The focus is on the second of two releases for Musicor with a monster from Wigan!

This old standard becomes highly infectious in the hands of this competent vocal group as they harmonise the hook line with great accuracy and ferment. It is just pitiful that the US had all these fabulous groups (too many in fact) and in Europe we got the 'watered down' copyists.

Top 500 Position: **280**
Original Label: **PAP**
Current Value: **£100**

'One of the first big money 70's anthems

Dennis Turner, Soul Fan, South Wales, UK

Daybreak

I Need Love

One of the most active and talented producers in soul music during the last 25 years, Patrick Adams was a melody maker who was cut from the same cloth as the Philly and Salsoul producers.

Daybreak did little apart from a few plays by Jeff Troy on WWRL in New York. During my time as a record dealer the song was nothing more than a sweet soul sound that I remember as a new release. The UK however latched onto the side which received plays from Richard Searling at Wigan covered up as 'Tyrone Edwards'. The mystery of cover-ups is of course is common place in England, but totally confused Pat when I told him!

Incidentally, as an aside, Adams 'cut his teeth' in the studio in 1967 working for Bobby Robinson on The Carletts- 'I'm Getting Tired', which locally came out on BR, before being leased to Capitol. Patrick went on to produce Four Below Zero plus really making his name as Disco King with Fonda Rae and many others. His real soul connections with Black Ivory make the man a totally unsung hero of Soul.

Top 500 Position: **281**
Original Label: **Ashford**
Current Value: **£30 issue**
£300 Demo

'A bad dancer you might be, but this is the 45 to help you find some rhythm

Dave Evison, DJ, Stoke-on-Trent, UK

Eddie Parker

Love You Baby

Recorded by Jack Ashford for his Ashford label in 1968, the song ridicules the need for a different approach á la 'Cloud Nine' and other hits of the year. Ashford and his wife Lorraine Chandler were accomplished musicians and had worked for Kapp, RCA amongst others. Parker had a single on Awake called I'm Gone', which is a massive rarity.

The history? Well it was discovered at the Golden Torch in 1972, and the Exciters covered it at the request of Ian Levine. Dave Evison has since 'adopted' the tune has his own anthem. Absolutely ferocious in tempo, but forsaking a great melody, Parker was a real screamer and pretty damn good too.

Top 500 Position: **282**
Original Label: **Verve**
Current Value: **£10 Issue**
£15 Demo

'The duo are legendary, but the band more so on the scene'

Keith Wallers, Soul Fan, Merseyside, UK

The Righteous Brothers Band

Rat Race

Talk about unusual! The rhythm band for Bobby Hatfield and Bill Medley chose the old Richard Maltby track to cover in 1966. The influx of copies at Bradford market allowed the single to be exposed at nearly every soul night in the early 70's thus rapidly gaining a toe hold on the scene. This is pure stomp and with instrumentals in general falling from grace it's nice to hear it occasionally.

Yet another Wigan Casino great - this one was absolutely tailor-made for Station Road!

Top 500 Position: **283**
Original Label: **Rouser**
Current Value: **£5,000**

'RARER than rare'

Steve Mikowski, Soul Fan, USA

The Butlers with Frankie Beverly

Because Of My Heart

Very expensive today on Fairmount, 'Because Of My Heart' was in fact originally released on local label Rouser, however there is only one known copy. The reverse 'I Want To Feel I'm Wanted' is yet another classic, if underplayed track, from the Maze front man whose voice just seems to get better and better with age.

The Rouser release is arguably the rarest Northern Soul 45 on its original imprint.

Top 500 Position: **284**
Original Label: **Toxsan**
Current Value: **£300**

'An exceptional 60's dancer with anthemic overtones'

Mark Liddell, Soul Fan, West Midlands, UK

Herb Johnson and the Impacts

I'm So Glad

Although better known on the nationally released Brunswick label, Johnson recorded this in '66 for Wally Osborne's indie label from Philadelphia - his backing group, the Impacts, featured Major Harris - who appears earlier in the chart.

The artist had a few cracks at success with further singles on the label and one for Arctic. What makes this 45 stand out is 'oh whoa whoa oh' hook that ripples through the track. The beat to is irresistible and was one of many classics first aired at the Golden Torch all-nighter.

Top 500 Position: **285**
Original Label: **ABC**
Current Value: **£25 Issue**
£50 Demo

'The multi-talented Earl Nelson I presume?'

Tom Levin, Chicago, USA

Jackie Lee

Darkest Days

The Mirwood production team leased this 1967 rarity to ABC, but sadly the act couldn't repeat the success of 'The Duck'. Picked up by the Twisted Wheel DJs, the scene was still in its infancy when we were first treated to this most uplifting of Soul sounds.

At one time it could be counted as the country's biggest in-demander. Regarded now as a 'cheapie' it is typical of the kind of disc that is, in fact no longer knocking around in the States - so that if demand again rises you can expect the value to rocket!

Top 500 Position: **286**
Original Label: **Columbia**
Current Value: **£70**

'It was only a matter of time before Helen's obscurities surfaced'

Andrew Topping, Soul Fan, London, UK

Helen Shapiro

Stop And You'll Become Aware

One of the better pop discoveries at Wigan Casino, Shapiro was the youngest female chart topper when at 15 years of age she had realised two No. 1 hits!

She headlined the first UK tour on which the Beatles appeared as her support act. Outside of the hitmaking period, Shapiro flirted with all manner of releases and this mock-Motown groove is one of the results of the singers' attempts to gain favour with EMI who stayed faithful to her throughout the 60's, despite her having no hits after 1964.

The all-nighters loved this in the 70's and she certainly is one act to have remained in the hearts of a large number of fans with widely-differing musical tastes.

Top 500 Position: **287**
Original Label: **Verve**
Current Value: **£25 Issue**
£40 demo

*'To some this was
THE Torch anthem'*

Gary Holland, Soul Fan, Sheffield, UK

The Shalimars

Stop And Take A Look At Yourself

From a label conception by Norman Granz and distributed by MGM from 1958, Verve mixed Jazz, Folk, Pop and Soul together with many failures. Here is just one that for me is one of the best Northern sides ever. The group from New York were fronted by 'Sari' who later used herself as the official leader on a single for Veep in 1968.

The commerciality of the 45 is glaringly obvious with a piano riff to die for, stunning background vocals and a lead reminiscent of Shirley Alston.

Top 500 Position: **288**
Original Label: **Skyway**
Current Value: **£50**

*'Another storming dancer
from Miles Grayson'*

Brenda Smith,
Soul Fan, West Midlands, UK

Louise Lewis, Miss LL

Oo Wee I'll Let It Be You Babe

A great track to DJ with in the 70's. The single from 1966 is pure Motown meets Mirwood with former opera singer Lewis squealing over a delicious Miles Grayson groove.

A Simon Soussan find with yours truly and Russ Winstanley on it big style at the Station Road venue.

Maybe out of step today, but the catchiness of the melody makes this a worthwhile chart edition for Miss Double-L. A simultaneous release by Karl Evans faired no better commercially.

Top 500 Position: **289**
Original Label: **Canterbury**
Current Value: **£10 Issue**
£25 Demo

'Just a little understanding - it was bound to succeed!'

Bob Crichton, Soul Fan, Los Angeles, USA

The Younghearts

A Little Togetherness

This group also features in the chart under their alternate name, the Tempos.

A monster Torch anthem and now used as the theme tune for the increasingly popular Togetherness Allnighters at Stoke's King George's Hall.

The Los Angeles group led by James Moore later gave up their dual identity and went on to record as the New Younghearts.

'A Little Togetherness' was also released later on the Zea label credited to the 'King Of Hearts'.

Top 500 Position: **290**
Original Label: **United Artists**
Current Value: **£100 Issue**
£25 Demo

'It started out as a theme tune for a TV car commercial'

Robin Holland, Soul Fan, Leicester, UK

The Steve Karmen Band featuring Jimmy Radcliffe

Breakaway

Karmen was a new generation band leader, who later composed the 'I Love New York' promotion theme when the city was considered by some to be unsafe during the 70's. Radcliffe on the other hand was a first class vocalist famous for his work on Musicor and others.

Here we have a big production matched by a mammoth vocal and a blaxploitation type song that Isaac Hayes would have approved of. DJ Colin Curtis was first out of the trap with this one and, it sort of allowed more non-traditional sides to get played. An innovative but unusual record.

Top 500 Position: **291**
Original Label: **Col-Soul**
Current Value: **£300**

'On hearing this I realised Northern Soul could always hold it's head high'

Tom Luccino, Collector, Maryland, USA

The Chandlers

Your Love Makes Me Lonely

Ohio's attempt at group Soul harmony and certainly bagging a few thousand listeners here in the UK. Sadly, the single from 1966, was far too dated for the US market.

They recorded a further single on local label Bleu Rose in 1969, but that too sank without a trace.

Amazingly this record started its rise to fame in Accrington at the British Legion/Band Club nights there - an unglamorous but typically truthful beginning for a Northern Soul record!

Top 500 Position: **292**
Original Label: **Impact**
Current Value: **£75 Demo**
£100 Issue

'Popularised in the 70's, soaring upwards today'

Leanne Holly, Soul Fan, USA

The Lollipops

Loving Good Feeling

This cutesie girl group recorded for Smash, RCA, Motown's V.I.P and Detroit's Inferno.

Label owner Harry Balk had a great production partner in Duke Browner and together they made the label one of the most sought after in Britain.

This is the group's best dancer with a typical young lead joined by a nice chorus.

Drifting in and out of popularity since 1973.

Top 500 Position: **293**
Original Label: **Volt**
Current Value: **£30**

'I'd like to have a Pow-Wow with this lady!'

Kev Sowerby, Soul Fan, Cumbria, UK

Linda Lyndell

Bring Your love Back To Me

A stunning effort from Lyndell, a full-blood American Indian, which allegedly was recorded in Texas with the Crazy Cajun production team. It was released on Volt in 1968 with a UK release here on Stax. She later found minor fame with the much sampled 'What A Man' before disappearing into further obscurity.

A perfect Motown type waxing that made its mark at the tail end of the Twisted Wheel and played extensively by its last DJ, the late Les Cokell.

The groove is insatiable and would make an ideal song to cover today.

Top 500 Position: **294**
Original Label: **Harthon**
Current Value: **£20**

'Lovingly produced by the legendary Harthon crew'

Gary Allen, Soul Fan, Philadelphia, USA

The United Four

She's Putting You On

As I play back my answer phone a voice appears 'hey Kev this is Weldon Arthur McDougall the third, calling from Philadelphia'.

Weldon is one of Philly's great mouthpieces, championing the great music from the city. Why, he should get into politics, but he's too modest for that, simply going about his business recording the local black talent of the day. His association with Styles, Randolph, Holman, Gamble, Huff is well documented, and on this occasion we turn to a 45 first played in 1974 by DJ Ian Levine.

The track is probably the most energetic and entertaining of all the productions he made. Vocals coming at you from all directions, typical Virtue type groove cooking in the background and the quality hook you come to expect from the team.

A thousand pound sound for twenty - the stockbroker says BUY!

Top 500 Position: **295**
Original Label: **American Arts**
Current Value: **£75 Issue**
£50 Demo

'Increasingly popular internationally'

Joe Roccini, Soul Fan, New Jersey, USA

Bobbie Smith

Walk On Into My Heart

The 45 produced by the Balk/Browner tie up, has steadily grown into one of the definitive sounds of the last 20 years. Picking up the slack on the scene from the likes of Lainie Hill, Dena Barnes etc, the 1965 recording did poorly in the US except for Pittsburgh where it became a minor hit.

The disc strolled into Stafford becoming one of their first monster sounds - even generating a 'lookalike' reissue that caught many a collector out.

Bobbie was originally part of a girl group called Bobby and the Dream Girls.

Top 500 Position: **296**
Original Label: **Jay Boy**
Current Value: **£6**

'Massively in-demand with dancers, despite having no collector appeal'

Rob Jeffries,
Soul Fan, Northamptonshire, UK

The Bob and Earl Band

My Little Girl (Instrumental)

Released in the UK when sister company President held the UK rights to Mirwood, the backing track amazingly overtook the popularity of the already released vocal by Bobby Garrett. The scene makes it's 'own' sounds and while DJ's suggest and coerce, the dancer will have the final word.

Record company and punter forced the turntable terrors to play it, and why not, the groove is irresistible with Fred Smith and company doing the usual. Randy Wood's production line was simply sensational and it's a real shame he's not alive to still see the enthusiasts 'go to work'.

Top 500 Position: **297**
Original Label: **ABC**
Current Value: **£80**

'In the scheme of things this is pretty awful - unless of course you are an expert dancer'

Mark Welsh, Soul Fan, Kent, UK

August and Deneen

We Go Together

Major labels issued 'what's happening at the time' one shot wonders. The obvious Sonny and Cher influence via the lyrics and concept is evident. The 45 became another statistic, failing to arouse anyone outside of the promo team at ABC. Years later and the scenes thirst for new 'stompers' saw this manic pastiche become a major part of the culture at Wigan Casino.

Today's DJ's of course frown on such a single, but hang on guys, you were not playing to crowds of 2,000 week after week.

In those days the bigger the dance floor, the faster the tempo, and this little romp from '67 was for a time on everyone's wants list.

Top 500 Position: **298**
Original Label: **Loma**
Current Value: **£100 Issue**
£60 Demo

'Mythology again, as one wag insisted it was the vocal to Bok to Bach'

Chris Lever, Soul Fan, Northamptonshire, UK

Ben Aiken

Satisfied

Ben Aiken had a minor hit with an alternate version to Brenda and The Tabulations 'Stay Together Young Lovers' in 1965 on Roulette. Following his departure and new signing to Warner Brothers, he saw himself on their new Loma label (a soulish spin-off).

The vibe and harp tingling 'Satisfied' exploded onto the scene in May 1973, the reason for the accurate account of 'first play' comes as I was at the Top Rank, Hanley the night of discovery.

For many years Aiken was hailed as a genuine blue-eyed soulster - due to a mix up with Ben Atkins of Memphis. Aiken is of course the genuine article - 'Satisfied' now?

Top 500 Position: **299**
Original Label: **Green Dolphin**
Current Value: **£250 'L' Allen**
£300 as 'Larry'

'A thin, but infectious production'

Steve Harris, Soul Fan, Wiltshire, UK

Larry/L. Allen

Can't We Talk It Over

Larry Allen from Pittsburgh hoped to catch on with a thinly disguised attempt at a real Soul record. Critics aside, it really works in the North of England, or rather the South - it was first popular at Yate, possibly due to the tuneful piano riff.

Collectors love it of course, and while I personally remain unconvinced, the single has survived the variety of directions the scene has gone.

A single that sounds unfinished.

Top 500 Position: **300**
Original Label: **Paula**
Current Value: **£10 Issue**
£25 Demo

'Stunning'

Stan Lewis, Label Owner, Louisiana, USA

The Montclairs

Hung Up On Your Love

Phil Perry is without a doubt one of the Soul's most accomplished singer/songwriters. Even back in 1968 recording for Arch records in St. Louis the signs of greatness were emerging.

With two 'biggies' on Paula, the other being 'I Need You More Than Ever' penned by Bobby Patterson, it was 'Hung Up' that did it for the Montclairs getting the dancers 'at it' in the UK several months after its American release.

The bass riff intro and Perry's killer falsetto sell it magnificently!

Top 500 Position:	**301**
Original Label:	**ABC**
Current Value:	**£300 Issue**
	£200 Demo

'Lightweight pop with just enough vocal expertise to see it through'

Allan Pollard, Soul Fan, Stockport, UK

Jay Traynor

Up And Over

Blue-eyed John 'Jay 'Traynor was an early member of Doo-Wop group the Mystics. Furthering his career he formed Jay and the Americans and left in 1964 to pursue a solo career with ABC. The group which spawned the Northern hit 'Livin' Above Your Head' had new lead Jay Black fronting the group.

Wigan DJ, Richard Searling purchased 'Up And Over' in 1976 from Mecca main man Ian Levine, it subsequently went massive at the Casino, becoming a 70's turntable legend.

Today it continues to become even more popular and expensive to buy!

Top 500 Position:	**302**
Original Label:	**Kent**
Current Value:	**£10**

'A superlative cover-up that became folk law for 20 years or so'

Brian Harris, Soul Fan, Lancashire, UK

Little Ann

What Should I Do

Recording for Dave Hamilton's Topper label before signing to Ed Wingate's Ric-Tic, Ann Bridgforth could never imagine the intensity surrounding her unreleased track (at the time) 'What Should I Do'.

The fact is that the 'master of cover-ups' Richard Searling created one of the scene's best kept secrets. According to the former Casino DJ, the acetate was supplied by record dealer John Anderson. Searling promptly covered the title and artist (it revealed Ann Bridgforth on the label) and exposed it to the all-nighter faithful, under the guise of Rose Valentine - 'When He's Not Around', showing the DJ's smartness and the scene's willingness to embrace the mystery surrounding it!

Top 500 Position: **303**
Original Label: **Crimson**
Current Value: **£100 Issue**
£70 Demo

'A storming dancer with full-on commerciality'

Jeff Hollis, Soul Fan, Australia

Lee Andrews and the Hearts

I've Had It

Put together by Tommy Bell and Billy Jackson, the five piece from Philadelphia lead by Arthur Lee Thompson recorded this fabulous fingersnapper in 1968.

Released on Lost Nite's Crimson label as the follow up to the equally remarkable 'Nevertheless' the side was picked up by DJ Pep who popularised it in the Midlands.

In fact it is one of the first regional-regional hits!

The group were a remarkable 50's act and kept on going through the 60's on RCA and Lost Nite before fading away in 1969.

Top 500 Position: **304**
Original Label: **Smash**
Current Value: **£6**

''Ready or not here I come', they sang, and I flipped'

Jerry Ross, Producer, Philadelphia, USA

Jay and the Techniques

Apples, Peaches, Pumpkin Pie

This is a tale of two countries.

Firstly, in the US, where the song became a million seller in August, 1967. Then in the UK, where it became a cult rarity after bombing out when released on Philips.

As the Twisted Wheel revellers loved it, the song crossed over to more mainstream clubs and, while the scene today is fairly dismissive of the song, it was incessantly played for around 5 years.

I met Jay Proctor in the 80's and he was amazed of the discs failure to hit in the UK and the interest in a few other oddities that definitely did not sell in the US.

For the group from Allentown, PA this was their finest hour, and another success for the prolific production team of Ross/Renzetti.

Top 500 Position: **305**
Original Label: **Marton**
Current Value: **£1,000**

'A tempestuous offering from young Tamala'

Harry Crossley,
Soul Fan, Greater Manchester, UK

Tamala Lewis

You Won't Say Nothing

George Clinton had been in Detroit for a spell while still keeping a variety of recording contacts in New Jersey. He captured the whole Motown thing with youngster Tamala Lewis, who probably looked and sounded good but obviously did not have the Gordy conveyer belt at her disposal.

Still, we have an incredibly energetic 45 here, and I for one am still yet to own a copy even though my last offer for one in 1981 (£80) was considered a 'little' too low!

Discovered in the US by former record dealer George Greco.

Top 500 Position: **306**
Original Label: **Page One**
Current Value: **£30**

'Up to the peak of popularity and straight back down again!'

John Grover, Soul Fan, Southampton, UK

Muriel Day

Nine Times Out Of Ten

Larry Page was bemused when I told him how popular this 1969 ditty had been. The Troggs and Kinks manager vaguely remembers the flip 'Optimistic Fool' as an Irish Eurovision entry. Imagine the pauses on the phone as I am describing a back drop, cartwheel, maple wooden floors and a £30 single!

Page remained unconvinced and promptly dismissed the conversation as nothing more than a minor fad. He ought to be right, except the song has filtered into the mainstream and while presenting a daily show for EMAP's 'Magic 828' in Leeds, I dread to think of the amount of requests we had from West Yorkshire. Soul NO - Northern Soul YES !

Top 500 Position: **307**
Original Label: **Compass**
Current Value: **£100**

'Rough and ready - and coming 'atcha like a driverless car!'

Keith Hunt,
Soul Fan, Greater Manchester, UK

The Adventurers

Easy Baby

A Va-Va's discovery, championed by resident DJ Richard Searling. Had the need for pop stompers had not been upon us in 1974 then the 45 would have been right up there in our chart.

The group from New York featured Greg Perry who later recorded for Chess, Alfa and Casablanca. They had great 45's on Ran-Dee, Music World and Blue Rock.

Unusually, the intro starts with a sort of bagpipe effect before launching into a really good soulful offering laced with a rolling back beat.

Top 500 Position: **308**
Original Label: **Riverside**
Current Value: **£30 Issue**
£50 Demo

'One of the best starts to a 60's floorshaker, ever'

Ian Ryles, Soul Fan, Yorkshire, UK

The Gems

I'll Be There

A 'toot-toot' intro rips into a dancer of some repute from Manchester's legendary Pendulum nights. Here the New York based Riverside label attempts to gain some soulful credibility, with the Gems masterpiece and their stable mate, Lou Courtney, to an otherwise Jazz oriented label.

Originally known as the Lovettes, Minnie Ripperton became lead singer before joining Rotary Connection. The girls originally recorded for Chess, and folded shortly after this last ditch, furious attempt at success.

In 1966 this was too fast for its own good, but a few years later - across the Atlantic the kids loved it!

Top 500 Position: **309**
Original Label: **Decca**
Current Value: **£40**

'The Cindy Scott cover-up name at least gave it a purpose...'

Martin Vincent,
Soul Fan, Montreal, Canada

Joey Heatherton

When You Called Me Baby

It is as if this 45 has followed me around permanently for over 20 years! Originally played by Richard Searling on a Belgian Brunswick copy he had covered as Cindy Scott.

I found my own copy shortly after in New Jersey, from a flea market dealer who revealed he knew the writer John Madara (Formations, Len Barry etc). Tracking him down, I discovered that Johanna from New York had a brother who he believed was a Disc Jockey.

Four years later (anorak that I am) I visit WCBS in NYC, and, after a brief introduction to the programming department, I visit the studio to find afternoon drive jock Dick Heatherton in full throttle. Expecting me to 'have the hood totally up' Dick and I chatted, the conversation predictably turned to Northern Soul whereby the link was established. Dickyboy, as he was affectionately known, tried to call his sister Joey, to no avail. She now realises at least someone likes her 1966 effort. She did in fact have a minor chart flurry in the early 70's with a song called 'Gone'. OK, can I take down the hood now?

Top 500 Position: **310**
Original Label: **Decca**
Current Value: **£20 Issue**
£40 Demo

'The revealing intro of... 'where is my baby', sets the scene for a truly frantic jaunt'

Philip Smith, Soul Fan, Leicestershire, UK

Earl Grant

Hide Nor Hair

The cool keyboard player and actor saw this song as his final attempt at major success. He did have a No. 7 hit in 1958, but further chart action was to elude him, and he died in a car accident in 1970.

The disc is pure Soul beat and totally in keeping with what was happening in 1966, it tells quite a story and in that respect can be likened to 'The Snake'.

A Blackpool Mecca spin in '73, the 45 proved real popular until the pop dross of twelve months later froze it out.

Top 500 Position: **311**
Original Label: **Ric-Tic**
Current Value: **£5**

'One of the first big Ric-Tics'

Brian Rae, DJ, North Wales, UK

Al Kent

You Got To Pay The Price

Born Al Hamilton, Al Kent, along with Edwin Starr, put the Ric-Tic label right on the map, with many eager collectors searching for every number.

The UK sought fit to release the side on Track in 1967.

A nifty guitar lead groove that Duane Eddy would be proud of, Kent recorded a few worthwhile tracks with Ed Wingate and even managed a tour with the Ric-Tic revue in the early 80's.

Massive at the Wheel, the tune even realised a vocal version too by Gloria Taylor on King Soul and Silver Fox.

Top 500 Position: **312**
Original Label: **ABC Paramount**
Current Value: **£150 Issue**
£100 Demo

'A lounge classic long before the new cult revival'

Gavin Lacey, Soul Fan, London, UK

Eddie Bishop

Call Me

During the 70's the all nighters certainly tested all formats of dance. From the new releases more in keeping with London, to off-the-wall pop stompers, Soul temporarily went on the back burner... Cue oddities such as saxophonist Eddie Bishop's 'Call Me'. The Tony Hatch thingy covered for about the thirtieth time, but the dance floor had it sewn to the holdall and Bishop did at least score somewhere.

Perennially popular amongst the Scooter scene, quite what this Hatch composition that was even recorded by Lulu has to do with Northern Soul, I am still trying to work out!

Top 500 Position:	**313**
Original Label:	**Brunswick**
Current Value:	**£10 Issue**
	£15 Demo

'A hazy, fuzzy dancer that seemed to work hand-in-hand with the pills'

Bob Tinsley, Soul Fan, West Midlands, UK

Johnny Jones and the King Casuals

Purple Haze

Hendrix rock masterpiece given a full Soul workout by Atlanta's Johnny Jones.

The year 1972, and with the Torch firmly installed as the top venue, a mixed bag of weird 45's were still knocking around (Scratchy, Put It Where You Want It etc), Purple Haze was no exception!

It really does work though, with the group chanting the lyrics almost demanding audience participation. Remember back in those days the Casino 'clobber' had not yet fully surfaced and it was not uncommon to be standing outside the Hose Street venue with an afghan coat or two!

Top 500 Position:	**314**
Original Label:	**Tower**
Current Value:	**£25**

'The enormity of the first few bars will live forever'

Tony Michaelaides, Soul Fan, London, UK

World Column

So Is The Sun

Not too many 45's are massive on the scene at first play... this Soul single with a distinct Sly Stone flavour was for Ian Levine.

The hook and lyrics are fairly meaningless, it's the 'pap pap pap pap pap pap pa pa' that whips the dancers to a frenzy. The original 'b' side is a Deep Soul classic incidentally, but the mayhem created by 'sun' makes it one of the scenes most exciting discoveries ever.

Northern fans of a younger generation will no doubt remember UK Mod revival band the Jam's shameless rip-off, (or is that 'tribute' or 'homage'?) 'Trans Global Express'.

Top 500 Position: **315**
Original Label: **Tay-Ster**
Current Value: **£500**

*'What is Northern Soul?...
Look no further!'*

Sharon Levesly, Soul Fan, London, UK

Lillie Bryant

Meet Me Halfway

Coming straight out of The Isley's - 'This Old Heart Of Mine', Bryant debuts for Jack Taylor's Tay-Ster label with a masterpiece.

Originally with New York pop duo Billie and Lillie who had two top twenty hits in the US during the late 50's, she tried the solo route with a really good commercially sounding Soul side. Instigated by DJ Barry Tasker at Manchester's short lived Pendulum venue, it failed to attain greater popularity due to the lack of originals in circulation, the one illustrated is in fact the original copy spun by Barry all those years ago!

Top 500 Position: **316**
Original Label: **Wind-Hit**
Current Value: **£1,000**

*'The true original is
SO hard to find!'*

Mark Levesly, Soul Fan, London, UK

Servicemen

Need A Helping Hand

The value may look odd considering many DJ's had it at their disposal in the mid 70's! The fact is the original on Wind Hit featuring the excellent flip 'Are You Angry' is <u>very rare</u>.

Danceability-wise this is the business and to be honest I can't understand why the group never made it after supplying us with 3 excellent 45's - the further 2 are on Chartmaker and Patheway.

DJ Colin Curtis got this one away in 1974. An irresistible vibe intro leaps into a frenzied groove that no self respecting dancefloor should be without!

Top 500 Position: **317**
Original Label: **MGM**
Current Value: **£150 Issue**
£75 Demo

'The Soul of the Carolinas'

John Swain (deceased),
Hillsborough, North Carolina, USA

Top 500 Position: **318**
Original Label: **MGM**
Current Value: **£150**

'A great double header from a massive artist on our scene'

Bernie O'Brien, Soul Fan, Lancashire, UK

The Embers

Watch Out Girl

In 1978 I visited Raleigh, North Carolina to meet up with record dealer John Swain (deceased) who appeared to be the main contact for Soul outside of the Wax Museum in Charlotte. I certainly knew I was in the right town when the following morning of my arrival, I was subjected (while eating eggs benedict) to a background tape of 'Watch Out Girl', 'I've Been Hurt', 'Be Young, Be Foolish, Be Happy'. I noticed a distinct wiggle from the waitress (who obviously knew the tunes) and asked if she liked the music. As straight faced as you like she hollered 'ah love to shag'. Napkins were quickly ordered as the coffee spill was burning a hole in my Soul!

The Carolinas obviously have a scene that is parallel with our own and thoroughly enjoyable, with DJ's discovering dance sides that sit well within their parameters. The Embers, who are white, are legendary down there and Jackie Gore's outfit are not without a spin or two here with rarities on Bell, Atlantic and EEE. The stock copy incidentally appears to be incredibly rare although it sold fairly well in the South Eastern part of the US. Maybe, that's where they all are!

Dean Courtney

Love, You Just Can't Walk Away

Courtney could be forgiven for thinking that he was making singles for the north of England during his 60's career.

The RCA and MGM efforts are terrific and outside of his other anthem 'I'll Always Need You', this late 70's spin has been nearly as popular in some quarters. A very well produced disc it would appear not to have actually been issued for some strange reason.

On a recent visit to the UK combining a licensing deal for some of his unissued RCA material with a PA at the 1999 Northern Soul Convention in Blackburn he was a great hit with the Soul crew.

Top 500 Position: **319**
Original Label: **Brunswick**
Current Value: **£30 Issue**
£50 Demo

'A groovy irresistible dancer that just about EVERYBODY loves'

Weldon Arthur McDougall III,
Harthon Records

The Cooperettes

Shing-A-Ling

Allnighter classic from 1972, and very difficult to quantify against other more unusual but popular discoveries of recent times. Everything is here, the Harthon groove, great lead, commercial song and lotsa gloss!

The unreleased demo by Irma titled 'You Need Love' received a few plays in the 80's and remains the collectors choice, but the old timer is the one that wins hands down.

Snare drums, strings and that hook, turn it into something special.

Top 500 Position: **320**
Original Label: **Constellation**
Current Value: **£15 Issue**
£30 Demo

'I'm proud to have the contributed to Northern Soul...'

Gene Chandler, Artist, USA

Gene Chandler

I Can Take Care Of Myself

Two different eras of popularity for this monumental mid tempo side from the ever popular Eugene Dixon. Firstly towards the tail end of the Wheel returning as a monster revival spin at the Casino.

A terrific double sider with the classier 'Care' just ahead of 'I Can't Save It', it saw a British label release on Action in 1969 two years after its original US outing on Constellation in '67.

Today it is massive once again following a much needed revival by DJ Richard Searling.

Top 500 Position:	**321**
Original Label:	**Brunswick**
Current Value:	**£10 Issue**
	£15 Demo

'Haunting, slick vocals turn an average lyric into something special'

John Moore, Soul Fan, Leeds, UK

Fred Hughes

Baby Boy

Not to be confused with Freddie Hughes who recorded for Wee in California the Chicago based singer recorded a few sides for Brunswick during the 60's. Born in Arkansas, he quickly established himself as a quality Soul singer signing to Vee-Jay in 1965, and scoring a major R&B hit with 'OO Wee Baby I Love You'.

The 1968 recording 'Baby Boy' took off at the Torch all-nighter and has been a classic revival tune ever since.

Top 500 Position:	**322**
Original Label:	**Sure-Shot**
Current Value:	**£50**

'The bass intro is enough for dancers to start the movements'

Steve Roberts,
Soul Fan, Gwent, Wales, UK

The Malibus

Gee Baby (I Love You)

Lead by Monroe Powell. From the Duke/Peacock stable comes this 1967 record from Houston. A dark sort of production with the group groovin' along to an irresistible rhythm track, leaving the hook to sink into your subconscious. DJ Ian Levine discovered and played the first copy in late '73.

The band went on to record three other singles for the label, as well as one for Duke.

Top 500 Position: **323**
Original Label: **Nite Life**
Current Value: **£300**

'You must experience this at an all nighter to fully enjoy it

Jeff Holland, Soul Fan, Australia

The Jades

I'm Where It's At

Attempting to establish the band's origins has drawn a blank. Groups with the same name have seen releases on MGM, Cherry Red (definitely not them), Mode, Tower, Poncello, Imperial and Verve!

Anyway, whoever the Jades really are they should 'take a bow' as this is their entrance to Northerndom. A frantic pop dancer, with a startling intro popularised by Richard Searling and, in its day, his biggest spin as a one-off at the Casino. In a fit of generosity he loaned it out to be copied for a fanzine, the publisher of which proceeded to leave it on top of the hot range in a Fish and Chip on the way home with dire consequences - Ooops!

Top 500 Position: **324**
Original Label: **Breakthrough**
Current Value: **£4,000**

'Rare, rarer... and nearly the rarest'

Mark Villiers, Soul Fan, Suffolk, UK

The Inspirations

No One Else Can Take Your Place

A fabulous group 45 that everyone wants - on both sides of the Atlantic.

Discovered in 1974 by dealer Bob Cattaneo in San Francisco, the record (a one sided demo) started at the customary £100 and turned in one mighty investment for some.

Producer and label owner Joey Jefferson did remix the record in the late 70's and added the instrumental on the flip, but this is a true collector's dream - that has only ever turned up on 3 or 4 occasions.

The group are not to be confused with other bands of the same name, although it is likely they had involvement with other acts on main label Mutt and Jeff.

Top 500 Position: **325**
Original Label: **Verve**
Current Value: **£30 Issue**
£40 Demo

'The gospel feel makes it a worthy addition to the scene'

Tony Lee, Soul Fan, Yorkshire, UK

Clara Ward

The Right Direction

Absolutely fantastic, taken from the acclaimed 'Hang your tears out to dry' album. Jackson had one the best Gospel choirs in the land 40 years ago, and in 1966, decided to be more contemporary and signed to Verve to make a Soul album. Following minor success on the label with a cover of Lennon and McCartney's 'Help' (a good northern 45 too) Verve had a stab with 'Direction' and suddenly found themselves the purveyors of new gospel, releasing the Robert Banks classic 'A Mighty Good Way' in the same vein.

Direction was the operative word for we niter goers in 1972 as the real Soul of 'Gospel Hummingbird' Ward rippled through the Torch perfectly after a dose of Sam and Kitty! A rare version by Herman Griffin and Gerry Jackson exists on the Stone Blue label.

Top 500 Position: **326**
Original Label: **CBS**
Current Value: **£250**

'Northern Soul from the Lake District!

Gary White,
Soul Fan, Barrow-in-Furness, Cumbria

Chapter Five

You Can't Mean It

The Barrow-in-Furness (yes that Barrow), UK-based R&B band, signed with Mervyn Conn who in turn produced two singles for them on CBS.

One is a cover of Maxine Brown's 'One In A Million', preceded by this original composition by group leader Dave Girty. Discovered in Manchester at Granada's great Music Library by legendary 'Junk Shopper' Arthur.

It has had a reasonable amount of play dating back to 1978 and was especially popular amongst the Scooter Boys of the eighties - rising to ever greater heights at every Soul night over the next decade.

Top 500 Position: **327**
Original Label: **Tuff/Karisma**
Current Value: **£30 Tuff**
£300 Karisma

'Could this be the first unofficial rap?'

Tom Hooper, Soul Fan, Northamptonshire, UK

E Rodney Jones

R'n'B Time (Part 1)

As popular as the official sung version by Bobby Treetop ('Wait 'Til I Get To Know Ya'), former 60's DJ on WVON in Chicago was invited to 'cut a record', the idea being that he would play it on his show. Well, in certain quarters it worked with Jones backing up the disc all over the 'Windy City'. Latterly his other Tuff release, the considerably rarer 'Peace Of Mind' has found its own popularity.

It was common practice for DJ's to get in on the action with Tom Clay and Frankie Crocker recording potentially good sellers. Years later we got Chris Hill's 'Renta Santa'!

Top 500 Position: **328**
Original Label: **Date**
Current Value: **£40 Issue**
£50 Demo

'Northern Soul never sounded so good'

Steve Ripley, Sony, London, UK

Johnny Moore

Walk Like A Man

One of the very best records from the Torch era. DJ Tony Jebb played the song with real conviction almost weekly around the same time. A ferocious backbeat with Moore's yelling intro 'I may be down - I may be out' is a true delight.

Not to be confused with the Drifters' front man, Moore recorded for Blue Rock, Bright Star, Larry-O, Jadan and Brunswick.

You can now buy the song on the classic Sony CD 'Soul Time' Vol. 1, I urge everyone to own the it!

Top 500 Position: **329**
Original Label: **Date**
Current Value: **£50**

'Vibes and more vibes - the key ingredient of an all nighter classic'

Gill Warner, Soul Fan, Staffordshire, UK

The Sweet Things

I'm In A World Of Trouble

A spate of fabulous recordings on the Columbia spin-off Date in the 60's, meant the scene could get it's teeth into the excitement they created. A girl group sound from '66 with a typical New York production and oh-so-heavenly vocals.

Lead by Francine Barker who later became Peaches (and Herb) thus embarking on a successful career. The girls recorded two singles for Date with this being the undoubted winner. Tailor made for 60's dancing, the sax break, vibes and altogether polished production separate the side from other less obvious 45's.

A true Golden Torch anthem with DJ's Tony Jebb and Keith Minshull leading the way.

Top 500 Position: **330**
Original Label: **MGM**
Current Value: **£150 Demo**
£250 Issue

'Re-discovered in the 80's, which captured the texture of it perfectly'

Brian Wilks, Soul Fan, Manchester, UK

Andrea Henry

I Need You Like A Baby

Impossible to play this during the 70's due to the down tempo though the subtlety made it a great listen in any era. Detroit was the recording base for the Herman Griffin production at United Sound in March, 1966.

A cover by Janice on Roulette failed to stir any competition and Henry is just Tammi Terrellish enough to win the interest of a crowd who no longer expected (or indeed wanted) 100 mph stompers by the 1990's. If any record epitomises Northern Soul's new wave then this is it.

Top 500 Position: **331**
Original Label: **Brunswick**
Current Value: **£6 Issue**
£15 Demo

'The lead vocal is the man's finest hour

Peter Rose, Soul Fan, Hong Kong

The Artistics

I'm Gonna Miss You

Fronted by Marvin Smith, this in all probability is the classiest smoocher to arrive at the Twisted Wheel. A reasonable sized hit in the US, it failed on all fronts here, until Whitworth Street became the focal point for such brilliant music. Smith shows off his vocal range with a lovely falsetto that Eddie Kendricks would have been proud of.

The flip, 'Hope We Have', has also become a perennial oldies favourite in its own right.

The group also recorded for Okeh.

Top 500 Position: **332**
Original Label: **Despenza**
Current Value: **£200/**
£600 Wand

'60's Chicago that never goes out of fashion'

Brian Allen,
Soul Fan, Nottinghamshire, UK

The Ivorys

Please Stay

Lead by Anita Anderson and an excellent example of a record the 'never-quite-made-it' years ago soaring in demand and therefore price as the UK found out just how rare it really was.

Talking of value, the single was picked up for national release by Wand in 1966, but try finding that release!

A long time in the making, today 'Please Stay' is far bigger than when first it broke in the 70's at the Cleethorpes Allnighter.

A superb single from Chicago.

Top 500 Position: **333**
Original Label: **Caravelle**
Current Value: **£150**

'Swamped by better records during the golden era, it has now matured into a fine adult - albeit 25 years later'

Stefan Kryzwicki, Soul Fan, USA

The Chaumonts

I Need Your Love

Also on Bay Sound. A sort of love-hate relationship exists with this 1967 obscurity from Baltimore, MD.

The label had the great Nicky C record too, but the Chaumonts, probably due to the irritating girl chorus 'ooing and wowing', had the most commercial sounding cut of the label's releases amongst their 8 outings.

The Chaumounts is generally considered have been most popular on the East Coast of England and two of their Bay Sound releases have also had plays on the scene.

Top 500 Position: **334**
Original Label: **Veep**
Current Value: **£10 Issue**
£25 Demo

'This is a Randazzo-Pike composition, enough said!

Simon Wakely, Soul Fan, Australia

Little Anthony and the Imperials

Gonna Fix You Good

Although Mr. Gourdine from Brooklyn, New York is undoubtedly famous here for 'Better Use Your Head', this '66 outing was the first introduction to the group for the Northern scene.

The US No. 4 in '58, 'Tears On My Pillow' did not sell here hence the unknown quantity of the act. . Our first main all-night venue unearthed the gem from it's UK base of United Artists, and the disc became an absolute monster even getting bootlegged as early as 1970!

Top 500 Position: **335**
Original Label: **Share**
Current Value: **£8 Issue**
£15 Demo

'Writer Dave Godin's cementation with the North'

Tony Hallsworth, Soul Fan, Derby, UK

The Ad-Libs

Nothing Worse Than Being Alone

As a youngster reading Blues and Soul magazine, the tales of Northern Soul as portrayed by writer Dave Godin convinced me to investigate further and leave the mining town that had been my world for 14 years.

Godin was fully aware of the demand for obscure uptempo North American 45's, so, upon his inaugural visit to Whitworth Street in early 1970, he offered DJ Les Cokell 'first play' on a 1968 recording for Van McCoy's Share label by '65 hitmakers the Ad-Libs. Lead singer Mary Ann Thomas had lead the act successfully with the initial recordings on Blue Cat, with one release on Karen and the mighty 'New York In The Dark' on A.G.P. before a tie up with Van the man!

Oozing with class the production seems spot on and lyrically par excellence, surprisingly though as good as it is it did not become the monster that DG thought it should have been.

Top 500 Position: **336**
Original Label: **Soul**
Current Value: **£50**

'Superb Motown from the early days of Northern'

Richard Layton, Soul Fan, Worcester, UK

Frances Nero

Keep On Loving Me

Frances was a teenage singer who had one shot at success with Motown subsidiary, Soul, it failed despite - gaining radio airtime, especially in the Philadelphia area.

'Keep On Loving Me' is yet another gem of classy production from Berry Jnr's recording empire which is so 'happening' that it just mystifies me why it didn't hit!

This lady's story continues though courtesy of our own Ian Levine who tracked the lady down in Detroit and recorded 'Footsteps Following Me' which became a big hit some 25 years later, ironically as it happens because Ian who was one of the people responsible for the Northern popularity of her first release!

Top 500 Position: **337**
Original Label: **Queen City**
Current Value: **£1,500 Issue**
£2,000 Demo

'My worst seller - yet so popular'...

Sammy Campbell,
Lead Singer, Newark, New Jersey, USA

The Del-Larks

Job Opening

Discovered by DJ Ian Levine who not only turned his discovery into a monster floor filler but also went on to record the lead singer, Sammy Campbell, under his stage name of Tyrone Ashley on several disco cuts in the 70's.

Remaining very rare, yours truly found a black and silver demo in a store in Newark, New Jersey, in 1977... I sold it for £100 - I'll never make a stockbroker!

This is a superb East Coast group 45 that sounds unlike any other and that just about EVERYBODY wants!

Top 500 Position: **338**
Original Label: **Capitol**
Current Value: **£50**

'After hearing this I knew the meaning of 'keep the faith'

R, Soul Fan, Doncaster, UK

Jerry Cook

I Hurt On The Other Side

One of those Soul obscurities that makes you wonder how it failed to hit!

Written by Sidney Barnes who performed it on the Blue Cat label, the unknown but fantastic Jerry Cook (I feel this must be a pseudonym) became one of the most crucial discoveries after the Torch closed and Wigan opened. The scene, in a sort of limbo at the time, needed various new finds and this certainly fitted the bill.

A much better production than Barnes' version with a gloss and vivacity missing from the original take.

Top 500 Position:	**339**
Original Label:	**Wand**
Current Value:	**£10 Issue**
	£20 Demo

'Vibrant and compelling'

Ken Holmes, Soul Fan, Leeds, UK

Chuck Jackson

These Chains Of Love (Are Breaking Me Down)

'Chains' was originally a Country recording by BJ Thomas (remember 'I Don't Have A Mind Of My Own'?) on Hickory, but our man wins through in the end. Released here on Pye International it became one of the first big all-nighter sounds via the Twisted Wheel.

Much has been written and said about Jackson, suffice to say this is undoubtedly his best 60's Northern dancer.

Top 500 Position:	**340**
Original Label:	**Quinvy**
Current Value:	**£700**

'One of the most talked about and least successful floor fillers'

Rob Whitton, Soul Fan, Hertfordshire, UK

Don Varner

Tear Stained Face

When a record is discovered and pre-promoted as was this when Ian Levine played it as early as 1974, the dance floor expectancy was high to say the least. In real terms the song was a failure. During the 80's and 90's with more record collector involvement, the 45 from Alabama realised its true potential.

Varner hailing from the state, was produced by Quin Ivy, a local DJ and label owner. He recorded for Diamond, Downbeat, House Of Orange, Quinvy and sister label South Camp.

Top 500 Position: **341**
Original Label: **Sound Stage 7**
Current Value: **£40 Issue**
£30 Demo

'A vibrant piece of Soul group machinery'

Carol Frederick,
Soul Fan, Stoke-on-Trent, UK

The Valentines

Breakaway

Another 45 totally out of focus, with dealers finding it a tough cookie to sell. Try explaining that to the traders of rare singles 25 years ago!

A terrific sound from Nashville, that is simply a dancer of some repute. The group are not the ones who recorded for Rama in the 50's, but a quartet who cut two singles for Sound Stage 7 in 1969.

Once again, the fun element of the side takes centre stage as 'Breakaway' was an absolute giant 1972-74 and it is tricky to find original copies that do not jump!

Maybe a little too 'boppy' for today's market, but an important jigsaw piece in the make up of Northern Soul.

Top 500 Position: **342**
Original Label: **Sonday**
Current Value: **£20 Issue**
£30 Demo

'The energy level of this fresh sounding Northern side is second to none'

Bev Chalmers, Soul Fan, Coventry, UK

Leslie Uggams

Love Is A Good Foundation

The first time the UK had encountered Ms. Uggams was via DJ Ian Levine who yet again sniffed out a winner. Released on Dionne Warwick's label Sonday, the actress/singer from New York performed well on a dynamic song and arrangement. Later, the scene heard from the lady again with the 1966 recording for Atlantic - 'Don't You Even Care'. I foolishly asked Atlantic to re-press it for the UK market (which they did) only to discover it really wasn't that popular! Best return to the Highland Room circa '73 and the exhilaration of 'Love Is A Good Foundation'!

Top 500 Position: **343**
Original Label: **Verve**
Current Value: **£10 Issue**
£15 Demo

'Wild and crazy instrumental'

Dave Owen, Soul Fan, Doncaster, UK

The Triumphs

Walkin' The Duck

The Duck of course was a Soul dance craze among African Americans in '65 and many producers jumped on the bandwagon with their own interpretation of it. Chips Moman a key figure on the Memphis music scene, took local combo The Triumphs to the task and record an instrumental variation of Jackie Lee's hit.

Scorching brass and neat lead guitar are perfect for dancing, helped on enormously by a reasonable supply of copies from the famous Bradford market in '72. The Golden Torch was the outlet for this thoroughly enjoyable romp.

Top 500 Position: **344**
Original Label: **Cadet**
Current Value: **£150**

'Another cut from the incredible Chess stables'

Bob Richards, Soul Fan, North Wales, UK

George Kirby

What Can I Do

A stylish sound that caught on in the 80's, this wonderful Chicago string laden cooler is perfect for the variety the scene now demands.

Kirby is obviously another gem that has not yet heard of our movement as he would I'm sure be amazed at the fond affection we have for this superlative side.

Sadly a further release for the Chess subsidiary Argo records also failed to make any impact in the American charts.

Top 500 Position: **345**
Original Label: **NYCS**
Current Value: **£30**

*'Refreshing to hear
even today'*

Colin Dilnot, Soul Fan, Merseyside, UK

Flame 'N' King

Ho Happy Day

An unusual sort of Gospel/Soul/Disco 45 from New York, '77. DJ Richard Searling played the single approximately two years after release, but even then it was impossible to get.

Developing out of the Fatback Band, the group were simply seeking to cash in on the delicate balance between Soul and disco of the time. As early as '68 the outfit were distributing their own label from their Queens, New York base (Gerry and Paul, The Puzzles), and this feel gooder seemed a natural throwback. The lead singer incidentally is Oscar Richardson.

Top 500 Position: **346**
Original Label: **Dejac**
Current Value: **£75**

*'One of only a small group
of latin 45's on the scene*

Stan Forbes, Collector, Dublin, Eire

Tommy Navarro

I Cried My Life Away

El Watusi by Ray Baretto ventured into Club Soul back in the mid-60's, Tommy Navarro continued that brief tradition.

The Top Of The World monster from the early 80's along with Bobby Valentin's Fania stormer 'Use It Before You Lose It' helped pave the way for more originality and diversity in the scene.

Unlike more overtly latin sounds of the period, Tommy Navarro's classic remains a favourite, having today spread from its more southerly following to be a nationwide floorfiller.

Top 500 Position:	**347**
Original Label:	**Lloyd**
Current Value:	**£40**

'One of the first real Northern sounds'

Mick Roberts, Soul Fan, Nottingham, UK

Paul Kelly

Chills And Fever

Miami based Kelly recorded the song in 1965 for a local Florida label before gaining a national release on Dial, which was distributed by Atlantic.

A reasonable success with sales over 10, 000, the single was released here on Black Atlantic and an immediate hit at the Twisted Wheel club. Kelly, became a revered vocalist in the States with product for Phillips, Happy Tiger and Warner Brothers amongst others.

More recent times have seen the prior release to 'Fever' break on the scene. 'The Upset' is a very rare item from a very well known artist - proving that there are still surprises in store for our scene!

Top 500 Position:	**348**
Original Label:	**Golden World**
Current Value:	**£400 Issue**
	£80 Demo

'Just impossible to get for many years'

Jan Smith, Soul Fan, London, UK

Tamiko Jones

I'm Spellbound

Born Barbara Tamiko Ferguson. First recording contract with Chess. Her first Detroit 45 was for Ed Wingate's Golden World in '66, later recording for Bell subsidiary December before a career with UK based Contempo finding a husband in the shape of label boss and founder member of Blues and Soul John Abbey. I found a yellow stock issue of the single in '78 and to this day can't remember why I would sell such a fantastic and super rare release.

Mostly, the singles are white demo copies, largely from a Soul Bowl haul some 20 years ago. The discovery was unearthed outside of Wigan/Blackpool by Midlands DJ Pep and became one of his 'exclusives',adding to the mystery and collectability at the time.

Written by Rosemary McCoy especially for Jones, it reflected what McCoy saw as her distinctly 'Witchy' sex appeal!

Top 500 Position: **349**
Original Label: **Thelma**
Current Value: **£35 Issue**
£100 Demo

Emanuel Laskey

I'm A Peace Loving Man

'A Detroit Soul brother that helped expose the great Thelma label to the UK

Richard Allinson, Collector, Detroit, USA

Recording for NPC, Wild Deuce and Thelma, Lasky was the top drawer singer who sadly did not breakout of the local scene, turning to Gospel instead. The 45 we are focussing on is the first play of any Thelma release, gaining minor plays at the Golden Torch.

The act himself was around the Don Davis set up as far back as '63 with a song called 'Welfare Cheese', and whilst a reasonable hit ensued, it is his later material on Thelma which saw his reputation grow in the UK.

Top 500 Position: **350**
Original Label: **Atlantic**
Current Value: **£20 Issue**
£30 Demo

Barbara Lewis

I Remember The Feeling

'I couldn't believe it! seeing Barbara Lewis performing at a flea market in Orlando!'

Ray at Rock 'n' Roll Heaven, Orlando, USA

A great cover exists too by Deon Jackson. This is one of Lewis' sleepers airing periodically over 25 years, but increasing of late.

Barbara was born in South Lyon, Michigan and discovered by WHRB DJ and later Karen (named after his daughter) records boss Ollie McLaughlin.

Written by Rose McCoy and recorded at Atlantic studios in June '66 the track is about as professional as you can get. Her earlier works including 'Someday We're Gonna Love Again' from '64 often included backing vocals from the mighty Dells.

Top 500 Position: **351**
Original Label: **Jamie**
Current Value: **£15 Issue**
£30 demo

*'Cool as you like for
the newcomer'*

Tony Leggett, Soul Fan, North Wales, UK

Marke (Chris) Jackson

I'll Never Forget You

Released in the US as Marke and here as Chris. The single recorded by Van McCoy in 1968 was the first in a series of demos recorded by Van and Billy Jackson. What happened to the Billy Jackson sessions we are not exactly sure, except according to (Billy) Jackson the singer 'skipped town' during a dispute. McCoy recorded a demo too titled 'Since there's no doubt' which did surface on acetate but never came out despite being scheduled to be released on the UK '444' label.

The single is as classy as you would expect from Van, and forgotten by a few, when reminded of it's existence, big smiles fill the room.

Top 500 Position: **352**
Original Label: **Theoda**
Current Value: **£150**

*'My northern Soul roots
started with this fantastic
Detroit dancer'*

Cath Lubinski, Soul Fan, London

Ann Perry

That's The Way He Is

First spun by DJ Pep, at Wolverhampton's Catacombs, the super quick tempo, fresh sounding female vocal (we know of no other record by her) and a glorious hook line make for an incredible dancer.

The record was released twice, once locally in Detroit and again in Los Angeles (identifiable by the Circa Distribution rosette on the light green, rather than light blue label).

Originally popular as an instrumental - famed for the way its beat ricocheted off the back wall at Wigan - today the vocal is a monstrous all nighter favourite!

Top 500 Position: **353**
Original Label: **Musicor**
Current Value: **£6**

'I sincerely hope you have as much fun dancin' to it as I did creating it'

Richard 'Popcorn' Wylie,
Producer, Detroit, USA

The Platters

Washed Ashore
(On A Lonely Island In The Sea)

When Sonny Turner replaced Tony Williams in the group everybody said 'what are they going to do now?', the answer was to start making top quality Soul music!

The traditional balladeers donned dancing shoes as they teamed up with Wylie and Hestor to make a new album in early 1967. Recording in New York and at the Terra Shirma studios in Detroit, Turner pulled in some of his best performances with the above, 'I Love You 1,000 Times' and 'With This Ring', as well as the cover of John Hampton's Northern monster 'Not My Girl' (unreleased at the time).

'Washed Ashore' has become <u>the</u> dancer even outsmarting the energetic 'Sweet Sweet Lovin', itself a major Northern item at the Wheel. While remembered as one of the first major Black groups, their 60's period for Soul lovers was by far the best.

Top 500 Position: **354**
Original Label: **Sidra**
Current Value: **£100 Red**
£60 Blue

'Just made for the Northern Soul dancers'

John Kirsten, Soul Fan, London, UK

'Instrumental' (Ronnie and Robyn)

Sidra's Theme

The more popular instrumental to a vocal by Ronnie and Robyn was discovered in 1974 and its popularity surged as both major venues at the time (Wigan Casino and Blackpool Mecca) were on it like a shot.

The vocal as you would expect is pop, but the instrumental is pure Detroit and pretty good too. The unusual harp intro builds to a great orchestral performance (the invoice for musician participation must have been staggering) and the beat relentlessly kicks throughout. To anyone hearing it from outside the UK, you might think you were listening to 'two way family favourites on short wave'. To the North it's another chapter in this most remarkable scene.

Incidentally Robyn went on to record for Motown subsidiary, VIP, as part of 'Rick, Robyn and Him'.

Top 500 Position: **355**
Original Label: **Hickory**
Current Value: **£8 Issue**
£15 Demo

'Still a terrifically exciting track'

Chris Johnson, Soul Fan, Hong Kong

The Newbeats

Run Baby Run

From the first wave of rare 45's to be played this major Stateside hit from 1966 shook the Twisted Wheel in the late 60's and everyone wanted it - so much so it charted in '71 and crossed over to every teen disco. The group assembled in Nashville featured the high falsetto of Texas born Larry Henley. the act also scored on the scene with 'Crying My Heart Out' .

Very forgotten and far too commercial to play in these times the track was on everyone's lips for around 2 years and was popularised by mobile discos everywhere.

Top 500 Position: **356**
Original Label: **Goldspot /GAR**
Current Value: **£200 Goldspot**
£100 GAR Issue
£50 GAR Demo

'A tricky intro but with enough panache to be a true original'

Kev Sowerby, Soul Fan, Cumbria, UK

Kenny Smith

Lord What's Happening To Your People

Originally in doo-wop group Otis Smith and the Charms. The disc had two almost simultaneous releases for the Cincinatti, Ohio labels.

The first on Goldspot has a church organ intro, the latter a more contemporary version in keeping with the time, 1972. Smith had recorded for RCA in the late 60's without any success and this great gospel groover was to become an anthem at Blackpool Mecca largely due to plays by resident DJ Colin Curtis.

The copies on Goldspot and the blue stock issue on GAR are incredibly rare, so check those collections immediately.

Top 500 Position:	**357**
Original Label:	**Soft/Coral**
Current Value:	**£50 Soft**
	£10 Coral

'This side displays all the hallmarks of a monster Northern sound'

Tom Wilkinson, Soul Fan, Scotland, UK

The Sons Of Moses

Soul Symphony

Major Bill Smith of the US Air force, upon retirement, eagerly wanted to get into the business and sources report over 3, 000 recordings were produced by the man in less than 15 years. With hits from Bruce Chanel and Paul and Paula under his belt he ventured into Soul music mainly inspired by Randy Wood of Mirwood whom he had met when Wood was owner of Dot records. During the period '65-69, Smith had Pic and Bill, Robert Thomas, Sunny and Phyllis (aka The Nomads) and others, recording alternate versions in many cases. In fact during '74 a collector from the Burnley area was almost being sent weekly new versions of the song by Ede Robin (a vocal) plus the Hammond Bros and Maggie(an instrumental).

Smith, ever the entrepreneur latched on to the Northern market custom pressing his 'rarities' to meet demand. Initially released on his own 'Soft' label, and later leased to Coral, 'Symphony' is simply a tuneful play on the works of Ramsey Lewis and, whilst largely forgotten, the 45 is still a floor filler when played.

Top 500 Position:	**358**
Original Label:	**Sound Stage 7**
Current Value:	**£20 Issue**
	£30 Demo

'Capturing the very essence of the 60's perfectly'

Tom Brewer, Soul Fan, Leicester, UK

Little Hank

Mister Bang Bang Man

First plays in the UK were as far back as '68 and, is credited as being one of the first rare 45's to be reissued. The UK release on London is incredibly rare and although acknowledged by the Record Collector price guide at £35, sources reveal it is more likely to be £100 as the single was withdrawn after only a week!

The US copy didn't fair much better, but the underground loved it. Coming off like a cross between 'Shotgun' and 'Shotgun Wedding' the song is heavy with metaphors of a different kind, Hank sounds pretty good with his one of only two releases on the label.

Saxes blaring all over the place, it programmes perfectly with the Willie Mitchell's and Robert Parker's. Very southern in it's feel, very Northern as an end result!

Top 500 Position: **359**
Original Label: **Columbia**
Current Value: **£300 YOP**
£200 JF Demo
£300 JF Issue

Youth Opportunity Programme / Jimmy Fraser

Of Hopes And Dreams And Tombstones

'The title may well have put dealers off even playing it'

Chris Little, Soul Fan, Lancashire, UK

A promo only from Columbia originally credited to the 'Youth Opportunity Programme', featuring sleeve notes by Senator Hubert Humphrey, it was subsequently issued as Jimmy Fraser.

Not surprisingly when you listen to the lyrics the song in fact has a strong social message, and indeed it was part of the same US government sponsored campaign that produced Brenda Holloway's 'Play It Cool, Stay In School'

The record originally surfaced in the late seventies with the instrumental side in favour. Twenty years later it was the R&B tinged vocal that had the dancers clapping to this memorable tune's perfectly timed breaks.

Top 500 Position: **360**
Original Label: **Brunswick**
Current Value: **£8 Issue**
£15 Demo

Gene Chandler and Barbara Acklin

From The Teacher To The Preacher

'A brilliant duet packed full of Marvin and Tammi overtones'

Gail Smith, Soul Fan, Hampshire, UK

Both hugely successful at Brunswick with Chandler already being charted in the Northern hall of fame.

Now we look at the late Ms. Acklin who enjoyed healthy sales on many 45's for the label, not least 'Love Makes A Woman' which peaked at no. 15 in '68 stateside. Barbara who recently passed away was cousin to Monk Higgins who recorded her both as Barbara Allen and Acklin for his Special Agent label out of Chicago. She married Eugene Record of the Chi-Lites and co-wrote 'Have You Seen Her' before signing to Capitol.

The classic 'Teacher' is an old school Wheel sound with a certain classiness that both artists generated on most of their recordings.

Top 500 Position: **361**
Original Label: **Okeh**
Current Value: **£75 Issue**
£100 Demo

'Okeh was undoubtedly the scenes' backbone, product wise'

Barry Wain, Soul Fan, London, UK

The Triumphs

I'm Coming To Your Rescue

Ferocious mover from the scene's favourite label. The group from Los Angeles were brought to Okeh by producer Arthur Wright and released another goodie 'Memories',but the winner is undoubtedly 'Rescue'.

Played extensively at the Golden Torch,'I'm Comin' To Your Rescue' takes a well earned position in the top 500 for the Triumphs, a group often mistakenly associated with the Verve combo of the same name who hailed from Memphis and also appear in the chart.

Top 500 Position: **362**
Original Label: **Imperial**
Current Value: **£40 Demo**
£100 Issue

'Blue Eyed Soul at its very best'

Brian Lea, Soul Fan, Greater Manchester, UK

Danny Wagner and the Kindred Soul

I Lost A True Love

After playing this and his version of Johnny Wyatt's 'This Thing Called Love', from the Kindred Soul Album, I discovered 'I Lost a True Love' was indeed a single too!

Fortunately this invigorating side was a instant hit at Wigan Casino when I first played it in March 1974. Barry White had a hand in the production and the record company saw Wagner as a new Johnny Rivers, who at the time had left the company and formed the U. S. Soul City label.

Top 500 Position: **363**
Original Label: **Bareback**
Current Value: **£150 Issue**
£200 Demo

*'One of the happiest Northern
sounds you're
ever likely to hear'*

Tony Gioe, DJ, New York, USA

Will Collins and Will Power

Is There Anything I Can Do?

A good friend of mine Tony Gioe was the A&R man for Midland International and had scored hits in the U. S. with Carole Douglas and Silver Convention, as well as the great Marboo 45 'What About Love'.

After lunch one afternoon in the late seventies, Tony asked if I wanted to take a few boxes of some new releases from their new sister label Bareback. I politely declined as I though what the heck am I going to do with new 70's releases! You can imagine how I felt when I discovered that DJ Richard Searling was playing a cover up by The Love Committee known to be by Will Collins on Bareback.

Somehow I wish the record was poor - fat chance! This one is straight from the top deck! Collins went on to record for Capitol and gave our spin off scene Jazz Funk the classic 'Where You Gonna Be Tonight'.

Top 500 Position: **364**
Original Label: **Music Merchant**
Current Value: **£10**

*'It was amazing to hear this
sampled so heavily in a new
track by Fat Boy Slim'*

Dave Carne, Soul Fan, Cumbria, UK

The Just Brothers

Sliced Tomatoes

This 1972 instrumental recorded for Music Merchant records first came to Northern Soul's attention courtesy of the Torch, remaining popular throughout the 70's.

Played as an almost brand new release, 'Sliced Tomatoes' with its twangy guitar reminiscent of a Surf instrumental soon became a major dancefloor filler in the Stoke venue already famed for such legendary instrumentals as 'Thumb A Ride' and 'Tracks To Your Mind'.

In more recent years, despite a bizarre burst of interest resulting from heavy sampling of the track by dance supremo Norman 'Fat Boy Slim' Cook, it is the duo's earlier vocal recording for Garrison 'Carlena', also an excellent (and today very pricey) dancer, that has supplanted the popularity of 'Sliced Tomatoes'... Though it will be sometime before it attains the longevity of its younger brother!

Top 500 Position: **365**
Original Label: **Tetragramatton**
Current Value: **£10 Issue**
£15 Demo

'The performance in Blackburn is discussed almost as much as his music'

Terry Mould, Soul Fan, South Wales, UK

Bobby Paris

Per-son-ally

Let's establish some interesting facts on New Yorker Paris who moved to California in the late 60's. On three different labels he has a trio of absolute hot-to-trot 45's of which this 1968 recording was his first actual play on the scene.

The excitement factor at the Golden Torch was paramount, and the one line hook followed by 'I Don't Give A Hang' (substituting 'Damn' which was still considered swearing at the time) has become one of the biggest Northern hits.

The single got a UK release on Polydor in 1968 which is much rarer than the U.S. copy (weighing in at around £60) and was covered by both the notorious Wigan's Ovation and Strawberry Jam - weak versions by comparison with our man Paris of course!

Top 500 Position: **366**
Original Label: **Verve**
Current Value: **£100**

'A total adrenaline rush hitting 9. 9 on the Richter scale!'

Martin Grimes, Soul Fan, Northampton, UK

Youngblood Smith

You Can Split

A total one-off from the man and sheer athleticism from the audience made it a top dancer during the Wigan era.

Re-issued far too early (1974) and with the misleading title 'Walk On Baby', which was it's original cover up name.

Unless you know otherwise, the 45 was never actually issued, whilst most of the demos ended up in the UK... No change there then!

An intro similar to 'I Can't Help Myself' by the Four Tops.

Top 500 Position: **367**
Original Label: **KKC**
Current Value: **£300**

'Many slants on the Philly Dog craze have appeared, Jimmy's interpretation is right up there'

Bill Esplen, Soul Fan, Northumberland, UK

Jimmy Raye

Philly Dog Around The World

Sticks Evans a New York session drummer, owned two labels Hype and KKC. The 1966 single on KKC is an earth shattering 45 that didn't click initially when played by DJ Ian Levine at Blackpool Mecca and it was down to Soul Sam to popularise the record at St. Ives and other venues of the time. Wigan eventually took its cue for a piece of dance ephemera almost tailor-made for its cavernous dancehall.

Owning an original copy is not quite as easy as you may think as a lookalike counterfeit is still floating around and in many cases masquerading as the original.

Top 500 Position: **368**
Original Label: **United Artists**
Current Value: **£70 Issue**
£100 Demo

'The epitome of big-beat'

Cal Sutton, Soul Fan, London, UK

Ray Pollard

The Drifter

As tastes have changed over the years, the appreciation of total quality has never lapsed. 'The Drifter' was also competently recorded by Long John Baldry on British United Artists.

Well turning full circle we can now honour the side which now ranks as one of the Top 5 'enders', and at least brings Pollard in from the cold.

Largely unknown here, he was the voice behind 50's/early 60's group The Wanderers, moving on to record for UA, Decca, with a version of Elvis' 'Wanderlust', and Shrine. 'It's A Sad Thing', also recorded for UA, also continues to receive attention, but the sheer craft of 'The Drifter', which received a British release, ensures it's popularity long into the new millennium.

Interestingly Ray has only one arm as a result of service in the Korean war, but that hasn't hindered a burgeoning career as a film extra - look closely and you'll see him in 'Ghostbusters'!

Top 500 Position: **369**
Original Label: **Mercury**
Current Value: **£6 Issue**
£10 Demo

'The all 'original' oldie that refuses to lie down!'

Gary Marsh, New Jersey, USA

Jerry Butler

Moody Woman

From Sunflower, Mississippi and the older brother of Billy, the 'Ice Man' started out life with the Northern Jubilee Gospel singers before joining The Quails and of course The Impressions in 1957.

'Moody' was his third to last hit which started back in 1958. The link with Gamble and Huff was a prudent move as the hits trawled out from '67 and continued until '72 before a second wind with Philadelphia International in the mid 70's - then off to Motown.

A remarkable career, with the UK embracing this minor hit from 1969 almost from initial release. However the 'scene' has championed the side in more recent times-to full effect.

Top 500 Position: **370**
Original Label: **Phoof**
Current Value: **£15 Issue**
£25 Demo

'A short lived Wigan anthem, that you either love or hate'

Barbara Teal, Soul Fan, Australia

James Coit

Black Power

When you are on a record buying trip and you find the most in demand single at the time of your enterprising venture it certainly puts a spring in your step.

During a trip to Long Island, New York in 1977, I had James Coit at the top of my wants list. Entering a store I had never been to before imagine my surprise at finding it there. Literally this became a triple figure record for about two months, and while the collector interest has waned over the years I have to reveal that on a closer listen it's not bad at all.

Wigan Casino was the obvious venue to test the water with such a frantic effort and the dancers were equal to it.

Top 500 Position: **371**
Original Label: **Keymen**
Current Value: **£40**

'Great as an instrumental or as a vocal'

Jeff Barry,
Soul Fan, Greater Manchester, UK

The Furys

I'm Satisfied With You

Led by Jerome Edwards the group was handled by James McKeachin (Jimmy Mack - not to be confused with the Palmer artist). A fantastic 1966 recording for an act who tried desperately for a hit via Mark IV and Liberty among others.

James Carmichael's arrangement is awesome as the strings and bass link with the lead's intro 'Hey Girl' into one of the all-time greats. By the way the instrumental take which was massive at the Casino in its own right is only to be found on the various reissues.

A note to collectors - this is a vastly underrated 45!

Top 500 Position: **372**
Original Label: **Capitol**
Current Value: **£20**

'A spate of 'kid' Soul started to infiltrate the scene in early 74, Garner was at the forefront'

Robert Taylor, Soul Fan, London, UK

Reggie Garner

Hot Line

Child TV star Reggie Garner had a brief career musically, scoring with a minor hit for Capitol titles 'Teddy Bear', before departing for ABC and the Northernesque 'Half A Cup'.

Slotting in to a new youthfulness that DJ Ian Levine was implementing i.e. Mark Copage, Leonard Kaigler, Garner's 'Hotline', was unashamedly commercial for an all-nighter monster in the first part of 1975.

Unfortunately he didn't hit the heights TV wise either, and Garner returned to singing under the identity of Reginald.

Top 500 Position: **373**
Original Label: **Impact**
Current Value: **£250 Issue**
£200 Demo

'A real sleeper from where else? - Detroit!'

Barry James, Soul Fan, Detroit, USA

Jock Mitchell

Not A Chance In A Million

Jock recorded two singles for Impact and one for local label Golden Hit which is extremely sought after. The clubs up North plumped for the danceable 'Not A Chance In A Million'.

Certainly a record in the 70's that could not get past around the £10 mark in saleability, the mid-eighties saw this disc recognised as a true classic of non-Motown Detroit Soul - with perhaps one of the greatest changes in tempo ever committed to vinyl!

Top 500 Position: **374**
Original Label: **Verve**
Current Value: **£100 Issue**
£80 Demo

'A superb vocal'

Gary Fisher, Soul Fan, Indiana, USA

Howard Guyton

I Watched You Slowly Slip Away

Former lead singer of Festival group, the Top Notes which also featured Derek Martin, Howard Guyton, recorded this terrific beat shuffler for Verve in 1966. Fellow New York recording artist Lou Courtney cut it for Philips too, but even though Courtney was the writer Guyton's version just edges it.

Amazingly this was the original 'cheap' 45 until the 80's, when tempos changed and the disc became a seriously sought after item, it now takes its place as something of a latter day classic.

Top 500 Position: **375**
Original Label: **UK Spring**
Current Value: **£10**

'A Mr M's classic'

Richard Thomas, Welling, UK

Millie Jackson

A House For Sale

Another delicious almost new release from Jackson who recorded it for her 1976 LP 'Free And In Love'.

A total Mecca play it caught on instantly with the scene as the transition from mono to stereo was well and truly under construction.

Settling in New York in the late 60's Ms. Jackson recorded her 1st single for MGM titled 'My Heart Took A Licking' which is now being taken seriously by collectors. 'House For Sale' meantime has become a household phrase at most commercial Soul Nights.

Top 500 Position: **376**
Original Label: **Imperial (LP)**
Current Value: **£30**

'To this day, hardly anybody knows the original name and title'

Alan Loxley, Soul Fan, Inverness, UK

Total Eclipses

6 O'Clock

The creativity of record dealer Simon Soussan, was arguably a turning point in the scene's makeup. Discovering odd 45's like 'Footsee' and adding instrumentation to Soul it up a little, gave the scene additional excitement. The Lovin' Spoonful recorded the vocal version and the orchestral cover by Total Eclipses sat on a obscure LP, until SS speeded it up, and gave it a new identity as 'Supertime' by the Golden World Strings.

A little cheeky perhaps, but an improvement on the bland original. This is where only the dancers become appreciative and is considered non-descript by collectors.

Top 500 Position:	**377**
Original Label:	**Goldmine**
Current Value:	**£5**

'Many of my fans rate this as my best - yet it was only a demo!'

Eddie Holman, Artist, USA

Eddie Holman

Where I'm Not Wanted/Hurt

Eddie is a legend of the scene, a writer of a host of classics for Philadelphia's finest, from Larry Clinton to Bernard Williams, he is of course most widely respected for his own golden voice and enormous solo recording output for Parkway, ABC, GSF, Silver Blue and Salsoul.

First finding favour in the North with the ultimate Mod feelgood sound 'Eddie's My Name', his 'Hey There Lonely Girl' became one of the first Northern driven pop hits in 1970.

'Where I'm Not Wanted' and 'Hurt' (also enormously popular by the Victors on Philips) were first played from a double sided Harthon studio demo acetate that still featured the count-ins. Broken by Richard Searling, both deservedly became all-time Station Road dancefloor classics.

Top 500 Position:	**378**
Original Label:	**Mirwood**
Current Value:	**£10 Issue**
	£15 Demo

'Stunningly original and atmospheric, and certainly energising'

Jim Moorhead, Soul Fan, Glasgow, UK

Jackie Lee

Do The Temptation Walk

Synonymous with the scene is Louisiana's Earl Nelson, better known as Lee. The period of 64' to 67' had Nelson working a conveyor belt of dance crazes and uptempo Soul nuggets.

He was possibly the most played artist in Soul Clubs during the late 60's, and we could easily have listed the 'B' side 'Shotgun And The Duck' as this also received adulation from the dancefloor.

His relationship with Randall Wood was critical and historically he was certainly the dance master of the mid sixties in the Los Angeles area.

Top 500 Position:	**379**
Original Label:	**Solid Hit**
Current Value:	**£800**

'The most in demand 45 from the Detroit based Solid Hit label'

Pat Lewis, Artist, Detroit, USA

Pat Lewis

No One To Love

First recording 'Deep Freeze' as part of the Adorables along with sister Diane and another set of sisters called Jackie and Betty (surname unknown). Pat and Diane became two thirds of Isaac Hayes' backup group Hot Buttered Soul. She featured on many Golden World releases and productions by George Clinton, Parliament and Funkadelic. Pat is still active today performing in clubs, in and around the greater Metropolitan Detroit area.

At first sight of the gaudy label you might assume this record was trashy 70s pop, but this sound which took a good while to break is a massively popular Northern Soul classic today.

Lewis recorded three other worthy releases for Solid Hit but for some reason this is by far the rarest.

Top 500 Position:	**380**
Original Label:	**Vee Jay**
Current Value:	**£10 Issue**
	£15 Demo

'A great platform for the lady to discover the UK, and see first-hand the interest in her'

Brenda Hollings, Soul Fan, Manchester, UK

Betty Everett

Getting Mighty Crowded

Born 61 years ago in Greenwood, Mississippi, typical gospel performer who moved to Chicago in the late 50's, recording for Cobra the Vee-Jay. Following the international smash hit of the 'Shoop Shoop Song' and 'Let it Be Me' with Jerry Butler, she recorded the very atmospheric 'Getting Mighty Crowded', which has been revived more recently after a cult following at the Twisted Wheel club.

She later recorded for Uni, with her album track 'You're Falling In Love' being a monster sound and 'Fantasy', she most certainly is an act who's work is cherished by Soul fans worldwide.

Top 500 Position: 381
Original Label: Champion/Doc
Current Value: £20 Champion
£250 Doc

'Now it's been re-discovered as a Motown acetate, interest is riding high again'

Kath Jones, Soul Fan, Sanbach, Cheshire, UK

Sandy Wynns
A Touch Of Venus

Professionally known as Edna Wright and former Honey Cone member. Originally in the Blossoms along with her sister Darlene Love, she recorded for Champion, Simco and Canterbury. The single released with its incredibly rare UK Fontana issue became a huge Catacombs, Mecca and Torch favourite.

A Jobete published song written by Motown staffer Ed Cobb (who produced it for Sandy), 'A Touch Of Venus' was in fact created for the great Marvin Gaye! Whilst Marvin never released it, a demo by Patrice Holloway is doing the rounds at this very moment. Mary Love did also record this classic, though it sadly remained in the can.

Top 500 Position: 382
Original Label: Swan
Current Value: £10 Issue
£25 Demo

'The General commands attention, whenever I hear his sublime voice'

Paul Simpson, Record Dealer, UK

The Showmen
Our Love Will Grow

From one of the best double siders of it's generation. Norman Johnson powers a lead that others dare to follow.

Roaming like a stealth bomber, this side has weaved continuously around the scene, though generally suffering from being 'too easy to get' during the heady 70's.

Finally, we all latched on and bravely played the 'cheapie' until mass overkill turned it underground once more.

The flip 'You're Everything' is now starting to draw attention and not a day too soon. One of the old Swan masters, cut at Virtue studios. Enough said!

Top 500 Position: **383**
Original Label: **Verve**
Current Value: **£100 Issue**
£80 Demo

'Listen to this when you've just split with the missus - it'll slay you!'

Dave Greenhill, Collector, UK

The High-Keys

Living A Lie

The group led by Troy 'Love Explosion' Keyes was typical of its big city production.

A Golden Torch discovery and fairly easy to find throughout the 70's. Eventually the constant demand for copies has forced the price up to reflect its quality as a dancer.

The flip is one of the all-time great 'Soul' sides too but 'Living A Lie' is the one that will never die.

Top 500 Position: **384**
Original Label: **Soozi**
Current Value: **£20**

'How I would love to tell the group what a fabulous track this is'

Julie Roberts, Soul Fan, Nottingham, UK

The Velvet Hammer

Happy

The 70's and Chicago are linked heavily to the charts with the Chi-Lites keeping the Windy City alive. Eugene Record may have been top dog but what about the wannabees such as Velvet Hammer?

Typical falsetto lead in an attempt to challenge the Russell Thompkins of their time, what makes this one shot wonder is the originality of the arrangement. The strings are superb, the song excellent, so one can derive from that, the record company were simply under financed, even more amazing then that this 45 was culled from an album!

One of the better 70's singles to still warm the cockles of many a true Northerner.

Top 500 Position: **385**
Original Label: **Crazy Horse**
Current Value: **£10**

'The second Northern hit for this Blue Eyed outfit"

Ed Philips, Soul Fan, Derby, UK

David and the Giants

Ten Miles High

Following on from their other chart entry, David Huff and The Giants who sound as if they are from New York (that Brooklyn accent gives it away). The Muscle Shoals, Alabama recorded single also failed to make it. DJ Ian Levine quickly found the single off the back of his initial play of 'Superlove'.

Although not quite as big as the former, it certainly did the business in 1974, and prompted Capitol in the UK to re-issue both sides back to back following the big oldies revival of 1975/76.

Top 500 Position: **386**
Original Label: **Minit**
Current Value: **£10 Issue**
£25 Demo

'The real meat 'n' potatoes of the scene'

Bill Snow, Soul Fan, Doncaster, UK

Homer Banks

Hooked By Love

Legendary song writer who provided much of the material for the Stax roster after 1968. He was born in Memphis in 1941, and made his debut on the Genie label recording 'Lady Of Stone'. As well as writing classics such as 'Who's Making Love' for Johnny Taylor, he signed to the Minit label and recorded some absolute dynamite stuff.

The Twisted Wheel club is credited with discovering the disc, and it's getting more plays today as newcomers realise the emotional attachment he had to all his performances- not bad for a singer with a lisp!

His other classic 'A Lot Of Love', also recorded and popular by Taj Mahal, was recently a major hit when covered by Simply Red.

Top 500 Position: **387**
Original Label: **AGC**
Current Value: **£30, £250 with rare flip**

Joe Hicks

Don't It Make You Feel Funky

'The Funk element is certainly missing, Northern Soulers are grateful for that'

Brian Hall, Soul Fan, North Wales, UK

Amazingly enough the record was played on radio by Wolfman Jack (American Graffiti), during his stint out in California. The record sold very little though.

Two separate releases with different flip sides exist, and the record was discovered in 1974 by DJ Ian Levine. Hicks went on to record for the Stax subsidiary Enterprise for whom he made an album, and listening closely to the largely unknown singer from LA he had much too offer.

Top 500 Position: **388**
Original Label: **St Lawrence**
Current Value: **£10 Issue £30 Demo**

Mamie Galore

It Ain't Necessary

'My personal introduction to the Northern scene, and what a record to start me off!'

Ann Roberts, Soul Fan, Stafford, UK

Outstanding 45 from April 1966, that was written by Jerry Butler and almost made the U. S. charts bubbling under at No. 132. Discovered by Monk Higgins, Mamie, born Mamie Davies, recorded for Sack, Thomas and Imperial (with Dee Erwin).

A cover version exists by The Embers on Bell and one by Brandy Alexander on Tangerine titled 'Do Right Man'.

Allnighter-wise it was one of the Top 5 discoveries of 1971.

Top 500 Position:	**389**
Original Label:	**Soul**
Current Value:	**£25**

'This one really gets them going at most venues'

Tim Greensmith, Soul Fan, Sheffield, UK

Junior Walker and the Allstars

Tune Up

Audrey deWalt Jnr. was discovered by Johnny Bristol. 'Tune Up' is one of Junior's first recordings for Motown after being signed to the company's Soul subsidiary. Junior joined the Hitsville roster after Berry Gordy bought out 'Harvey', the label owned by Harvey Fuqua on which the Allstars released 'Twist Lackawanna' and the incredible 'Brainwasher', a cut that makes 'Tune Up' sound like a stroll in the park!

The Northern of scene of late has been experimenting with earlier R&B sides and this unbelievable sax workout quite rightly is one of his most played tunes, even surpassing most of his mid-60's output.

Top 500 Position:	**390**
Original Label:	**Island**
Current Value:	**£20**

'One of the first Mod records to cross over to the Northern Scene'

Rob Glass, Soul Fan, Essex, UK

Wynder K Frog

Green Door

Michael Weaver from Colchester with a surprising Northern Soul hitster. The 60's instrumental version of Jim Lowe's 1956 hit was very popular in the late 60's and became a Wigan giant a decade or so later.

He recorded an album titles 'Out Of The Frying Pan' and worked with the Spencer Davis Group around the same time.

Very little to do with Soul, but a terrific dancer nonetheless.

Top 500 Position: **391**
Original Label: **Excello**
Current Value: **£100**

'Discovered as early as 1969, the collector confined the masterpiece to his bedroom'

Barry Kendrick, Soul Fan, Midlands, UK

Roger Hatcher

Sweetest Girl In The World

Brother to Willie Hatcher and cousin to Edwin Starr.

I was visiting a childhood friend in 1969 and he promptly played a few Twisted Wheel purchases made by his elder brother. Amongst them he spun this 45 which he had got from a Soul pack (very fashionable for collectors at the time), it was years before I actually heard this in a club and even longer before it approached anything like its enormous current popularity.

The Nashville label formed by Ernie Young had boasted some terrific blues music and amazing enough had licensed the flip side 'I'm Gonna Dedicate This Song To You' to UK President. The British indie sadly left off the real winner. Staking it's claim in our hall of fame, this Soul man recorded other 45's In his home town of Detroit on the Dotty's and aptly titled Northern De-La label and finally in the 70's released a very rare and obscure album for the Guiness label.

Top 500 Position: **392**
Original Label: **RCA Victor**
Current Value: **£60 Demo**
                 £300 Issue

'Chandlers' discs escalated in popularity during the 70's, here's another milestone'

Robert Steele, Soul Fan, Los Angeles, USA

Lorraine Chandler

I Can't Change

Despite the famous discussion on 'is she - or isn't she singing flat?' her superbly emotional deliveries ensure that her vinyl output really is top-notch.

The three singles recorded for RCA are quite simply mind blowing and long after the oddities have burned themselves out, these exquisite Jack Ashford productions will still be going strong.

This track also recorded by Yvonne Baker on Junior was first aired by Catacombs DJ and Midlands main man Pep.

Top 500 Position: **393**
Original Label: **Wand**
Current Value: **£150**

'Just one of a multitude of incredible Soul sounds from the boys'

Dallas Frazier, Producer, Texas, USA

The Masqueraders

Do You Love Me Baby?

The Masqueraders from Dallas, Texas are one of the great Soul groups, led by the wonderful voice of Lee W Jones and later by Lee Hatim, their recording career for a wide range of labels including Stairway, AGP, Bell, LaBeat, Amy, ABC and Bang, started with Soul Town, for whom their incredibly rare and extremely popular 'That's The Same Thing' was waxed.

This is yet another 45 that didn't quite make it in the venues of the 70's - it took another decade to appreciate the sheer quality of the recording - a tenfold increase in price has of course ensued.

Top 500 Position: **394**
Original Label: **Date**
Current Value: **£20 Issue**
£12 Demo

'An old-style girl group with a big city production and a lightning quick beat'...

Mitchell Waring, Soul Fan, Bedford, UK

The Charmaines

Eternally

Some 45's take your breath away during a particular time frame. One Saturday morning in February 1974 I received a package from record dealer Simon Soussan with this inside. The second the stylus hit the vinyl I just knew this would be tonight's number one at the Casino, I was not wrong.

Unfortunately the track petered out too early and was promptly re-issued. A mini revival is taking place for records of this ilk at the moment and I am pleased to say the single is once again the centre of attention.

Produced in Detroit by Herman Lewis, the record was quickly picked up by Columbia subsidiary Date for release in 1966.

Top 500 Position: **395**
Original Label: **Parkway**
Current Value: **£400 Issue**
£250 Demo

'A legendary 'cover-up''

Mark Leadbetter, Soul Fan, Sussex, UK

Vickie Baines

Country Girl

When DJ Richard Searling covered over this exquisite 45 on Parkway as Christine Cooper, the mystery became so wrapped up in 'scene euphoria' perhaps only the 'who shot JR 'saga on Dallas was bigger in the 80's.

The single saved Wigan from ridicule in the late 70's, with a subsequent uncovering in 1980.

Baines had two outings for Cameo Parkway both of which failed miserably being unsupported by the label and she moved on to Warner Brothers Soul label, Loma.

To this day the exposure of those initial plays has propelled the side to even greater heights.

But in the mire of 'Joe 90' and Muriel Day, thank heavens for the discovery.

Top 500 Position: **396**
Original Label: **United Artists (UK)**
Current Value: **£50**

'The second of three Northern discoveries by the man'

Alex Philpott, Soul Fan, Staffordshire, UK

Bobby Goldsboro

Too Many People

In similar vein to Paul Anka it was inevitable that Goldsboro from Marianna, Florida would sidestep his pop-country roots to go uptempo in the mid-60's. Strangely his biggest northern hit never saw the light of day in the US, and this is surprising because the 'Honey' man revels with the Soul groove of 1967.

As you would expect Wigan Casino was the stomp outlet for this nifty mover. An investigation of his 60's output reveals a surprising number of similar cuts.

Top 500 Position: **397**
Original Label: **Columbia**
Current Value: **£75 Issue**
£30 Demo

'Another 70's 45 that helped cement a new style within the scene'

Paul Veerhorn, Soul Fan, Holland

Lou Edwards

Talkin' 'Bout Poor Folks (Thinking 'Bout My Folks)

This single was the first sign of a totally new groove that was about to infiltrate the scene in 74'. Looking back the whole shaft style which in theory had nothing to do with Northern was beginning to impose it's style.

The record from 1972 absolutely bombed in the US probably due to an uncompromisingly 'black' style. Originally played by DJ's Ian Levine and Colin Curtis at the famed Highland Room , its Soulful style was very much in vogue at Blackpool Mecca though it is rarely heard these days.

Top 500 Position: **398**
Original Label: **Bell**
Current Value: **£10 Issue**
£20 Demo

'A classic from the early days of the scene'

Jeffrey Mitchell, Soul Fan, London, UK

The O'Jays

I Dig Your Act

A blockbusting side penned by the Poindexter brothers for one of the finest acts ever!

Eddie Levert leads the original Ohio group into ecstacy as they tear into this George Kerr production from late 1967.

Discovered by DJ Eddie O'Jay, their remarkable career dates back to 1958 when they were known as the Mascots. The group recorded for Apollo, Wayco, King, Imperial, Minit, Bell, Neptune and Philadelphia International (the start of their real success), before some cool stuff for EMI's Manhattan.

A real good Northern night can't be complete without hearing this, or one of their many other floorfillers such as 'Hold On' 'I'll Never Forget You' 'Deeper (In Love With You)'.

Top 500 Position: **399**
Original Label: **Candi**
Current Value: **£1,200**

'The introductory church organ makes way for a fantastic Doo-wop, Soul beat'

Mick Plant, Soul Fan, Cumbria, UK

The Empires

You're On Top Girl

James Chavis the label owner, dumped around 1,000 45's to a thrift store near Willmington, Delaware in 1976. I managed to find multiple copies of the in-demand 'Like A Bee' by The Spidells, I also found a copy of this wonderful mover from 65, did I leave a bulk quantity?...

An absolute stormin' dancer far too dated even at the time for success but cherished by collectors and dancers alike resulting in today's massive price tag.

Top 500 Position: **400**
Original Label: **Liberty**
Current Value: **£50 Issue**
£75 Demo

'The emotion ripples through the dance halls as this great balladeer really delivers'

Gary Holland, Soul Fan, Leeds, UK

Gene McDaniels

Walk With A Winner

Eugene McDaniels has just celebrated his 65th birthday.

Originally from Kansas City he moved to Omaha and sang in choirs before signing to Liberty in 1961. In his first two years he had no less than six hits, he also recorded a good follow up to 'Winner' with 'Hang On', before disappearing and performing as Universal Jones in 1972.

Popular for many years, this record is still one of the truly great 'enders'.

Top 500 Position: **401**
Original Label: **Palmer**
Current Value: **£300**

'Firing on all cylinders'

Keith Leadbetter, Soul Fan, Norfolk, UK

The People's Choice

Savin' My Lovin' For You

Not to be confused with the Philadelphia group who recorded for Philips, Phil-LA-Of Soul, PIR etc. Rumours abound that in fact Al Green was in the group, though a recent interview with writer/producer 'Popcorn' Wylie revealed that he certainly <u>didn't remember</u> such a famous minister in the lineup!

In terms of quality, well it's yet another powerhouse group sound that features that rolling Detroit groove made the way only Wylie and Hester know how!

Top 500 Position: **402**
Original Label: **Buttercup**
Current Value: **£30**

'A real Casino anthem'

Graham Leavitt, Soul Fan, Scotland

Sheila Anthony

Livin' In Love

From a label owned by Teddy 'You Don't Need A Heart' Randazzo, comes this Soul beater that doesn't sit too well with any audience except for northern England.

I am as surprised as anyone at the popularity of such an obscurity and DJ Russ Winstanley played the single with a conviction which finally got it a UK release on Route records after Ian Levine broke it at Blackpool Mecca.

Top 500 Position: **403**
Original Label: **Swan**
Current Value: **£10**

'The condensation from the walls of the Twisted Wheel went straight on my mohair suit'

Ray Monks, Soul Fan, Merseyside, UK

Mickey Lee Lane

Hey Sah-Lo-Ney

From Pittsburgh, PA comes this 1965 dancer in similar vein to Mitch Ryder's outings. The record sold fairly well in the states as it slipped out almost unnoticed on UK Stateside. There was talk of Itzy being it's first label, this is false as Swan bought the master from Itzy who then promptly manufactured some copies a couple of years later, Lane went on to have another mediocre hit pop wise with 'Shaggy Dog'.

Also recorded by UK Mod group the Action (who performed at the Mojo), Mickey's original was first played at the legendary Twisted Wheel by Les Cokell - who had tracked it down after he heard it one Sunday afternoon on Radio Luxembourg!

Curiously, Cobblestone a subsidiary of Buddah, best known for the Vonnettes, released a remixed instrumental version in 1968, entitled 'Tracks To Your Mind' by the Sounds of Lane, which was so popular at The Golden Torch.

Top 500 Position: **404**
Original Label: **Soul**
Current Value: **£10 Issue**
£30 Demo

'Resurfacing again after all these years'

Gary Shelton, Soul Fan, West Midlands, UK

Gladys Knight and the Pips

Just Walk In My Shoes

One of the first rare Motown plays from the Twisted Wheel. Almost impossible to get in the late 60's, it quite simply sold nowt on Soul or on the UK TMG logo.

Several covers exist too including Gary Glenn (CO & CE) and the Outsiders (Capitol) which were both played at the Casino. Eventually the one true stunning version is back on the turntables from where the professional singer of some 48 years can well and truly be saluted.

A fantastic record that everyone adores!

Top 500 Position:	**405**
Original Label:	**Kent (UK)**
Current Value:	**£10**

'The unreleased tracks now being played are as good as the classics of yesteryear'

Robert Lee, Soul Fan, New York, USA

Carla Thomas

I'll Never Stop Loving You

Daughter of Rufus, she recorded with her father as early as 1960.

The wonderful Carla Thomas needs very little introduction to Soul fans. Although her material has always been considered a little too harsh for the Northern scene, the fantastic tape discovery by Kent records as licensor of Stax in the UK is a truly remarkable find.

The vibes and strings are not in any way in the tradition of the Memphis label, but quite frankly who cares, Thomas puts in a performance as if to outdo her massive 'Gee Whiz' hit. How on earth did it fail to gain release?

Top 500 Position:	**406**
Original Label:	**Ric-Tic**
Current Value:	**£10**

'Our Edwin just keeps on coming up with them!'

Peter Whitney, Soul Fan, Cumbria, UK

Edwin Starr

I Have Faith In You

The flip to 'Stop Her On Sight' - and what a performance from the UK's favourite Soul man.

A truly wonderful sound, 'I Have Faith In You' has traditionally been an 'ender' though today its quality makes it a popular spin at any time of the night!

Also covered by 'Bari Track' man Doni Burdick on Sound Impression, in recent times the unissued 'Detroit Sound' instrumental has also been enormously popular.

Top 500 Position: **407**
Original Label: **St. Lawrence**
Current Value: **£10 Fatman**
£75 Batman

Butch Baker

The Fat Man/Batman At The Go-Go

'Working off the hit TV series the obscurity works well'

Kerry Holmes, Soul Fan, Scunthorpe, UK

Like the Mylestones 'The Joker', Monk Higgins tried his hand with this play on the Batman series. In fact the single came out twice using first using 'Bat Man', which is very scarce indeed, and then 'Fat Man' as the lead words in the title.

Played at most of the all-niters in 73', you usually find that any cash-in on a TV series is necessarily contrived, that is not the case on this young singer's gem from Chicago.

A Blackpool Mecca spin from 1973.

Top 500 Position: **408**
Original Label: **Jamie**
Current Value: **£200 Issue**
£150 Demo

Pookie Hudson

This Gets To Me

'The heartbeat of a hare'

Kev Sowerby, Soul Fan, Cumbria, UK

James 'Pookie' Hudson was the lead with Doo-Wop group the Spaniels. Like all front men he decided to go it alone and teamed up with Jamie's house producer Bob Finiz. The result was this vibe laden groover from 1966.

The song is simple but effective and has a large following dating back to the mid 70's whereby it became a monster tune - largely due to plays from the East Anglia area

Subsequent collector's items by Hudson's band have been unearthed on Calla and North American, whilst Pookie went on to make a career for himself on the oldies revival circuit in the US.

Top 500 Position: **409**
Original Label: **Jubilee**
Current Value: **£10 Issue**
£15 Demo

'Coming off like Reginald Dixon meets Motown'

Tom Tynan, Soul Fan, Tyneside, UK

The Baltimore and Ohio Marching Band

Condition Red

The A side 'Lapland' sold fairly well in the States, enough so that it was released on UK Stateside.

The flip is the dance hit over here, the perfect model for the perverse side of Northern Soul, with the customary 2.5 minutes of pumping base lead track with a whistling organ.

Absolutely monstrous in 1974, long forgotten now it is a track guaranteed to confuse those trying to understand our music from outside the scene.

Top 500 Position: **410**
Original Label: **Kent (UK)**
Current Value: **£10**

'This song ought to have been on her album 'The Fabulous Sound Of..."

Ben Chambers, Soul Fan, London, UK

Maxine Brown

It's Torture

Discovered by Tony Bruno who signed her to his Nomar label, and scored immediately with 'All In My Mind'. The fan base for the lady from Kingstree, South Carolina has never been more evident, largely due to the unearthing of this track from the Wand vaults and her appearance at The Cleethorpes Weekender a few years ago.

Total Big City, a great singer, and an instant four figure single had it been released on some tiny label somewhere.

Top 500 Position: **411**
Original Label: **Fame**
Current Value: **£150 Issue**
£100 Demo

'A drum roll, an infectious beat combine with Barnett's bragging vocal'

Roger Wilson, Soul Fan, London, UK

James Barnett

Keep On Talking

The first single on Fame created by Dan Penn and Spooner Oldham in the company's Florence, Alabama studios.

The sensational backing vocals and the chorus is bouncy. Arthur Conley and Philip Mitchell also covered it, but here's by far the best version whose popularity is founded on the spins it first saw at the Torch in 1972.

The intro is about as dynamic as you can get.

Top 500 Position: **412**
Original Label: **Minit**
Current Value: **£20**

'The 'Heatwave' beat kicks'

Bev Thatcher, Soul Fan, California, USA

Jimmy Holiday and Clydie King

Ready Willing And Able

Jimmy Holiday rewrote a song that he had produced for Pamela Beatty called 'Talkin' Eyes' twelve months prior.

This potent item comes from two top quality singers with Holiday a seasoned pro recording for Everest, Diplomacy, Minit, crossover to name but a few, and the delightful Clydie King who made a series of great solo records for Imperial, Lizard, Speciality and Philips before assuming the identity of Brown Sugar on Polydor.

Top 500 Position: **413**
Original Label: **Verve**
Current Value: **£40 Issue**
£50 Demo

'Production hero from New Jersey who tells it like it is'

Robert Jackson,
Soul Fan, West Midlands, UK

Robert Banks

A Mighty Good Way

Robert Banks is a legendary Soul producer who worked with a variety of quality performers, on this occasion he turns to his gospel roots to record a thrilling single for Verve.

Almost too Soulful for the drug fuelled all-niters of the early 70's, this 45 made its way high up the Golden Torch playlist in 1972.

Collectors will find the man's name on many east coast rarities.

Top 500 Position: **414**
Original Label: **Smash**
Current Value: **£30 Issue**
£50 Demo

'A fantastic double sider'

Fred Willars, Soul Fan, Newark, USA

The Ambers

Potion Of Love

Robert Rhoney and Billy Chinn from New Jersey led the group to a nine year recording career without a hit. Signing for Greezie, New Art, Verve, Smash (Mercury) and finally Jean.

DJ Ian Levine discoverer of so many of the scenes' top sounds turned this into an absolute giant first play at Blackpool Mecca in 1973, today its flip 'Another Love' is also getting plays.

Top 500 Position: **415**
Original Label: **Fee**
Current Value: **£75**

'One of the hottest almost new releases'

Martin Evans,
Soul Fan, Cardiff, Wales, UK

Carol Anderson

Sad Girl

Carol who died tragically young was a bit part player on the Detroit music scene, recording for Big Tree, Whip, Expansion, Mid Town, Soulsonic and Fee. UK based Soul Bowl records made the discovery and supplied DJ Richard Searling 'who made the record his own'.

Interestingly this enormously popular sound was regularly selling at mid-eighties all nighters for up to £10 a copy on John Anderson's Grapevine label - when his import business, Soul Bowl, still had loads of genuine Fee originals for the same price! It just goes to show - check those record lists!

Top 500 Position: **416**
Original Label: **Hawk Sound**
Current Value: **£10 Issue**
£25 Demo

'Short lived and long overdue a revival'

Pete Haigh, DJ, Blackpool, UK

The Mylestones

Sexy Lady

An early 70's sweet Soul performance with a beat.

Championed by DJ Ian Levine at Blackpool Mecca the record failed to make an impact in the states despite being on former hitmaker Johnny Otis' Hawk Sound label.

Whilst possibly having a connection to producer Myles Grayson, the group are <u>not</u> the ones who recorded 'The Joker'.

In fact this group have one hell of a falsetto lead.

Top 500 Position: **417**
Original Label: **Kool Kat**
Current Value: **£350 Issue**
£400 Demo

'A great stomping classic'

Carl Matthews, Soul Fan, Warrington, UK

Joe Matthews

Ain't Nothing You Can Do

DJ Colin Curtis was the first to expose this Detroit rarity to the ever faithful Blackpool Mecca crowd in 1974. Matthews was no stranger to the scene recording excellent sides for Thelma.

The scarcity of the original has somewhat stumped its growth on the revival circuit but it is a masterpiece among collectors. The 'no no no no baby' intro reveals a slick bass bomber that becomes a joyous groove on the floor.

The one factor against the classic is that it was discovered in the 'Golden Era' (71-75) when there were too many fantastic discoveries. Today though it has risen to be a 45 of some repute.

Top 500 Position: **418**
Original Label: **Simco**
Current Value: **£1,000 Issue**
£700 Demo

'Massively popular after failing in the 70's'

Glyn Smith, Soul Fan, Warrington, UK

Gene Toones

What More Do You Want

An obscure spin by Ian Levine, Gene Toones took a good many years to gain mass popularity.

The New York based Toones following his departure from the independent Simco label he formed a group called Chapter IV and released a single on Wand titled 'Baby Boy' in 1975.

Just about everyone is searching for this single today, including many who, like me, sold the darn thing for £5 twenty five years ago!

Top 500 Position: **419**
Original Label: **Wheel City**
Current Value: **£700**

'A class act at the controls of that drivin Detroit rhythm'

Chris Fletcher, Soul Fan, Warwickshire, UK

Melvin Davis

Find A Quiet Place

Melvin who later joined Invictus group 8th Day recorded a variety of singles including product for Mike Hanks in the mid-60's. Melvin indeed almost made it in 1968 with 'Save It' for Mala which garnered a lot of airplay in the States.

Davis recorded this single in 1965 for Hanks' Wheel City label. Those lucky collectors who snapped up this rarity in the 70's for around £10 are now smiling sweetly as it will now set you back around £700!

A fabulous Detroit rarity!

Top 500 Position: **420**
Original Label: **Mar-V-Lus**
Current Value: **£10 Issue**
                   £25 Demo

'One of the first big girl group singles from Blackpool Mecca'

Nick Moore, Soul Fan, Preston, UK

The Du-ettes

Every Beat Of My Heart

Barbara Livsey later formed Barbara and The Uniques (Arden) and together with Mary Francis Hayes made several singles for the Chicago Mar-V-Lus group of labels.

Initially discovered and played at Blackpool Mecca in 1971, the record was re-issued in England on President therefore dampening DJ enthusiasm but leaving a melodic legacy which never quite leaves the subconscious.

The group's only success was 'Please Forgive Me' in 1965.

Top 500 Position: **421**
Original Label: **Ric-Tic**
Current Value: **£10 Issue**
£100
Demo

'An underrated act'

Jimmy Knowles, Soul Fan, St Helens, UK

Al Kent

The Way You Been Acting Lately

First propelled into the Northern limelight by his instrumental 'You've Got To Pay The Price', Al Kent Hamilton and the Ric-Tic label have become permanent fixtures on the scene and whilst his Wheel sound was the first played, it is 'The Way You've Been Acting Lately' that has proved the most popular and enduring. Discovered as early as 1971 it became a massive Blackpool Mecca spin and went on to become a key sound in the Casino oldies revival of '77.

Al's performance in the early 80's at Chris King's Hinkley Allnighter as part of the Ric-Tic revue is still talked about today... forget the instrumental - this guy can really sing!

Al is apparently working with 'Popcorn' Wylie in the States - we await the results with interest!

Top 500 Position: **422**
Original Label: **Fraternity**
Current Value: **£400 Issue**
£200 Demo

'A fabulous group and the scene relished it'

Steve Andrews, Soul Fan, North Wales, UK

Imaginations

Strange Neighborhood

First spun as a cover up at Wigan's Casino by key player, Richard Searling, this is another one of those singles that was 'recorded too late'. Released in 1967 when the whole Detroit/Group thing was already disappearing, the record sold poorly, even in it's Ohio locality.

The Imaginations, not be confused with the group from Philadelphia or the 70's outfit on Twentieth Century, did record another single on Fraternity in 1968, but this bombed out too - a pity for such a soulful combo.

Top 500 Position: **423**
Original Label: **Scepter**
Current Value: **£600**

'THE beat ballad anthem'

Mark Cosgrove, Soul Fan, York, UK

Johnny Maestro

I'm Stepping Out Of The Picture

Former lead singer of The Crests who recorded another fantastic Northern record twelve months after this on Parkway with 'Heartburn'. Later he had hits with the group Brooklyn Bridge on Buddah.

New York through and through, this Brooklyn born white singer is held in high esteem by Soul and Doo-Wop fans alike and this somewhat late (1980's) discovery is still extremely popular resulting in the high value of this scarce 45.

Top 500 Position: **424**
Original Label: **Pye**
Current Value: **£5**

'The record companies had finally discovered Northern Soul'

Dave McAleer, Soul Fan, London, UK

Nosmo King/The Javells

Goodbye/Goodbye Nothing To Say

Sitting in the Pye records A&R department one day in 1974 Dave McAleer discovered a single that had been released a few weeks previously on their own label by an act called Nosmo King (this was a creation of signing Steve Jameson who had formed a group called No Smoking).

Dave Mac was a Soul fan who knew the Northern scene was hot to trot and subsequently ordered some acetates renaming the group The Javells. Most of us were duped but the kids did not care, hence a UK chart position of No. 26 in 1974 on the Pye Disco demand label.

Top 500 Position: **425**
Original Label: **Motown**
Current Value: **£10**

'White hot right now'

Gavin Hallister, Collector, Arizona, USA

The Supremes

He's All I Got

It was bound to happen, the group originally known as the Primettes, with a number 9 hit 1966 in the US revisit the Northern Soul scene with the B side to 'Love Is Like An Itching In My Heart'.

Amazingly it looks as if they are back in fashion as DJ's are already playing another track by them (Stormy) from the 1987 Motown CD 'Never Before Released Masters'.

When the flipsides of Motown hits can make it over 30 years later in the quest for something 'new' there is proof positive that the scene will last forever!

Top 500 Position: **426**
Original Label: **Fontana**
Current Value: **£50**

'Hideously unfashionable now, but let's remember just how big it really was'

Mark Lethory, Soul Fan, Dublin, Eire

Kiki Dee

On A Magic Carpet Ride

Born Pauline Mathews 53 years ago in Bradford, she was signed to Fontana as early as 1963 and pretty much stayed with the label until a brief excursion to Motown in 1970.

Her international success of course was with Elton John. This is in fact her second Northern single (the first a cover of Tammi Lynn) but certainly the most popular. Totally Wigan it even inspired yours truly to record a cover version on my own Destiny label back in 1979. It didn't sell!

Top 500 Position:	**427**
Original Label:	**Fontana/ Teri-De**
Current Value:	**£75/£1,000**

'A legendary producer and writer with his own song'

James Conwell, Singer, Los Angeles, USA

Len Jewell

Bettin' On Love

Sadly passing away in 1996, Leonard Jewell Smith, sometimes credited as 'His Imperial Highness Sir Leonard Jewel Smith', is highly rated by most Northern Soul fans.

His involvement as partner in the Soulville production company with Leonard Graham and Jimmy Conwell were just part of this very talented guy's output. Fronting various groups in the mid 60's including The Styles on Modern, he recorded this song for his own Teri-De label gaining national release on Fontana and eventually re-issuing the record on a blue Teri-De label due to UK demand.

Top 500 Position:	**428**
Original Label:	**Columbia**
Current Value:	**£10**

'A bizarre instrumental that could only be recognised as a Northern 45'

Phil Woodley, Soul Fan, Carlisle, UK

Phil Coulter

A Good Thing Going

Recorded in the UK but surprisingly released only in the US, Coulter is a Northern Ireland producer who has worked with Billy Connelly and Sandie Shaw amongst others.

Together with partner Bill Martin he wrote the Eurovision hit 'Puppet On A String'.

'Good Thing' represents the obscure side of Coulter's massive output which perversely became one of 'The Heart Of Soul's' biggest sounds in 1978.

Top 500 Position:	**429**
Original Label:	**Veep**
Current Value:	**£100 Issue**
	£80 Demo

'One of the true unsung heroines of 60's Soul'

Rob Thomas, Collector, Lincolnshire, UK

Cindy Scott

I Love You Baby

Simply a great dancer, 'I Love You Baby' is just the tip of the iceberg when it comes to this little lady's talent.

Ben-lee, Arctic and an extensive list of backing vocals as well as 'Time Can Change A Love', also on Veep, have made her a household name in Northern Soul circles.

Despite the widely held belief that she is the vocalist on current unreleased monster sound 'World Of Happiness' this is merely a convenient cover-up name.

Top 500 Position:	**430**
Original Label:	**Constellation**
Current Value:	**£15 Issue**
	£30 Demo

'The Duke of Soul with another Northern hit'

Jenny Galloway, Soul Fan, Suffolk, UK

Gene Chandler

Mr. Big Shot

Gene took his stage surname from the actor Jeff Chandler.

'Mr Big Shot' was probably his worst selling single. DJ Ian Levine promoted the record to the faithful at Sale's Blue Room Soul Night and it became extremely popular across the North until it was overtaken by the rarer discs coming on stream at the time.

In terms of rarity this is possibly his hardest Constellation 45.

Top 500 Position: **431**
Original Label: **Shrine**
Current Value: **£1,500**

'One of the rarest Northern collectors' labels ever'

Jim Moore,
Soul Fan, North Carolina, USA

The Cairos

Stop Overlooking Me

Fantastic discovery around 20 years ago from the wonderful Shrine label.

The group lead by Kenny Lewis who sometimes used Shirley Edwards as female background later formed The Dreams ('They Call Me Jesse James').

Prior to the Shrine output he had a brief period as lead singer of the Enjoyables on Capitol, before a one off on Buddah with 'What's Her Name' and a 45 on De-vel.

In terms of musical content this stomper has a real identity of its own, utilising a burbling bass man in the manner of the Rivingtons a few years before - this Doo-Wop style is further reinforced by an interesting unissued acapella version.

The label has been popularised by the efforts of collector Andy Rix.

Top 500 Position: **432**
Original Label: **Class**
Current Value: **£100 Issue**
              £150 Demo

'Raspin' duet that's a real floorshaker'

Jack Bollington, Soul Fan, Derby, UK

Buster and Eddie

Can't Be Still

Buster is Tommy Williams and together with his brother Eddie who starred in some of the great Doo Wop groups such as the Aladins, Velvetones, Fortunes and The Colts recorded this Soul 45 in 1965 in LA.

The recording itself sound remarkably like a lot of the Renfro singles. A Wigan Casino spin in 1974, unjustly it was discarded by DJ's far too early but the plays between 1973 and '81 warrant a chart position.

An immortal sound if only for the unforgettable lyric 'I'm like a man with ants in his pants - I can't be still'.

Top 500 Position: **433**
Original Label: **Shrine**
Current Value: **£1,500**

'The legendary DC label hits the spot again'

Graham Steele,
Soul Fan, West Midlands, UK

Eddie Daye and the Four Bars

Guess Who Loves You

Originally played by DJ Richard Searling during the latter part of Wigan masquerading as Frank Wilson!

Eddie Jasper Daye had knocked around the DC recording scene for many years and was a key lounge act in the area.

Although Shrine was started in order to revive the black music industry in Washington DC along the lines of Motown, the productions have a unique quality. Almost messy and over-busy they win through by virtue of sheer power as is the case case with 'Guess Who Loves You' - despite a complete lack of melody.

Top 500 Position: **434**
Original Label: **Capitol**
Current Value: **£100 Issue**
£75 Demo

'A big late Twisted Wheel discovery, that the whole of Manchester was searching for'

Kelvin Lee, Soul Fan, Greater Manchester, UK

Patrice Holloway

Love And Desire

Sister of Motown diva Brenda who was signed to Capitol and Motown (although until recently the material remained in the vault) and finally back to Capitol.

A topsy turvy career which for a time looked fruitful as she joined the Hanna Barberra cartoon band 'Josie and the Pussycats' working alongside former Charlie's Angel, Cheryl Ladd.

Her final song for the label was 'Black Mother Goose' which is now better known by Sam Nesbitt. Recently 'Stolen Hours' has become a firm favourite too, but the activity surrounding this great double sider from '66 wins the race.

Top 500 Position: **435**
Original Label: **Elf**
Current Value: **£30 Issue**
£25 Demo

'Emerging from the very origins of the scene'

Mark Thatcher, Soul Fan, Reading, UK

Clifford Curry

I Can't Get Hold Of Myself

Boy has he been around. Formerly with The Five Pennies, Four Jokers, The Chimes, The Hollyhocks, and The Contenders.

The Tennessee singer had a few sides that were relatively popular but this was his finest hour.

An extremely big sound at the Wheel in 1970, a UK release on Pama further added to it's popularity.

A stop-start production and a thoroughly compelling hookline add up to a real charmer that just keeps coming back on the oldies circuit.

Top 500 Position: **436**
Original Label: **Okeh**
Current Value: **£20 Issue**
£30 Demo

'That screaming reverend just sends me Tutti-Fruitti - 'Poor Dog' that I am!'

Frank Waller, Soul Fan, Merseyside, UK

Little Richard

I Don't Want To Discuss It

Born Richard Penniman, the wild man of Rock 'n' Roll recorded a series of 45's for Okeh in 1967. Recorded in California, the official 'A' side 'Hurry Sundown' was the title of a 'B' movie of the same year. The flip though is a fantastic rockin' Soul cut.

'I Don't Want To Discuss It' was a key record in putting the short lived Up The Junction allnighter in Crewe on the map whilst yet another of his Okeh sides, 'A Little Bit Of Something' also created something a stir in the early 70's.

Top 500 Position: **437**
Original Label: **Solid Hit**
Current Value: **£750**

'Those water damaged labels could be the only ones in existence"

Tom Cottan, Soul Fan, new York, USA

Debonairs

Lovin' You Takes All Of My Time

Later becoming Dawn with lead singer Tony Orlando, Joyce, Vincent Wilson and Telma Hopkins were recording for Golden World in Detroit in 1964 before signing to Don Davis at Solid Hitbound productions in 1966.

Originally discovered by record dealer Martin Koppel the scarcity of this disc has somewhat hindered its play. Very commercial and totally Supremes influenced.

The flipside 'Headache In My Heart' was released again and even got release on UK Track, the sheer rarity of 'Lovin'' would suggest that it was withdrawn for some specific reason.

Top 500 Position: **438**
Original Label: **Tamla**
Current Value: **£50**

'Belting unreleased Motown that has deservedly been issued in CD'

Chris Jenner, Motown expert, London, UK

Marvin Gaye

Love Starved Heart

Marvin Pence Gaye Jnr, recorded a wealth of material with Norman Whitfield in the mid 60's.

This is one that almost got away until being discovered on a acetate that came into Richard Searling's possession in 1979 with no known title at the time, it became popular as 'It's Killing Me'.

In recent times the persistence of DJ Chris King in his dealings with Motown have seen a fluke US promo release and finally a release on CD in the UK.

Top 500 Position: **439**
Original Label: **Gordy**
Current Value: **£10**

'Motown megalomania'

Sheila Brunt, Soul Fan, Lincolnshire, UK

Martha Reeves and the Vandellas

One Way Out

The flip of 'Love Bug Leave My Heart Alone',and Reeves' top tune on the Northern scene.

Fairly common, it became a massive oldie in the 70's and remains very popular today.

A US hit in '67, the group have weathered all storms and are still performing today. With a track record spanning almost 40 years (dating back to '62 with the Del-Phis) Martha may not have too many more pleasant surprises, the hard driven 'One Way Out' may just be one of them.

Top 500 Position: **440**
Original Label: **Omen**
Current Value: **£150**

'A big beat groover, that never ceases to amaze'

John Givens, Soul Fan, Warley, UK

Brice Coefield

Ain't That Right

In and out of many R&B groups starting with The Savours, Coefield's only solo single was in 1966 recording for the A&M subsidiary Omen.

First popular at venues like the Cats, Torch and Mecca, 'Ain't That Right' is one of the unsung heroes of early 70's playlists that has retained credibility through the years becoming even bigger now then when it was first played.

One of those rarities from the 70's that wasn't reissued, booted ensuring the longevity of a song with such immortal lines as 'money can buy the Mona Lisa and money can straighten the Tower of Pisa'.

Top 500 Position: **441**
Original Label: **Capitol**
Current Value: **£50**

'To old timers this is one of the best Northern records ever!'

Jim Barratt,
Soul Fan, Greater Manchester, UK

Bobby Sheen

Dr. Love

Long, long before his superb Warner Brothers winner was ever thought about, the Twisted Wheel had already embraced this great version of the Whispers' original.

A typical big time West Coast production making full use of the Vine Street orchestration. An immensely popular sound around 1970, part of the legendary Discotheque '66 series this classic British collector's item received a UK reissue in 1972 as a result of its enduring popularity.

In more recent times Sheen has toured with the Coasters and has worked with a variety of top producers including Phil Spector and Terry Woodford.

Top 500 Position: **442**
Original Label: **Liberty**
Current Value: **£5**

'Unashamedly kitsch

Lee Shanklin, Soul Fan, Dublin, Eire

Gary Lewis and the Playboys

My Heart's Symphony

After being discovered in 1964 as the house band at Disneyland California, the group signed to Liberty and had a spate of hits through to 1968. Gary, born Carie Levitch is the son of comedian Jerry Lewis.

The song was a hit in 1966 in the US and reached the UK Top 40 in February 1975.

Popularised by every DJ on the scene at the time after initial "Play it for a dare" spins by DJ Richard Searling, it is almost certainly the only Allnighter spin to prominently feature a Hawaiian guitar!

Top 500 Position: **443**
Original Label: **Mercury**
Current Value: **£100 Issue**
£75 Demo

'I don't understand what Northern Soul is but this is a good record I didn't want to sell to England'

Steve Kolanjan, Collector, New York, USA

Burning Bush

Keeps On Burning

Championed by DJ Ginger Taylor, this white record from New York, the creation of ace producer Artie Kornfeld, became massive at the tail end of the 70's.

Fast and furious, this one could only have made it in the 70's due to its tempo and blatantly white vocals - so white in fact that this was covered up as the 'Gems' (a female group). Nonetheless one of the real biggies of '76/'77, and in terms of danceability is a first class mover.

Top 500 Position: **444**
Original Label: **Mir-A-Don**
Current Value: **£200**

'That group harmony sells it so well'

Melvyn Christie, Soul Fan, Australia

The Ascots

Another Day

Archie Powell and Pat Thompson are the leaders of this Washington DC group, they also had a popular duet single on the same label, 'Darling, Darling'.

A true sleeper that was around for years prior to taking off in the late 80's. Very quickly it became apparent that copies were not available and the price soared.

Compare the understated production and great harmonies with the previous track by Burning Bush to understand where the scene has gone in recent years.

Top 500 Position: **445**
Original Label: **Wand**
Current Value: **£10 Issue**
£20 Demo

'The London influence surprisingly made this a Northern monster'

Gary Carlton, Soul Fan, Cambridge, UK

Chuck Jackson

Hand It Over

Once a massive influence on the Beatles, with John Lennon sighting Jackson as one of his favourite singers in an interview in NME in 1963.

Chuck is cousin to Walter (yes that Walter Jackson!) and his brother Senator, and perennial black presidential candidate, Jesse Jackson and to Ann Sexton. Following initial success with doo-wop legend The Del-Vikings, he first recorded solo for Beltone in 1960.

'Hand It Over', recorded in 1964 was a US Hot 100 No. 92 hit. This superb Wand recording, was an early favourite at clubs like the Wheel DJ's Rob Bellars & Phil Saxe, and Sheffield's Mojo that disappeared for many years until its deserving resurrection by Harborough Horace and the boys at London's legendary 100 Club.

Top 500 Position: **446**
Original Label: **Jetstar**
Current Value: **£15 Issue**
£25 Yellow
vinyl demo

'A solid 45 from one of the scene's favourite artists'

Clive Holland, Soul Fan, London, UK

Bobby Patterson

My Baby's Coming Back To Me

Bobby has recently sprung to prominence via the Blackpool Soul Weekender. Patterson and his band the Mustangs had several great sides for Jetstar which incidentally was the inspiration for UK distributor of the now same name, following owner Carl Palmer having his own UK label - Pama, which in fact released one of the very first UK cover-ups via Wheel DJ Rob Bellars.

The side was Bobby's 'What A Wonderful Night For Love', which is popular again today along with 'Im In Love With You' - a mid tempo lovely from 1970. Writing for the Montclairs and recording for Paula and now his own label, Proud. Bobby is one of R&B's super Soul guys.

Top 500 Position: **447**
Original Label: **Nasco**
Current Value: **£15**

'Superb 70's sounding as fresh as the the sea breeze at Cleethorpes'

Bill Hamilton, Soul Fan, Grimsby, UK

Bits 'n Pieces

Keep On Running Away

Also known as Brothers, Sisters and Cousins. The emergence of the Winter Gardens, Cleethorpes in 1975 posed the first real threat to Wigan Casino and this was one of the key 45's to cement the rivalry.

Like the No. 1 venue they raced out of the trap with new names DJ wise and a fresh playlist which consisted of some obscure new releases. Not all were good, but a gem or two emerged like this Tennessee recording from 1974.

Features an absolutely wild falsetto lead with a thumping bass and rhythm combo.

Top 500 Position: **448**
Original Label: **Challenge**
Current Value: **£40**

'Longevity never really materialised for what it is ostensibly a true Northern gem'

Carol Lerning, Soul Fan, New Jersey, USA

Ron Holden

I'll Forgive And Forget

The R&B vocalist from Seattle later worked as a DJ for Art Laboe and his 'Oldies But Goodies' nights around the East LA area before sadly passing away in 1997 .

Without wishing to become an A&R man you can hear the let down in the final mix as the chorus is outstanding and the verse so weak.

Massive at Wigan for a short time it seems likely that 'I'll Forgive And Forget' was never actually released as no one seems to have seen an issue!

Top 500 Position: **449**
Original Label: **Warner Brothers**
Current Value: **£60 Issue**
£80 Demo

Linda Jones

I Just Can't Live My Life (Without You Babe)

'Absolutely brilliant'

Martin Porterhouse, Soul Fan, Canada

Sadly passing away in March 1972, the sheer brilliance of this lady is well documented. Starting her recording career with Cub records she moved on to Atco, Blue Cat, Loma, Warner Brothers, Neptune, Turbo and Stang.

To many she is THE all-time great Soul voice. It was Ian Levine that first treated us to this truly magnificent George Kerr masterpiece.

It is a great dancer, but the rhythm is irrelevant - paling into the background as Linda delivers the vocal of a lifetime!

Top 500 Position: **450**
Original Label: **MGM**
Current Value: **£100 Issue**
£30 Demo

The Jewels

We Got Togetherness

'The ultimate 'countdown' sound!'

Martin Waterfield,
Soul Fan, West Midlands, UK

I hold my hand up to this one! This is where a DJ discovers a single lurking in a colleague's box knowing full well he could make it massive!

It really is a frantic 200 mph dancer that takes no prisoners!

In Max Millward's shop in November 1973 I purchased it from him for £15 - and promptly hammered it at the Casino. It was tailor made for that environment.

The group remain a mystery, sources reveal they were the Jewels on Dimension and Four Jewels on Dynamite and hail from New York. The flip side is a rendition of 'I'm Forever Blowing Bubbles' - I stopped short of airing that one due to my soccer loyalties being in Sheffield and not the East End of London!

Top 500 Position: **451**
Original Label: **Dunhill**
Current Value: **£300 Issue**
£150 Demo

'Perhaps the greatest Northern double-sider of them all!'

Clive Hall, Soul Fan, Yorkshire, UK

Willie Hutch

The Duck/Love Runs Out

One time boyfriend of Brenda Holloway, the former singer in the Phoenetics of 'Just A Boy's Dream' fame, Willie Hutch is a legend on the scene. I first played this in March 1974 after acquiring it from dealer Simon Soussan. Simon ensured that 'The Duck' was to make its debut as Richard Temple on Stephanye - 'Love Runs Out' was left to go massive in '77.

Both sides are simply too good for words and made for a label like Mirwood. Dunhill obviously intended to cash in on Jackie Lee's dance craze.

Two totally different recordings, one a million seller the other sunk without trace. But as far as the scene is concerned Soul hero Willie Hutchinson with his work for Motown and RCA as well as with groups like the Marvellos is OUR choice North of Watford!

Top 500 Position: **452**
Original Label: **Impel/**
Seventy 7
Current Value: **£200 Impel**
£40 Seventy 7

'A really classy dancer'

Ted Jennings, Soul Fan, New Jersey, USA

Ann Sexton

You've Been Gone Too Long

This delicious 70's play from Blackpool Mecca was yet another of DJ Ian Levine's masterstrokes. Smack in the middle of the customary 'stomper' set comes this easy groover which did sell locally around Tennessee.

Originally released on Impel Ann Sexton's classic was later picked up by Seventy 7 records. A relative of Chuck Jackson, Ann went on to become a cult figure in the Southern States, performing at many Soul and Blues concerts.

Top 500 Position:	**453**
Original Label:	**Gordy**
Current Value:	**£10 Issue**
	£25 Demo

'Megadacious Motown'

Sharon Davies, Writer, London, UK

Kim Weston

Helpless

If not so easily obtainable we might be looking at the biggest record ever. The scene's obsession with rarity can easily stunt a records' growth!

Born Natalie Wilson, Kim was formerly married to William 'Mickey' Stevenson, the great Motown writer/producer. She has appeared with Marvin Gaye and Johnny Nash on vinyl and has a plethora of immaculate material in and out of the Motown vaults.

Helpless is true M-Town, with a irresistible groove, magnificent vocal and glossy production. Oh, not forgetting one of the best sax breaks ever.

If on a small label with 2 or 3 copies known, say hello to a five grand price tag!

Top 500 Position:	**454**
Original Label:	**MB**
Current Value:	**£500**

'One of my all-time favourites!'

Horace Ott, Arranger, New York, USA

Bobby Kline

Say Something Nice To Me

I secured a few copies of this sublime 45 from the great producer/arranger and label boss Horace Ott in the 70's. Sadly at the time it was considered far too slow and I promptly off-loaded them for £6 each!

During the intervening 20 years tempos have changed and today the popularity of sounds of this quality is at a peak.

The release itself is on the local label MB which was out of Queens, New York, sadly it sold poorly despite the support of local black radio station WWRL who stayed with the cut for a month or-so.

Top 500 Position: **455**
Original Label: **Sedgrick**
Current Value: **£3,000**

'A legendary big ticket item'

Mark Evans, Collector, South Wales, UK

Top 500 Position: **456**
Original Label: **Fantasy**
Current Value: **£6 Issue**
£10 Demo

'Totally out there in left field'

Steph Keeley, Soul Fan, Stafford, UK

Don Gardner

Cheatin Kind

This is the type of investment we all wish we had made!

Sold for just £50 in the 70's , the price tag raced up to £300 in the 80's, today? Well it's a year's mortgage payments for some to buy this little gem!

This is a terrific piece of Chicago production by Jimmy Vanleer on a song executed to perfection by Gardner who had been kicking around the Windy City scene with a number of creditable 45's to his name.

Ever growing in stature, this is a fantastic haunting mid-60's cut!

Roger Collins

You Sexy Sugar Plum

The Bay area produced many a fine recording artist and Roger Collins is up there with the best.

His finest hour is the self penned 'She's Looking Good', later to be covered by Wilson Pickett.

The Northern scene had other ideas when a recent release from '74 set the UK on fire which culminating in a UK hit.

Collins himself is the all original showman, playing guitar even doing comedy!

He still writes material today for Buddy Ace and Sugar Pie Desanto among others, and obviously still receives royalties for his UK one hit wonder!

Top 500 Position: **457**
Original Label: **Mowest**
Current Value: **£10**

'Hey Mr. DJ, have you got the 'animal song'?'

Lionel Richie, Artist, USA

The Commodores

The Zoo (The Human Zoo)

This is about as freaky as you can get within the scene, as a really strange Gloria Jones/Pam Sawyer song capitalised on the changeover from traditional 60's to 70's almost new releases.

Yes, we are talking Lionel Richie here as the 'nighter patrons' warmed to the bizzare feel of the track while still doing the back drop thingy!

The record is good. A mesmerising and totally original Motown single that confirmed a perception of 'oddness' from those of the 'out crowd'. At the time we needed a few sounds of this ilk to confirm their ignorance of the truth!

Either way I love it and surprise, surprise it has been played at a few venues recently. Remember how big this really was.

Top 500 Position: **458**
Original Label: **Capitol**
Current Value: **£8 Issue**
£15 Demo

'Wreckless and totally invigorating'

John Mellor, Soul Fan, Indiana, USA

Human Beinz

Nobody But Me

A US hit in 1968 although written and recorded by the Isley Brothers several years prior. The group from Youngstown, Ohio have always remained somewhat of a cult garage band.

On these shores however they found themselves in the middle of the Ruffin's, Carr's, Mitchell's and other Soul icons to be found at the Twisted Wheel.

Well this IS a strange sort of 'Soul', but how many would be forced to admit having rushed to the dancefloor after that first guitar chord and the clarion call 'No, no, no-no-no, no no-no' from the lead 'Bein'!

Top 500 Position: **459**
Original Label: **Palmer**
Current Value: **£500 Issue**
£400 Demo

Jimmy Mack

My World Is On Fire

'Martha's bloke sure can sing!'

Nick Leeds, Soul Fan, London, UK

Many rumours have circulated as to the identity of this man. It is true that Martha Reeves did comment about a guy who was a friend of Lamont Dozier and the Holland brothers, and yes Jimmy IS from Detroit...

One thing is for sure - he is NOT the Jimmy Mack of the Furys' fame, that's James McKeachin. Palmer A&R boss of the time, Joey Welz once told me he was just some local act that label boss Palmer James had signed up for a one-single deal.

Whatever the answer, if you are out there Jimmy, this is one 45 you can be really proud of!

Top 500 Position: **460**
Original Label: **Soul**
Current Value: **£10 Issue**
£30 Demo

The Velvelettes

These Things Will Keep Me Loving You

'Yet another class act from the incredible production line'

Peter Jeffries, Soul Fan, Leicester, UK

We never seem to be on a level playing field with Motown, they were indeed the Man. Utd of Northern Soul.

Even their poorest sellers are better than your average 'big money rarity'.Quite why this was never a stateside hit I do not know, but the UK saw sense and on re-release it reached the top 40 in 1971. A '66 recording from the stunning Norman Whitfield handled act it demands attention.

The group, originally known as the Barbees, were signed in 1963 and left Motown in '69, before reactivating via Motor City in 1990.

Top 500 Position: **461**
Original Label: **Cameo**
Current Value: **£10 Issue**
£20 Demo

*'Discos were never the
same after hearing this'*

Steve Stone, Soul Fan, Nottingham, UK

Chubby Checker

At The Discotheque

Ernie Evans sure found some club action post-Twist, and he re-confirms his multiple Top 500 entries with the first of his 1965 recordings for Parkway.

The production is all too familiar as are the lyrics, the effortless ease of his vocal is superb. Many doubted Checker's vocal ability maybe possibly because of his fortuitous discovery by Dick Clark. The mid-60's really showed what he could do, and this Feldman-Goldstein-Gottehrer production confirmed his position as a top quality Soul singer.

One of THE Twisted Wheel anthems, the song symbolises the first wave of US imports to hit our scene.

Top 500 Position: **462**
Original Label: **Dotty's**
Current Value: **£800**

'A killer rarity'

Richard Lea, Soul Fan, Coventry, UK

Johnny Hampton

Not My Girl

Also recorded, though unissued, by the Platters, for me Hampton's is the definitive version. Recorded in 1965 at Ernie Stratton's Detroit studio, the label released a few 45's hoping to make their mark with the likes of the great Roger Hatcher.

This sound though was far too raw for the radio and without airplay it promptly sank. The Platters version has cropped up on a few CDs in recent times but had to wait for a 100 Club Anniversary single to hit vinyl at long last, unsurprising then that it is the Dotty's release that continues to receive the most plays at all nighters despite its rarity.

Top 500 Position: **463**
Original Label: **HFMP**
Current Value: **£15**

'THE 70s anthem!'

Mick Kozluk, Soul Fan, Sussex, UK

Larry Houston

Let's Spend Some Time Together

A local Chicago act like so many desperately trying to break out nationally, Houston would no doubt be amused to hear that his 70s classic was covered up as 'Top Cat'!

Quite why the name arose we are not sure - perhaps DJ Richard Searling has a secret love for Hanna Barberra cartoons! But joking apart, this is the type of 70s local Soul release that offered the scene some real passion - very much in the Bobby Hutton - Larry Saunders or Nate Evans bag.

Houston turned in a truly creditable performance that remained very popular for quite a while - but it is definitely now overdue for a revival!

Top 500 Position: **464**
Original Label: **Tamla Motown**
Current Value: **£10**

'Motown once again leading the field'

Johnny Bristol, Producer, USA

The Isley Brothers

Tell Me It's Just A Rumour

Taken from the 'Soul On The Rocks' LP, belatedly issued as a single in 1973 due to demand, this blockbusting stormer saw the veterans convert a new army of fans.

Sure, we all bought the hits, but this nifty dancer recorded in '67, surprised us all with it's phrenetic tempo.

I once interviewed Johnny Bristol who co-wrote it and he not only remembered the track, but liked it too!

The brothers from Cincinnati go back as far as the late 50's, but to us young 'uns it is the Motown period we most cherish.

Ronald Isley is absolutely top notch and belts the song out like he knows it's a smash. Eventually it was - but it took the North of England to make it!

Top 500 Position: **465**
Original Label: **Wand**
Current Value: **£10 Issue**
£15 Demo

'Appearing in Grimsby (Cleethorpes?) made me realise how popular I am!'

Maxine Brown, Artist, New York, USA

Maxine Brown

One In A Million

The great songwriter Rudy Clark was in the middle of a purple patch in his career following the roaring success of 'The Shoop, Shoop Song' with Betty Everett along with several other R&B hits.

His lyrical skills are most certainly evident on this New York production of 'One In A Million', a song which was incidentally covered by a number of UK acts including Karol Keyes and Northern favourites Chapter Five.

Top 500 Position: **466**
Original Label: **Soul**
Current Value: **£10 Issue**
£20 Demo

'A truly unsung Motown heroine'

Eddie Singleton,
Shrine Label Owner, USA

Barbara Randolph

I Got A Feeling

You can identify the backbone of the northern scene quite easily by listening to records like this.

A non-hit from 1967, that surfaced just one year later in the North of England to joyous delight.

We may have eventually concined this one to the local discos, but only after we had worn out the grooves during the early days of the scene!

Randolph sank under Berry Gordy, but later found another Motown connection marrying Eddie Singleton, ex-husband of Berry's first wife Raynoma Gordy.

Top 500 Position: **467**
Original Label: **Mod**
Current Value: **£30**

'This track stayed with me through 13 years of absence from the Northern scene'

Brian Reynolds, Soul Fan, UK

Madeline Bell

Picture Me Gone

It's not often that the cover version outstrips the original, in this case the by former Blue Mink lead singer, instantly recognisable in the UK as a major ('I could do with a 'D'') commercial singer.

'Picture Me Gone' is the flip to her cover of Dee Dee Warwick's 'I'm Gonna Make You Love Me' which became a US hit for Maddy. If we were compiling this chart in 1975, or indeed the days of the Wheel, then we would undoubtedly be saluting the original Evie Sands. However it is the later day popularity of this version both at Soul nights and on the eighties Scooter scene that has pushed Ms. Bell to the fore.

Top 500 Position: **468**
Original Label: **Immediate**
Current Value: **£100**

'Pat gracefully holds the rejected 'Stone' demo together'

Keith Allison, Soul Fan, Newark, UK

PP Arnold

Everything's Gonna Be Alright

Ex-Ikette PP Arnold found herself slap-bang in the middle of London's swinging sixties scene back in '67. Turning to Britain's finest sessioneers she soon scored with 'First Cut Is The Deepest', conversely 'Everything's Gonna Be Alright' did not enjoy 'immediate' (ouch!) success and this joyous pounding number was left in deletion boxes before the Torch club in Stoke-on-Trent made it an anthem some 4/5 years later.

A surprisingly rare non-US release.

Top 500 Position: **469**
Original Label: **Columbia**
Current Value: **£6 Issue**
£15 Demo

'What a mover from the Clapping song girl'

Carol Chadwick, Soul Fan, Oldham, UK

Shirley Ellis

Soul Time

A comeback record following her success with the 'Clapping Song' for mid-sixties hitmaker Shirley Ellis a singer /songwriter from New York.

Her husband (Lincoln Chase) also wrote most of her material and the sexy 'Soul Time' has knocked around the scene for nigh-on 30 years or more.

Simple, infectious with a wonderful brass laden groove, Ellis has a voice that is not too dissimilar to Marlena Shaw and while Shaw has continued recording and retained immense credibility Ellis has disappeared, leaving us with this fine 'bopper' to wipe the dust off occasionally. Hey, I'm not downsizing the appeal, this was super big at one stage.

Top 500 Position: **470**
Original Label: **Karen**
Current Value: **£75 Issue**
£50 Demo

'A haunting Detroit melody from the ever popular 'Popcorn''

Ian Savoury, Soul Fan, London, UK

Richard (Popcorn) Wylie

Rosemary What Happened

Discovered by DJ Ian Levine, Wylie's attempt to cash in on the Roman Polanski movie 'Rosemary's Baby' failed miserably in the American charts.

However the Northern scene of 1974 took it to heart and, with Daddy's kids on backing vocals, the legend adds another cherished collector's item, albeit on the wrong side of the Atlantic!

Top 500 Position: **471**
Original Label: **Dial**
Current Value: **£6 Issue**
£15 Demo

'The sheer energy makes it a dancers dream'

Barry Hart, Soul Fan, Yorkshire, UK

Joe Tex

Show Me

The Commitments was the platform on which the song became immensely popular worldwide with the stage act that developed from the hit film - it also created a bit of a stir on initial release in 1967. However the Northern scene took it to heart via the incredibly popular Mr. M's oldies sessions at Wigan Casino. Never really considered as anything except a good Soul single until DJ Dave Evison re-invented it in the late 70's.

Tex was born Joseph Arrington Jnr in Texas and sadly left us in 1982.

Whilst it was a US hit peaking at No. 35 it bombed here, but since the Commitments launch, the song has become a firm favourite with karaoke fans and Saturday night TV hosts!

Top 500 Position: **472**
Original Label: **Parkway**
Current Value: **£8 Issue**
£15 Demo

'What a great version of Shirley and Lee'

Stefan Kurz, Soul Fan, Austria

Bunny Sigler

Let The Good Times Roll and Feel So Good

Walter (Bunny) Sigler recorded one hell of an album for Parkway in 1967. With at least 3 Northern monsters to his credit, the Philly man took on these two old standards and made them work second time around.

One of the great pioneers of Northern Soul, Sigler together with Leon Huff created many Soul classics of which this is definitely one.

One of the first real dancers at the Twisted Wheel.

Top 500 Position: **473**
Original Label: **Hot**
Current Value: **£200**

'The song that kick-started the Casino'

Mike Rollo (deceased),
DJ, Wigan Casino, UK

The Sherrys

Put Your Loving Arms Around Me

The first record played at Wigan, this was a popular wartime hit given the makeover by the daughters of Little Joe Cook, who had his own popular alternate take entitled 'I'm Falling In Love With You Baby' which was credited as 'Against My Will' on its subsequent reissue.

The girls had a minor 1962 hit on Jamie with 'Pop, Pop, Pop-Pie' but unfortunately this 1966 release featuring lead vocal by Dina Cook failed miserably and indeed proved to be their last recording.

Top 500 Position: **474**
Original Label: **Goodway**
Current Value: **£400**

'A delight to open the album and find it in there!'

Rich Rosen,
Record Dealer, Las Vegas, USA

The Silhouettes

Not Me Baby

A promo only 45 that was distributed with the group's 1967 comeback album, this single is absolutely top-notch. Whilst Doo-Wop fans remember the group for their 1958 classic 'Get A Job', it is the Motownesque Goodway recording that we view as the peak of the group's recording career - Northern Soul-wise.

A great dancer, 'Not Me Baby' features a wonderfully controlled lead vocal by Bill Horton that at time soars up to total perfection!

Originally played by DJ Colin Curtis.

Top 500 Position:	**475**
Original Label:	**Tamla**
Current Value:	**£25 Issue**
	£50 Demo

*'Big-boss Motown
in full effect'*

Lol Charles, Soul Fan, Detroit, USA

The Marvellettes

I'll Keep Holding On

Working it's way into the chart is the totally credible 'I'll keep holding on', which has ventured in and out of Northern play for the last 32 years!

The group from Inkster, Michigan, also recorded as the Darnells, and have the distinction of having a no. 1 in the US.

In terms of Northern action, the group are near the top of the tree with absolute stunners such as 'Reachin' For Something I Can't Have', 'Only Your Love Can Save Me' amongst many others.

This 1965 Ivy Joe Hunter/Mickey Stevenson penned goodie, totally rocks your world if you are a true Motown and Northern fan.

Top 500 Position:	**476**
Original Label:	**Palmer/LaBeat**
Current Value:	**£1,200 Palmer**
	£900 LaBeat
	£1,500 LB Demo

*'One of the ultimate
Northern SOUL records'*

Clive Jones, Soul Fan, Warwickshire, UK

Al Williams

I Am Nothing

A Lou Beatty production as Detroit reigns supreme once again with a 45 that was issued on two separate labels - but either is rarer than snake's ears!

The vocal is typical of the time within R&B but the groove - like so many from Michigan is irresistible! DJ Richard Searling first aired the single in the late 70's and it was released in the UK on grapevine in 1979.

At most Northern Soul nights this is one of the most credible singles you're ever likely to come accross!

Top 500 Position:	**477**
Original Label:	**Magic City**
Current Value:	**£125 Issue**
	£200 Demo

'A thundering Detroit Express Train sound'

Alan Riding, Soul Fan, Barnsley, UK

Thelma Lindsey

Prepared To Love You

A stupendous romper from Detroit that Blackpool Mecca unleashed on us in 1973 - although the Casino revelled in the tempo for longer.

The flip 'Why Weren't You There' is a pearl too! - Making the disc a fairly unbeatable double header. Brass and bubbling bass line force Lindsey into overdrive and her performance surely warranted an album?

Today the side is very sought after with the DJ copies in particular fetching a high price.

Top 500 Position:	**478**
Original Label:	**A&M**
Current Value:	**£200 Issue**
	£125 Demo

'A gifted white artiste from LA'

Ed Cobb, Producer, Los Angeles, USA

Toni Basil

Breakaway

A lady who went on to become an ultra-famous choreographer, she had her own bubblegum punk hit with 'Mickey' in 80s.

Toni's career started with US TV's 'Shindig' series and it was in her cheerleader influenced dance style that she really made her mark, eventually being appointed as Janet Jackson's choreographer in the 80's.

'Breakaway', a 1965 recording credited to Ed Cobb and Lincoln Mayorga is typical of the period's white Teen-Soul with a Motown beat - but with that little bit extra!

Discovered languishing in a forgotten corner of Ian Levine's massive collection when Ian first sold some of his records, it was first exposed to the scene by Soul Sam in 1978.

Top 500 Position: **479**
Original Label: **Gordy**
Current Value: **£10**

'One of Edwin's true greats'

Keith Randolph, Soul Fan, Delaware, USA

Edwin Starr

My Weakness Is You

Edwin was originally in the Futuretones This is undoubtedly his best 'feel good' dancer of the 60's but was a poor seller!

Quite why Gordy released this as a 'B' side is anyone's guess

If you are a dancer, then listening to the first eight bars of this song conjure up thoughts of the spectacular twists and turns that have everybody in the club reeling with admiration.

If you are a record buyer, then the next announcement from you is SOLD! Tom Toms, girlie back up and Edwin's inimitable style all add up to another winner.

Yes we have seen him a hundred times but he is like no other. The biggest Northern Soul act ever - END OF STORY!!!.

Top 500 Position: **480**
Original Label: **MGM**
Current Value: **£150 Issue**
£75 Demo

'A neat working'

Jim Smith, Soul Fan, Michigan, USA

The Velours

I'm Gonna Change

Though originally by the Four Seasons, for whom it was bigger on the scene in 1973, the Velours' version of 'I'm Gonna Change' has been far more popular ever since.

Changing their name to the Fantastics, the Velours embarked on a brief but successful career in the UK scoring with 'Something Old Something New' in 1971 having previously recorded in the UK for MGM.

This is a brilliant version of the song which was discovered by respected Midlander - Pep, a regular DJ at the Catacombs, Wigan and a host of other classic venues.

Top 500 Position: **481**
Original Label: **MGM**
Current Value: **£20 Issue**
£30 Demo

'Can I have half a pound of Victory Vs... Oh and a copy of the Tymes!'

Nick Moore, Soul Fan, New York, USA

The Tymes

What Would I Do?

The group led by George Williams, who apparently now lives in Kent, hit the chart for the first time (see 490) with this remarkable dancer.

The appeal of this Tommy Bell penned MGM Torch monster was undoubtedly bolstered by a wealth of copies that appeared on Bradford market in 1972 so allowing every aspiring DJ to spin it in his local Soul Night!

The hook 'What would I do without you baby' makes it.

Top 500 Position: **482**
Original Label: **Epic**
Current Value: **£10 Issue**
£15 Demo

'A love song with great depth'

Brenda Halley, Soul Fan, Winchester, UK

Nancy Ames

I Don't Want To Talk About it

Out of the same stable as Lainie Hill, Lynne Randell and the like, comes a lightweight pop singer who after two other near-misses nosedived into obscurity.

A key fashion item in the 70's, 'I Don't Want To Talk About It' gave the girls a chance to twirl their flared skirts to Ames' heartfelt plea to 'I don't wanna talk about it, now we are thru'.

Totally unfashionable today, it was a veritable monster back in the mid-70's.

Top 500 Position: **483**
Original Label: **Jay Boy**
Current Value: **£125**

'A late-comer to the scene, how on earth did we miss it?'

Mick Glover, Soul Fan, Gloucester, UK

Ray Merrell

Tears Of Joy

Another unlikely Northern hitmaker as a contemporary performer of Irish Folk music! He joined Pye in 1964 moving to the indie label Windsor in 1966 before a brief career with Columbia in 1968, finally arriving at Jay Boy for his finest hour in 1970.

The 45 slots into the big beat movement well and imagine how surprised I was to receive a call from the man recently.

A massive British collector's item.

Top 500 Position: **484**
Original Label: **MGM**
Current Value: **£150 Issue**
£100 Demo

'Paris Blues and this - there's nothing more to say!'

Jimmy Smith, Soul Fan, London, UK

Tony Middleton

To The Ends Of The Earth

The old Nat King Cole number, also covered by Frank Sinatra, is really given the treatment by former Willows lead singer Tony Middleton.

Amazingly it actually received an excruciatingly rare UK Polydor release which weighs in at around the £400 mark.

Claus Ogerman's 1966 production is typical of New York R&B of the time and whilst this great cut was pretty much a non-starter in the 70's it has become one of the scene's most loved sounds in more recent times.

'Hopelessly pricey today'

Jeff Lealing, Soul Fan, London, UK

Eddie Parker

I'm Gone

A frighteningly rare record that has emerged as a major player both on and off the turntable.

First discovered in the mid-70's it somehow became caught up in the plethora of quality nighter sounds. Finally when the euphoria of the time died down it was the Soul 45's like this Detroit outing that remained to take their rightful place in the Northern Soul Hall of Fame.

If you are determined to own 'I'm Gone' on vinyl but don't get paid like a professional footballer, and don't want a reissue you'll find that Billy Sha-Rae's version is pretty good as well (he also recorded a very good alternative vocal to the equally sought after September Jones track entitled 'Do It').

'The 'Sweetest One' by a great vocal group'

Gary Leeds, Soul Fan, London, UK

The Metros

Since I Found My Baby

This is the group's second release from their 'Sweetest One' album which also includes a brilliant cover of the O'Jays' 'I'll Never Forget You' which has become very popular in its own right.

This is the group led by Percy L. Williams and should not be confused with the combo who worked for 1-2-3 and Ra-Sel. A Detroit based outfit, the group actually had a 80's outing for Soul King, but further investigation reveals this to in fact be a 1970 recording. Tracked down by Goldmine Soul Supply recently, this later recording can be heard on 'Detroit Soul From The Vaults'.

Top 500 Position: **487**
Original Label: **Money**
Current Value: **£10**

'To many this is the finest Soul record EVER'

Dave Godin,
Journalist and Soul Fan, Sheffield, UK

Bettye Swann

Make Me Yours

Simply irresistible. The single released here on CBS, didn't fair too well although it attained a Top 30 hit in the US in 1967.

The Wheel were the first to champion the classic, not without comment from journalist Dave Godin who went on record to say that it is his favourite 45 ever. Born Betty Jean Champion in Louisiana, she found fame recording for Money an independent label from Los Angeles.

Prior to the 1967 sessions in LA, she was a member of The Fawns who had recorded for Chancellor at the time. Scene wise it's now played regularly, although impossible to find a place for it during the stompified 70's. Bobby Montgomery, ZZ Hill and High Inergy have all done covers of the vintage song.

Top 500 Position: **488**
Original Label: **Argo**
Current Value: **£250**

'A stunning vocalist'

Trevor Wheatstone, Soul Fan, Yorkshire, UK

Herb Ward

Strange Change

Discovered by the legendary Harthon team of Randolph Styles and Weldon McDougall III, Philadelphian Ward recorded for Argo in 1965 before moving onto Buddy and of course RCA Victor where he released another true Northern classic 'Honest To Goodness'. A recent revelation is that Herb is in fact Herb Johnson who recorded for Toxsan, Brunswick, Tyler and Arctic and the like.

Fans of Herb's wonderful voice will find some interesting alternate versions of his City of Brotherly Love output on Goldmine Soul Supply CD 'The Northern Soul Of Philadelphia Vol. 2'.

Top 500 Position: **489**
Original Label: **Impact**
Current Value: **£200**

'A real oddity from Detroit'

Mick Bradley, Soul Fan, Derbyshire, UK

Nabay

Believe It Or Not

Odd is being kind to this real esoteric piece of nonsense.

I believe the rarity of the disc to be the platform for it's popularity, however I confess to loathing it.

The Impact waxing, recorded in 1966 - where else but Detroit, is still one of THE choice collectors' items and with the constant harmonized chant it has become a perennial favourite.

Nabay was in fact a Lebanese singer who was finally released from Impact records because owner Harry Balk owed him a favour!

Top 500 Position: **490**
Original Label: **Parkway**
Current Value: **£15 Issue**
£30 Demo

'Terrific group harmony'

Billy Jackson, Producer, USA

The Tymes

Here She Comes

From 1964 one of the 'old' sounds is saluted as George Williams, the lead singer, follows the beat to the anthemic conclusion that 'here she comes walking down the street'.

The label was certainly on a hot streak at the time with masses of hits from Dee Dee Sharp, The Orlons, Chubby Checker etc.

Maintaining a positive association with producer Billy Jackson, the band had a stop start career but did make some wonderful records on Cameo, Winchester and Columbia.

Sadly the band finally split up in the 80's, shortly after their comeback which produced 'You Little Trustmaker' and 'Miss Grace' for RCA.

Top 500 Position:	**491**
Original Label:	**Duke**
Current Value:	**£10 Issue**
	£20 Demo

'Mr Blue with arguably his best Soul 45'

Bob Hall, Soul Fan, Manchester, UK

Bobby Bland

Shoes

Robert Calvin Bland from Rosemark, Tennessee is no stranger to the scene despite being world renowned as a Blues master. His recordings go back as far as 1949, and with several other classic Duke singles ('Call On Me', 'Yum Yum Tree', 'Good Time Charlie' and 'I'm Not Myself Anymore') he has a fair fan base within our world too.

'Shoes' represents his true anthem, after originally becoming a constant play at the 100 Club, London in the 80's.

Top 500 Position:	**492**
Original Label:	**La Beat**
Current Value:	**£1,500**

'A meaty Detroit bounder'

Barry Williams,
Soul Fan, Greater Manchester, UK

Lester Tipton

This Won't Change

Lou Beatty formed a label par excellence in 1965. Nearly all the releases are sought after, and as for the talent, well try these for size, Al Williams, Nelson Sanders, The Masqueraders, Don Hart and James Shorter, who all contributed to the labels creativity. Club wise, Tipton's effort is first class, with the usual Detroit backtrack and a strong vocal.

As usual, great record, but with no promotion - thank heavens for Northern Soul. Tipton moved to LA later where he was unfortunately the victim of a murder in the late 80's.

Top 500 Position: **493**
Original Label: **Oliver**
Current Value: **£50 Issue**
£60 Demo

'Vintage Wigan'

Beth Stevens, Soul Fan, Wigan, UK

The Steinways

My Heart's Not In It Anymore/ You've Been Leading Me On

Yvonne Gearing, who went on to front the Glories, here sings lead with New York group The Steinways on this fabulous double sider.

'My Heart's' was the official Wigan A-spin but in recent years the flip has become the main play. Backed by abundant rich male harmonies the underrated Gearing really is firing on all cylinders on this one!

Top 500 Position: **494**
Original Label: **Smoke**
Current Value: **£300**

''Misery has finally trapped me and it's tearing me apart'… Just brilliant!'

Dave Makin, Soul Fan, Stafford, UK

George Blackwell

Can't Lose My Head

A truly massive New Jersey Soul beater from local legend and label owner George Blackwell.

Discovered by the Frost brothers in Loughborough of all places, it was promptly sold on to Ian Levine for the princely sum of £3! Of course Ian turned it into pure Northern Soul gold - the rest is history!

Smoke is a sought after collector's label, recorded in 1966 in Newark, N.J. 'Can't Lose My Head' is a real jewel in this label's crown.

Top 500 Position: **495**
Original Label: **Motown**
Current Value: **£10 Issue**
£20 Demo

'About as sublime as you can get'

Gary Walsh, Soul Fan, Wichita, Kansas, USA

The Spinners

Sweet Thing

It is all too easy to compile Motown 45s, they single handedly inspired the scene. The Spinners have their contributions well aired by the North and this 1964 recording is one of many. Bobby Smith breezes through the song (probably in one take) without breaking sweat, Henry Famborough, Pervis Jackson and Billy Henderson routinely perform the background.

The rhythm as you can imagine is 'top drawer',with Earl Van Dyke and the Soul Brothers rhythmically creating another 'hot ticket'.

The Twisted Wheel grabbed hold of it and not surprisingly the 45 is one of the first you might manage to own as your collection builds.

Top 500 Position: **496**
Original Label: **Roulette**
Current Value: **£6 Issue**
£10 Demo

'A slick female groover'

Mark Mason, Soul Fan, Derby, UK

The Fuzz

I'm So Glad

Formerly the Passionettes on Path records and hanging around the scene as a 'B list' item in 1974, the Blackpool Mecca was its official home with DJ Ian Levine working to death. Far too slick for the stomp-stomp niters, it's the groove that makes this a single that helped change the course of the scene.

The group's other single for Calla was 'I Love You For All Seasons' which became a big US Soul hit.

Top 500 Position: **497**
Original Label: **Atco**
Current Value: **£10 Issue**
£15 Demo

'Pioneering the youth culture'

Wayne Kennedy, Collector, UK

Tami Lynn

I'm Gonna Run Away From You

Recorded in 1964 it took 7 years to finally make it, peaking at No.4 in '71. Old hand Bert Berns took control of the typical girl group outing and engaged 19 year old Tami a young New Orleans singer to smother the song in kisses.

The ultimate 'dance 'round yer 'andbag' 45 which every disco in town got behind when re-released on Mojo.

Amazingly it also got a release on UK Atlantic in 1965.

Lynn was first discovered by Harold Battiste and signed to his AFO label, fronting a studio band called the AFO Executives. In more recent times a new discovery entitled 'Runaway' from a rare French EP has simmered along, and with an obvious connection to her longer title, it reprises the massive hit which we adore so much.

Top 500 Position: **498**
Original Label: **Spring**
Current Value: **£40 Issue**
£20 Demo

'The big sing-a-long song of '75'

John Matthews, Soul Fan, Birmingham, UK

Flower Shoppe

You've Come Along Way Baby

Phil Flowers from Washington, DC was a noted performer, writer, manager etc. He recorded a couple of killers for Dot in 1966 amongst many other labels.

Resurfacing in the early 70's, he secured a deal for his new band the aptly named Flower Shoppe. Recording one single for the Spring label with very risqué lyrics about 'the hairs below your waist' - no-wonder it totally bombed leaving the way open for us to once again at least give it a good funeral!

Top 500 Position: **499**
Original Label: **Mirwood**
Current Value: **£6 Issue**
£12 Demo

'One of the true 60's dance crazes'

Karen Grayson, Soul Fan, Upminster, UK

The Olympics

Baby Do The Philly Dog

From the great Mirwood label, 50's hitmakers The Olympics from Compton, California, rip it up with this 'club classic' from 1966.

Fred Smith the chief architect behind the great Mirwood sound cultivates a terrific performance from lead singer Walter Ward.

The song is typical of the time, and I find it difficult to understand how it missed the boat, especially after the success of 'Cool Jerk' among other dance anthems.

Whenever I hear it, fond memories of the legendary Rick Ricardo's record store in San Francisco spring to mind, with shop owner Rick executing the dance to perfection!

Top 500 Position: **500**
Original Label: **Evolution**
Current Value: **£50**

'A pumping bass treat'

Jon Maxtead, Soul Fan, London, UK

Larry Santos

You Got Where You Want Me

This typical Bobby Paris type stomper from 1970 is a pure one-off for Santos.

The intro makes it and, combined with gravelly vocal and killer hook we have the perfect scenario for the one shot wonder.

Though first popular when baggy trousers, bowling shirts were the order of the day, the song still receives a healthy following, but 1975 was undoubtedly it's golden year. Larry himself went on to record for legendary disco label Casablanca in the Seventies.

A reasonable cover version exists by Jon Ford on Philips, but if you can't get enough of Santos, get the LP version - it's a whole verse longer!

bubbling under

Every Soul Boy and Girl has their favourite sounds, I'm sure that as you read the Top 500 that you were surprised not to see a record that is particularly close to your own heart, I have my own personal favourites many of which didn't make it either, however you may well find it in this list of 100 spins that nearly made the chart...

1.	Billy Arnell	Tough Girl	Holly
2.	Bob Brady and the Concords	Everybody's Going To A Love In	Chariot
3.	Marsha Gee	Baby I Need You	Uptown
4.	Jackie Wilson	I Get The Sweetest Feeling	Brunswick
5.	George Lemons	Fascinating Girl	Gold Soul
6.	Tommy Ridgley	My Love Is Getting Stronger	International City
7.	George Pepp	The Feeling Is Real	Coleman
8.	Ollie Jackson	The Day My Heart Stood Still	Magnum
9.	Gwen Owens	You're Wanted (And Needed)	Velgo
10.	Linda Jones	My Heart Needs A Break	Loma

*Below: Linda Jones considered by many to
be the greatest Soul singer of them all.*

LOMA

LINDA
JONES
Produced by
George Kerr
For Tra-San
Productions

(L8...
Arra...
Condu...
Robert...

MY HEART NEEDS A BREAK
(Sammy Turner)
Three T Pub. Co. & J. T. Music Co.
ASCAP - 2:38
MADE IN U.S.A. WARNER BROS. RECORDS INC. ®

317

11.	**Bob Wilson**	Suzie's Serenade	Sound Stage 7
12.	**Channel 3**	The Sweetest Thing	Dakar
13.	**Dee Edwards**	All The Way Home	D-Town
14.	**Paris**	Sleepless Nights	Doc
15.	**The Four Larks**	Groovin' At The Go-Go	Tower
16.	**Donna Coleman**	Your Love's To Strong	Avin
17.	**Elbie Parker**	Please Keep Away From Me	Veep
18.	**Joanie Sommers**	Don't Pity Me	WB
19.	**Benny Spellman**	Fortune Teller	Minit
20.	**The Ellusions**	You Didn't Have To Leave	Lamon
21.	**JJ Barnes**	Sweet Sherry	Volt
22.	**Steve Flannagan**	I've Arrived	Era
23.	**Marv Johnson**	I Miss You Baby	Gordy
24.	**John Leach**	Put That Woman Down	Lawn
25.	**Danny Monday**	Baby Without You	Modern
26.	**Marvin Holmes**	You Better Keep Her	Brown Door
27.	**Jimmy Ruffin**	He Who Picks A Rose	Motown Acetate
28.	**The Brooks Brothers**	Looking For A Woman	Tay
29.	**Lorraine Chandler**	I Cant Hold On	RCA
30.	**The Trammps**	Hold Back The Night	Buddah
31.	**The Fiestas**	Think Smart	Old Town
32.	**Jnr Walker and the Allstars**	I Ain't Going Nowhere	Tamla Motown
33.	**Edwin Starr**	Backstreet	Ric-Tic

Opposite: Bob and Earl, the Mirwood duo who recorded many Northern classics. Earl Nelson (left) was of course also Jackie Lee and recorded a host of Northern Soul sounds of his own, including 'Would You Believe' and the wonderful 'Darkest Days'.

Left: Another great Harthon production... 'Groovin At The Go-Go' from the Four Larks also features 'I Still Love You (From The Bottom Of My Heart)' on the reverse which has also become popular in recent years.

319

34.	**Terry Callier**	Ordinary Joe	Chess
35.	**Dalton Boys**	I've Been Cheated	VIP
36.	**Johnny Honeycutt**	I'm Coming Over	Triode
37.	**The Twans**	I Can't See Him Again	Dade
38.	**The Trends**	Thanks For A Little Lovin	ABC
39.	**Bobby Womack**	So Many Sides Of You	Beverly Glenn
40.	**Bunny Sigler**	Follow Your Heart	Parkway
41.	**Jackie Wilson**	I Don't Want To Lose You	Brunswick
42.	**Danny Woods**	You Had Me Fooled	Correc-Tone
43.	**Martha Starr**	Love Is The Only Solution	Thelma
44.	**The Belles**	Don't Pretend	Mirwood
45.	**International GTOs**	I Love You Baby	Rojac
46.	**Jimmy Robins**	I Just Can't Please You	Jerheart
47.	**Just Brothers**	Carlena	Garrison
48.	**The Elgins**	Heaven Must Have Sent You	VIP
49.	**Williams & Watson**	A Quitter Never Wins	Okeh
50.	**Lew Kirton**	Heaven In The Afternoon	Alston
51.	**Charles Johnson**	Never Had A Love So Good	Alston
52.	**The Construction**	Hey Little Way Out Girl	Sync 6
53.	**Jay D Martin**	By Yourself	Tower
54.	**The Magnificents**	My Heart Is Calling	Dee Gee

Left: The Magnificents' 'My Heart Is Calling' has been 'bubbling under' in the popularity stakes for many years. Its was co-written by Marc Gordon and Frank Wilson and despite the misspelling of Jobete it was in fact a Motown published tune.

The Doo-Wop influenced 'B' side 'On Main Street' has also received plays over the years.

55.	**Lynne Vernado**	Wash And Wear Love	Gator
56.	**Yvonne Vernee**	Just like You Did Me	Sonbert
57.	**Mickey Moonshine**	Name It You Got It	Decca
58.	**The Gypsies**	It's A Woman's World	Old Town
59.	**Moses Dillard**	I'll Pay The Price	Mark IV
60.	**Major Lance**	Investigate	Okeh
61.	**Florence Devore**	Kiss Me Now	Phi-Dan
62.	**Benzine**	Village Of Tears	Parkway
63.	**Norma Jenkins**	The Airplane Song	Maltese
64.	**Bud Harper**	Wherever You Were	Peacock
65.	**Little Eddie Taylor**	I Had A Good Time	Peacock
66.	**Margaret Mandolph**	Something Beautiful	Planetary
67.	**The Parliaments**	Heart Trouble	Revilot
68.	**Barbara Lynn**	Take Your Love And Run	Jetstream
69.	**Vala Regan**	Fireman	Atco
70.	**Phil Terrell**	Love Has Passed Me By	Carnival
71.	**André Brasseur**	The Kid	Palette
72.	**The Wonderettes**	I Feel Strange	Ruby
73.	**Damon Fox**	Packin' Up	Fairmount
74.	**Rita and the Tiaras**	Gone With The Wind Is My Love	Dore
75.	**Mandrill**	Never Die	Polydor
76.	**The Formations**	At The Top Of The Stairs	Bank
77.	**Donald Lee Richardson**	You Got Me In The Palm Of Your Hand	Soulville
78.	**Jean Carter**	Like One	Decca
79.	**First Choice**	This Is The House (Where Love Died)	Scepter

Left: Moses Dillard, the man behind 'I'll The Price', 'Pretty As A Picture' and many more great tracks both common and very rare.

Opposite: Edward Hamilton who with the Arabians recorded many Soul gems for the likes of Grand Prix and Mary Jane. Note that though this is a Mary Jane release it is written by Melvin Davis and produced by Lou Beatty of La Beat fame.

Left and Below: Marvin Smith, lead singer of the Artistics has had some major Northern sounds in his own right, most notably 'Baby Boy' for Brunswick.

80.	**The Whispers**	Remember Me	Soul Clock
81.	**Donna King**	Take Me Home	Hot Line
82.	**Edward Hamilton and the Arabians**	I'm Gonna Love You	Mary Jane
83.	**Jesse Johnson**	Left Out	Old Town
84.	**Yvonne and the Violets**	Cross My Heart	Barry
85.	**Marvin Smith**	Have More Time	Brunswick
86.	**The Soul Brothers Six**	Thankyou Baby For Loving Me	Atlantic
87.	**Debbie Dean**	Why Am I Lovin' You	VIP
88.	**Sandra Philips**	World Without Sunshine	Broadway
89.	**The Petals**	You Can't Close The Windows To Your Heart	Mercury
90.	**Bobby Williams**	I've Only Got Myself To Blame	Sure-Shot
91.	**Bobby Jason**	Wall To Wall Heartaches	Ranwood
92.	**Cajun Heart**	Got To Find A Way	Warner Brothers
93.	**Cliff Nobles**	My Love Is Getting Stronger	Atlantic
94.	**The Isley Brothers**	My Love Is Your Love	MFP LP
95.	**The Inspirations**	Your Wish Is My Command	Midas
96.	**Charles Sheffield**	It's Your Voodoo Working	Excello
97.	**The Ambassadors**	Too Much Of A Good Thing	Pee-Vee
98.	**William Powell**	Heartache Souvenirs	Power House
99.	**Bobby Treetop**	Wait 'Til I Get To Know Ya	Tuff
100.	**Lorraine Silver**	Lost Summer Love	Pye

321

essential cd purchases

If you are returning to Northern Soul after a break or are new to the scene and wish to learn more you will no-doubt be wanting to track down those sounds that give you a buzz. But if you have looked in a sales box recently you'll probably have had a shock! Today records that cost a few cents each when they were first pressed are frequently, tens, hundreds and sometimes even thousands of pounds each!

If you are a serious vinyl junkie this is of course of no surprise and will probably just slow you down a little! However for the majority of us most rare vinyl is today beyond our means, however in recent years an enormous amount of classic Northern Soul, rare and not-so rare, has become available not as the notorious bootlegs of old but as legitimate releases on top quality CDs from companies like Kent and Goldmine/Soul Supply as well as the Majors who have at last woken up to the true quality of those subsidiary label 'turkies' they have buried in their vaults!

Here's 20 excellent CD purchases that contain most of the Top 500 - to get you started!...

1.	Out On The Floor	*(GOLDMINE/SOUL SUPPLY)*
2.	The Wigan Casino Story	*(GOLDMINE/SOUL SUPPLY)*
3.	The Golden Torch Story	*(GOLDMINE/SOUL SUPPLY)*
4.	Big In Wigan	*(KENT)*
5.	Jumping At The Go-Go	*(BMG)*
6.	Soul Self Satisfaction	*(UNIVERSAL)*
7.	Gettin' To Me	*(KENT)*
8.	This Is Northern Soul	*(DEBUTANTE)*
9.	Soul Time	*(SONY)*
10.	The Wigan Casino 25TH	*(GOLDMINE/SOUL SUPPLY)*
11.	Rare, Collectable And Soulful	*(KENT)*
12.	The Essential Northern Soul Story	*(GOLDMINE/SOUL SUPPLY)*
13.	Turning My Heartbeat Up	*(BMG)*
14.	Northern Soul Floorshakers	*(BMG)*
15.	Shrine, The Rarest Soul Label	*(KENT)*
16.	It's Okeh Up North	*(XCLUSIVE)*
17.	The Twisted Wheel Story	*(GOLDMINE/SOUL SUPPLY)*
18.	Out on The Floor Again	*(GOLDMINE/SOUL SUPPLY)*
19.	For Millionaires Only	*(GOLDMINE/SOUL SUPPLY)*
20.	Soul Underground	*(SEQUEL)*

Left: Northern Soul continues to develop and grow, 'Allnighter' from Goldmine/Soul Supply captures the essence of today's scene with a host of top current sounds including the massively popular unissued Harthon version of Cliff Nobles' 'Love Is All Right' by Jesse James.

ERICA RECORDS

Moa-Lah Pub. Co. B.M.I. Time

Arr. J. Cameron Prod. B. Watkiss

"I REALLY LOVE YOU"
(R. NEWSOME)
JIMMY BURNS

BLUE STAR RECORDS

45 RPM 45 RPM

Hemisphere Music (BMI) (TM-1000-A)
Time 2:45

TM-1000
Dist. by MALYNN ENTERPRISES, INC.

PROMOTIONAL COPY

SILENT TREATMENT
(Ernest J. Lucas)
ARIN DEMAIN
A Thomas R. Morgan Production

ROUSER RECORDS
WASHINGTON, D.C.

Pecle Music BMI

F-1017 A
Produced by Frankie Beverly & Tommy Rouse

BECAUSE OF MY HEART
(Beverly)
THE BUTLERS WITH FRANKIE BEVERLY
A QT Production

Prophonics STUDIOS

2029-A
45 RPM
Time: 2:45
Arrangement by: Larry Johnson

Prophonic Music Pub-BMI
Written By: Bill Tuthill
Produced by: William Latchaw

I DON'T LIKE TO LOSE
THE "GROUP"
Featuring
CECIL WASHINGTON

PRODUCED AT PROPHONIC STUDIOS — MT. MORRIS, MICHIGAN - PHON 232-965

SOUND IMPRESSION RECORDS

Jobete Music BMI
Time: 2:56
Produced by: Tom Cohen

SIR 6808
Directed by: Brian "Funk" Dombrowski INSTR.

BARI TRACK
(Peachy Art)
DONI BURDICK
"A SOLID SOUL SOUND"

HEM

HM-1091S

1000
VOCAL
Pub. Cashmere-Haven, BMI
Time: 2:05

SHOW STOPPER
(Jefferson)
THE CASHMERES
Arr. by Fred Perry

Party time

Clairlyn Pub. Co. BMI
Engr. by Joe Tarsia

Time: 2:25
Arr. & Cond. by Joe Thomas
Produced by Kip Gainsboro

I'M NOT STRONG ENOUGH
(Steals-Thomas-Steals)
THE FOUR PERFECTIONS
PT-1001

SHRINE RECORDS

Ramitary Mus. Corp. BMI

SR -112-1
2:00
Produced by Harry Bass

GUESS WHO LOVES YOU
(H. Bass-C. Kidd)
EDDIE DAYE & 4 BARS
Arranged by Dale Warren

eskee

Bilde Music, Inc.
Time: 1:45

ESKEE 10.001
6570
Arranged by Frank Owens & Syd Shaw

PROMOTIONAL COPY

YOU DON'T MEAN ME NO GOOD
(Charles Thomas)
THE JELLY BEANS
AN ESCULATOR PRODUCTION
DIST. BY BELL RECORDS, N.Y.

Goodway

11401 Roosevelt Boulevard Philadelphia, Pa. 19154

Goodway Music BMI
(45-1502)

Time: 2:25
For Promotion

From "The Original & New 58/68 Silhouettes" Album #GLP-100

NOT ME BABY
G101

SEDGRICK RECORDS

Vanieer Music BMI

No. 3001
Time 2:35
Side Two

CHEATIN KIND
Don Gardner
Wr. & Prod. J. Vanleer
For Vanleer Productions

TIE RECORDS

Tietom Music
Time 2:04

T-101-A

CAN'T GET OVER THESE MEMORIES
(Pinkard - Hendley)
JOHN and THE WIERDEST

Wonderful rarities!... Classic floorpackers that cost a king's ransom!

Above: 'Ciao Baby' grooving with hip white Australian Ms. Lynne Randell!

Right: The wonderful Barbara Lynn, her first ever UK performance at Blackpool Weekender 1999, supported by Snake Davies and his band.

WASHPAN RECORDS

Side 1
Washpan Music
BMI
2:15

ST 372932
Eng. by Ed Wolfrum
at United Sound
WM 3125

I REALLY LOVE YOU
(Claude Williams)
THE TOMANGOE'S
Produced by Washpan Music
Arr. & Cond. by Randy Gibson
and G. Washington
WASHPAN RECORDS, 2715 CADILLAC TOWER, DETROIT, MICH.

PARKWAY RECORDS

177

Wemar Music
Corp.-BMI

Time: 2:10
Produced by
Stuart Wiener &
Mike Lewis

45-177

NOT FOR SALE
D. J. COPY

COUNTRY GIRL
(Joe Simmons)
VICKIE BAINES
P-966-A
© 1964 CAMEO-PARKWAY RECORDS, INC.

JOKER RECORDS

45 RPM   45 RPM

Jobete (BMI)
Time 2:35

(45-J-1)

MY SUGAR BABY
(Frank Wilson)
CONNIE CLARK
Prod. by Joker Enterprises
716

BREAKTHROUGH

Little Jeff
Time: 2:52

1001
(03)

**NO ONE ELSE
CAN TAKE YOUR PLACE**
(L. Ivey - L. Bell - H. Bell - J. Gibson)
INSPIRATIONS
Prod. by Joey Jefferson

FRANKIE KARL
AND THE CHEVRONS

Philtown RECORDS

PH-105-A
Prod. by
Dave Chackler
For M.H.B.
Productions
Arr. by
Joe Renzy

**"YOU SHOULD'O
HELD ON"**
(Herbert Holmes)
Ranbells Music Co.-BMI
PHILTOWN RECORDS DIV. OF PHILTOWN PROD.

GROOVE CITY RECORDS

Groovesville
BMI - 2:35

Record No.
101
(SI-C1004S-A)

THAT'S WHY I LOVE YOU
(Bruce, Jack & Leon)
THE PROFESSIONALS

VILLA RECORDS

Jokamp (BMI)
(4572-B)

705
Time 2:07

DOUBLE COOKIN'
(Campbell - Jones)
THE CHECKERBOARD
SQUARES
Prod. by Campbell & Jones

Yuppy RECORD

JACK HOWARD
PUB. - BMI
Time: 2:06

C-101-A
EXEC. PRODUCER
SONNY CASELLA

LOVER
(KEITH)
DE-LITES
(LAUREL PRODUCTIONS)

**SAVIN' MY LOVIN'
FOR YOU**
(Richard Wylie-Tony Hester)

palmer record company

Promotional
Not For Sale

P-5020-A
Ala-King
Music-BMI
Produced By:
"Popcorn" Wylie
For Palmer
Productions
Arranged By:
Mike Terry
Time: 2:49

**THE PEOPLE'S
CHOICE**
© 1967

La Beat RECORDS
Detroit, Mich.

Produced by
Johnny Mills
& Curtis Trusel

Mums Pub. BMI
Time: 2:20
P6607
17867

THIS WON'T CHANGE
(Mills - Trusel)
LESTER TIPTON
Orchestra LPT's
(LaBeat
Production Team)

TAY-STER

Dist. by Tay-Star Sales, Inc.
112 W. 70th St., New York, N.Y. 10024

TS 6015
Streetcar Music,
Inc.
BMI 2:10

Taylor-Gallo
Productions

MEET ME HALFWAY
(Jack Taylor)
LILLIE BRYANT

BONNIE Records

Gomba Music
BMI

ZTSC-107374
Time: 2:07

LADY IN GREEN
(B. Browner)
MAGNETICS

Wonderful rarities!... Classic floorpackers that cost a king's ransom!

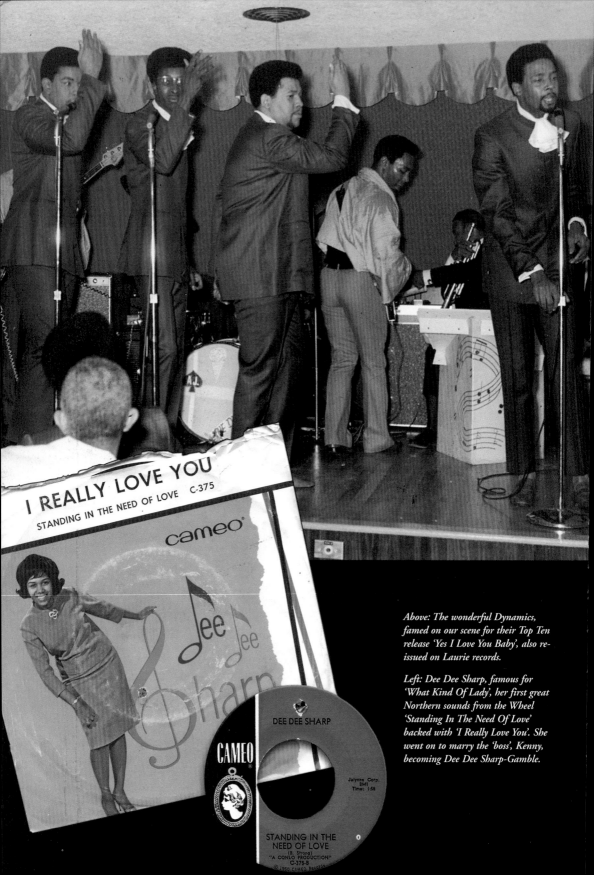

I REALLY LOVE YOU

STANDING IN THE NEED OF LOVE   C-375

cameo

Above: The wonderful Dynamics, famed on our scene for their Top Ten release 'Yes I Love You Baby', also re-issued on Laurie records.

Left: Dee Dee Sharp, famous for 'What Kind Of Lady', her first great Northern sounds from the Wheel 'Standing In The Need Of Love' backed with 'I Really Love You'. She went on to marry the 'boss', Kenny, becoming Dee Dee Sharp-Gamble.

DEE DEE SHARP

CAMEO

Jalynne Corp.
BMI
Time: 1:58

STANDING IN THE
NEED OF LOVE
(B. Strong)
"A CONLO PRODUCTION"
C-375-B
© 1960 CAMEO Records

Wonderful rarities!... Classic floorpackers that cost a king's ransom!

Above: Brenda Holloway (here live at Burnley Mechanics). A very likeable lady, when she finally performed on these shores courtesy of promoter Chris King in 1997 she took the scene by storm.

Left: Motown - responsible for an incredible number of Northern sounds - here on this one ad we see four classics (not counting Ms. Ross' effort!).

Left: Not you might think the most likely of Soul fans! Chris Tarrant, Bob Carolgees and the Phantom Flan Flinger seen here with Kev at a Soul Alldayer in Nottingham in the 1980.

Brunswick

Reg. U.S. Pat. Off. Marca Registrada Mfr'd by Brunswick Record Corp. New York U.S.A.

RECORD NO.
55330
(118,878)
(2:03)

Vocal With Instrumental Accompaniment

Wanessa Music, Inc. (BMI)

Promotion Copy Not For Sale

DON'T TAKE IT OUT ON THIS WORLD
(Ray Allen-Wandra Merrell)
ADAM'S APPLES
PRODUCED BY ALLEN and BROWN

SHE'S WANTED
(J. Solomon - E. Holman)

dynamo

Dandelion-Stilran Music (BMI)
D-LC430A
Time: 2:45

National Dist. Jamie / Guyden Dist. Corp.

J/G

A Horthon Production

D. J. COPY
NOT FOR SALE

LARRY CLINTON

Prod. by Randolph, Stiles, McDougal

300

IMPACT
RECORDS

Gomba Music Inc. BMI
VOCAL

IMPACT
#1032

Time: 2:37
Arranged by Theodore Coffey

'BELIEVE IT OR NOT'
(R. Kreisler - A. Bushaene)
NABAY
Produced by
A.N.B. Productions

Linda

121
(45-478-81)

Padua (BMI)
Time 2:25

(I LOVE HER SO MUCH) IT HURTS ME
(Arthur Robins)
THE MAJESTICS

SUEMI
RECORDS

PUSH SIDE

245 Lindberg
El Paso, Tex. 79922
Phone: 1-915-584-4110

Puntina-BMI
TIME: total 3:27
intro - 20 sec.
to fade 2:52

Produced By:
Kenneth Smith

ST 4567

PLAY SIDE

I'M COM'UN HOME IN THE MORN'UN
(George L. Pride)
LOU PRIDE

A DIVISION OF TASMIT ENTERPRISES

Green Dolphin

Time: 2:15

GAC 115-B
Gravenhurst Music (BMI)
65-6

A Jerry Reed Production

CAN'T WE TALK IT OVER
(L. Allen)
L. ALLEN

DADE

SHERLYN PUB BMI

D-235

I CAN'T SPEAK
(Reid, Clarke)
JIMMIE "BO" HORN
PRODUCED BY
BRAD SHAPIRO &
STEVE ALAIMO
(2025)

KING

PROMOTIONAL   PROMOTIONAL

45-
6148   K-12500
                    SOIL (BMI)
HIGH   TIME: 2:29
                    Vocal
          FIDELITY

I'M SLOWLY MOLDING
(Grant Burton)
CODY BLACK

MY WORLD IS ON FIRE
(M. Coleman, C. Hasentine, M. Valvano)

palmer
record company

PROMOTIONAL
Not For Sale

P-5019-A
Palmerton Pub. BMI and In-The-Pocket Music-BMI
Time: 2:24
Produced By: Coleman, Hasentine & Valvano

ACTION SIDE

JIMMY MACK
An In-The-Pocket Prod.
Arr. By: Mike Terry
© 1967

YOU'RE ON TOP GIRL
(Ira Thomas)

D. J. COPY
NOT FOR SALE

CA-2066

Vandever Music Co.
Time: 2:22

CADI

THE EMPIRES
Produced by James Chavis

IMPEL
A PRODUCT OF WASHINGTON SOUND

Artive Music
548 NE 42 St.,
Ft. Lauderdale, Fla.
(ASCAP)

A Washington Sound Production
SS-AS-103-B
2:26
Arr. by
Austin Campbell
Slide 2

YOU'VE BEEN GONE TOO LONG
(David W. Fry, Ann & Melton Smith)
ANN SEXTON AND THE MASTERS OF SOUL

PHELECTRON
RECORDS

LOS ANGELES   CALIFORNIA

45 RPM   45 RPM

Treasure Music
Co. (B.M.I.)
Time: 2:40

PH-382-B
Produced by
Cyril B. Roberts Jr.

NAUGHTY BOY
(Cyril B. Roberts Jr.)
JACKIE DAY

Wonderful rarities!... Classic floorpackers that cost a king's ransom!

... AND ANOTHER TOP TEN CANDIDATE FROM HITSVILLE, U.S.A.

I'LL ALWAYS LOVE YOU
by
THE SPINNERS

Motown 1078

TAMLA/MOTOWN/GORDY RECORDS
2648 W. Grand Blvd., Detroit, Mich.

Above: The incomparable Jackie Wilson turns in a thunderous performance.

Left: Perennial favourites the Spinners with their alltime classic 'I'll Always Love You' which is placed right up at number 64 in our chart.

La Beat RECORDS

Produced by
Bridges & Knight
Mums-BMI

-D.J. Copy

809L-6602DJ
LB-6602
Time: 2:10
TK4M-0044
NOT FOR SALE

I AM NOTHING
(Bridges-Knight)
AL WILLIAMS
Orchestra: THE LPT's /La Beat
Production Team

6072 14th ST. • DETROIT, MICH.

NOTHING CAN HELP YOU NOW
(Hall-Bateman-Levy)
Vixen Music Corp.

A Vixen
Production

BMI - 2:48

Prod. by
Benny Hall

961

LENNY CURTIS

Arr. & Prod. by
R. Bateman-R. Moseley

E-1127

A DIVISION OF ROULETTE RECORDS INC.

MADE IN U.S.A. BY ENO RECORDS

BELL RECORDS

Melston Publ. Co.
Delew Music Co.
Aye Bee Music
BMI

9064-BW

B-768
Time: 2:30

★

EVER AGAIN
(William Lucas)
BERNIE WILLIAMS
Arr. & Prod. by Joe Stevenson
and Saul Meloin

AMY mate BELL N.Y.C.

SITTING IN MY CLASS
(Ronnie McNeir)

De-To

DS 2878 A
Time: 3:07
Arranged by
F. Jones
Published by
Polk-Harding-Kyle
BMI

RONNIE McNEIR
Produced by
Jones & Kyle
DETROIT SOUND RECORDING CO.

Dotty's RECORDS

Produced by
Sonny Jones &
C. Marshall
Arranged by
J. Britton

Time 2:00

D-345-B
Snowdrift
BMI

NOT MY GIRL
(F. Johnson-C. Marshall)
JOHNNY HAMPTON

A PRODUCT OF DOTTY'S RECORD CO. . 5725 14th, DETROIT, MICH.

POWER-HOUSE RECORDS

Beechwood Music
(BMI)
Time 2:39

P-101-A

Arr. by Miles Grayson
Prod. by Wm. Powell

HEARTACHE SOUVENIRS
(William Powell)
WILLIAM POWELL
A Power-House Production

POWER-HOUSE RECORDS
4702 S. Hoover, L.A. 37, Calif.

La-Cindy RECORDS

225-B
BMI
Time: 2:35

Epitone-Pimlico
Produced By
Snookum-Hill
Arranged By
Lil Doll

STUBBORN HEART
(Eddie LaShea)
ERNEST MOSLEY

bareback records, inc.

D.J. Copy
Not for Sale

SIDE A
BB 131 A
STEREO
TIME:
3:40
Bareback
Music
ASCAP
Invisible
City Music
ASCAP
Master #
BMS-1097

Prod. by:
Art Polhemus
& Tom
Bridwell
Horn
Arrangement:
Mark Snow
Imagineer:
Art Polhemus

ANYTHING I CAN DO
(J. Wright, T. Bridwell, R. Weekes)
W/L COLLINS & WILLPOWER
©1977 by APO
All Rights Reserved.

BAREBACK RECORDS INC. 1650 BROADWAY, N.Y. N.Y. 10019

SMOKE RECORD CO.

KB-200-A
Time 2:30
Wellsound
House Co. B.M.I.

45 RPM
Arr. & Cond.
Bert DeChreaux
Produced by
Roy Thomas

CAN'T LOSE MY HEAD
(Kenneth Ruffin)
GEORGE BLACKWELL

NEWARK, N.J.

NO ONE TO LOVE
(Eddie Anderson)

LaBoyou Music
BMI
Time: 2:40
ZTSC-126479

-SH-109
Produced by
Taylor & Clinton

PAT LEWIS

Distributed by
Solid Hitbound Productions,
Detroit, Michigan

SHRINE RECORDS

Ramitary
Mus. Corp.
BMI

SR 111-2
2:21
Produced by
Eddie
Singleton

STOP OVERLOOKING ME
(Kent Lewis)
THE CAIROS
Arranged by
Dale Warren

fontana

PROMOTIONAL COPY   NOT FOR SALE

F-1599
1-35711
MRC Music
Inc. &
Delamiur
Music
(BMI) 2:42

Produced by:
L. J. Smith,
D. Wells,
J. Rose

BETTIN' ON LOVE
(L. J. Smith - J. A. Durke)
LEN JEWELL

Wonderful rarities!... Classic floorpackers that cost a king's ransom!

The late, great Junior
Walker making his
sax sing sax live on
stage in 1970.

TOP TENS
northern soul over the years

Over the years the scene has resonated to 1000s of different sounds, many like **PJ Proby's** 'Nicky Hoeky' or Elvis' 'Rubberneckin' popular at the **Wheel** in the late 60's or Spirogyra - played at Blackpool Mecca in the late 70's are completely out of step today. Massive in their day (though especially in the early days perhaps only locally as with **Billy Stewart's 'Exodus'** - the number one sound at the **Mojo** but little played at the **Wheel**), some do remain popular, but others are completely unplayable today.

Though the Twisted Wheel in fact opened in 1963 in Brazenose Street, Manchester, and only moved to the end of Whitworth Street in mid-1966, I have chosen 1967 as the starting point of the charts. This was a key year in the history of Northern (or rather at the time 'Rare') Soul with the move perhaps being the catalyst it became the period of sea change when in general the scene moved away from the hardcore R&B of Bo Didley and John Lee Hooker and, driven by Motown Stax/Atlantic and Mirwood, towards concentration on Soul. 1967 was basically the first year of recognisable Northern Soul.

This year by year series charts the most popular dancefloor sounds, as established by careful research and the recollections of fans and DJs of the time - it is as accurate as possible.

1967 THE TWISTED WHEEL/THE MOJO - The Inaugural Dance Chart

WADE IN THE WATER	RAMSEY LEWIS	*(CHESS)*
YOU'VE BEEN CHEATIN'	The IMPRESSIONS	*(ABC)*
DON'T MESS WITH MY MAN	IRMA THOMAS	*(RON)*
IT KEEPS RAININ'	FATS DOMINO	*(IMPERIAL)*
THE FIFE PIPER	The DYNATONES	*(ST. CLAIR)*
HEY-SAH-LO-NEY	MICKEY LEE LANE	*(SWAN)*
AT THE DISCOTHEQUE	CHUBBY CHECKER	*(PARKWAY)*
CALL ON ME	BOBBY BLAND	*(DUKE)*
LA DE DA I LOVE YOU	INEZ and CHARLIE FOX	*(SYMBOL)*
KICK THAT LITTLE FOOT SALLY	ROUND ROBIN	*(DOMAIN)*

1968   THE TWISTED WHEEL - We're Off And Runnin'!

GIRLS ARE OUT TO GET YOU	The FASCINATIONS	*(MAYFIELD)*
NOTHING CAN STOP ME	GENE CHANDLER	*(CONSTELLATION)*
LET THE GOOD TIMES ROLL	BUNNY SIGLER	*(PARKWAY)*
MR BANG BANG MAN	LITTLE HANK	*(SOUND STAGE 7)*
A LITTLE PIECE OF LEATHER	DONNIE ELBERT	*(GATEWAY)*
THE BEAT	MAJOR LANCE	*(OKEH)*
DUST MY BROOM	IKE and TINA TURNER	*(TANGERINE)*
EVERYBODY'S GOING TO A LOVE IN	BOB BRADY	*(CHARIOT)*
SOMEDAY WE'RE GONNA LOVE AGAIN		
	BARBARA LEWIS	*(ATLANTIC)*
GOOD TIME TONIGHT	The SOUL SISTERS	*(SUE)*

1969   THE TWISTED WHEEL - Getting Bigger...

THE RIGHT TRACK	BILLY BUTLER	*(OKEH)*
A LIL' LOVIN' SOMETIMES	ALEXANDER PATTON	*(CAPITOL)*
AT THE TOP OF THE STAIRS	The FORMATIONS	*(BANK)*
DO THE TEMPTATION WALK	JACKIE LEE	*(MIRWOOD)*
BREAKOUT	MITCH RYDER and the DETROIT WHEELS	*(NEW VOICE)*
SHE BLEW A GOOD THING	The POETS	*(SYMBOL)*
WHAT'S WRONG WITH ME BABY	The INVITATIONS	*(DYNO VOICE)*
AGENT DOUBLE-O SOUL	EDWIN STARR	*(RIC TIC)*
DR LOVE	BOBBY SHEEN	*(CAPITOL)*
THERE'S NOTHING ELSE TO SAY	The INCREDIBLES	*(AUDIO ARTS)*

Opposite: Laying the foundations... a selection of some of the pioneering sounds of our scene.

Left: Twisted Wheel Memberships came in an assortment of colours year by year, from Green to Purple, Orange and Red etc.

Below: Fontella Bass turning it on at the Wheel in 1970, though she had a limited number of Northern tracks she was always a very popular performer.

336

BOOM RECORDS

Dreamland Music, Inc. - Doraflo Music, Inc.
BMI - 2:56

BM 60,038
AMP 45-60,016-B

Produced by
Richard Gottehrer
for Sire
Productions

PROMOTIONAL
COPY
NOT FOR SALE

SKATE (Part I)
(Gottehrer, Parrish)
DEAN PARRISH
Arranged and Conducted by:
BURT KEYES

DISTRIBUTED BY ABC-PARAMOUNT RECORDS, INC. MADE IN U.S.A.

Hi

Pure East
Publications
BMI
HI 2460

45-2116
Time: 2:13½

LOVE IS AFTER ME
(Porter, Hayes)
CHARLIE RICH
Producer: Natalie Rosenberg

DISTRIBUTED BY LONDON RECORDS, INC.

PaMeLiNe

PAM-100-A
Ala King Music
BMI
Time: 2:30

Produced By
Richard
"Popcorn Wylie"
Arranged By
Mike Terry

GOIN' TO A HAPPENING
(Richard Wylie-T. Hester)
TOMMY NEAL
© 1967

ROMUR RECORDS

Scoebert Music Co.
(BMI)
Phy-4721A

RO011
Produced by
Roscoe Murphy, Jr.
Time: 2:27

D.J.   D.J.

LET'S COPP A GROOVE
(R. Murphy & R. Murphy)
BOBBY WELLS
Arranged by Leon Mitchell

ROMUR RECORD CO. © 1967 Phila., Pa.

YEW

N-1001-A
SIDE A
45 RPM

ODON &
NEIBURG
(BMI)
TIME: 2:50

IN A MOMENT
(THE INTRIGUES)
THE INTRIGUES
PROD. & ARC. BY MARTIN AND BELL
DIST. BY A. A. RECORDS, INC.
NEW YORK, N. Y. 10019

abc RECORDS

Chi-Sound
Corp., BMI
2:30

45-10831
AMP 45-13412

PROMOTIONAL
COPY
NOT FOR SALE

CAN'T SATISFY
(Curtis Mayfield)
THE IMPRESSIONS
Arranged and Conducted by:
JOHNNY PATE

A PRODUCT OF ABC-PARAMOUNT RECORDS INC. A SUBSIDIARY OF AMERICAN BROADCASTING COMPANIES, INC.

★★ **AIN'T NO SOUL**
LEFT IN THESE OLE SHOES ★★
(Arthur Resnick - Joe Levine)

SCEPTER
RECORDS

T. M. Music
(BMI)
Time: 1:57

SCE 12161 A
(60761)

RONNIE MILSAP
Produced by Huey P. Meaux
Arranged by Tommy Kaye

SCEPTER MUSIC INC., NEW YORK

GALAXY ®

Promotional   Not For Sale

TIME: 2:16
Cireco - BMI
Arranged by
Ray Shanklin

750
(F-2587)

SHE'S LOOKING GOOD
(Collins)
RODGER COLLINS

MY WEAKNESS IS YOU
(Whitfield, McMullen, Grant)

GORDY

G-7071
© 1967
Jobete, BMI
NUN 805592
2:19

Produced By
N. Whitfield

EDWIN STARR

A TRADEMARK OF MOTOWN RECORD CORP.

LIKE RECORDS

LK-10226

301
INSTRUMENTAL
Pub. Pronto,
Virdum, BMI
Time: 2:45

SOCK IT TO 'EM J. B. - PART I
(Dunn-Garvin-Holman)
REX GARVIN
(And The Mighty Cravers)
Produced by James Johnston
& William Shephard

DISTRIBUTED BY ATLANTIC RECORD SALES, 1841 BROADWAY NEW YORK, N.Y.

NORTH STATE RECORDS
Box 183   Goldsboro, N. C. 27530

1001
(SoN 56641)
Time - 2:35

North State Music
ASCAP
45 RPM

GIRL WATCHER
(Buck Trail-Wayne Pittman)
THE O'KAYSIONS

BILLY'S BAG
(Billy Preston)
BILLY PRESTON

45   45

VJ
VEE-JAY
RECORDS

PROMOTIONAL
COPY

VJ
VEE-JAY
RECORDS

PROMOTIONAL
COPY

45   45

VJ 653
64-6742 — Time 2:30
Greene Music Inc.
ASCAP
Arranged by Rene Hall

1970 THE TWISTED WHEEL /THE BLUE ORCHID-
The Imports Come Rolling In!

YOU GOT TO PAY THE PRICE	AL KENT	*(RIC TIC)*
LOVE, LOVE, LOVE	BOBBY HEBB	*(PHILIPS)*
FOLLOW YOUR HEART	BUNNY SIGLER	*(PARKWAY)*
GOING TO A HAPPENING	TOMMY NEAL	*(PAMELINE)*
YOU GET YOUR KICKS	MITCH RYDER and the DETROIT WHEELS	*(NEW VOICE)*
BACK STREET	EDWIN STARR	*(RIC TIC)*
NEVER FOR ME	The MILLIONAIRES	*(PHILIPS)*
TAKE YOUR LOVE AND RUN	BARBARA LYNN	*(ATLANTIC)*
COMPETITION AIN'T NOTHING	CARL CARLTON	*(BACKBEAT)*
THAT BEATIN' RHYTHM	RICHARD TEMPLE	*(MIRWOOD)*

1971 BLACKPOOL MECCA AND THE CATACOMBS -
Spreading The Word

HERE I GO AGAIN	ARCHIE BELL and the DRELLS	*(ATLANTIC)*
OUT ON THE FLOOR	DOBIE GRAY	*(CHARGER)*
LOVE ON A MOUNTAIN TOP	ROBERT KNIGHT	*(RISING SONS)*
CIGARETTE ASHES	JIMMY CONWELL	*(MIRWOOD)*
I'LL NEVER FALL IN LOVE AGAIN	BOBBY FREEMAN	*(AUTUMN)*
QUEEN OF FOOLS	BARBARA MILLS	*(HICKORY)*
YOUR GONNA MAKE ME LOVE YOU	SANDI SHELDON	*(OKEH)*
IN ORBIT	JOY LOVEJOY	*(CHECKER)*
THE NEXT IN LINE	HOAGY LANDS	*(LAURIE)*
THE WAY YOU BEEN ACTING LATELY	AL KENT	*(RIC-TIC)*

Opposite: Laying the foundations...
Further sounds from the early days of
Northern Soul.

Right: Inez and Charlie Foxx's frequent
live appearances across the UK at clubs
like the Wheel, the Mojo and the Blue
Orchid helped ensure the popularity of
their many cuts, 'Tightrope' was of course
particularly popular, but 'Come By Here'
is a classic that is largely forgotten today.

PHILIPS
FOR BROADCAST ONLY NOT FOR SALE
40400
PHW1-38236
Champion Music Co. & Double Diamond Music Co. (BMI) 2:50
Vocal Producer: Jerry Ross From PHILIP'S Album, SUNNY PHM-200-212
LOVE LOVE LOVE
(Ross-Renzetti)
BOBBY HEBB
Arranged by Joe Renzetti

Ric-Tic RECORDS
Mylo Music BMI Time: 2:42 ZTSC-107342
RT-107
Arranged by: Sanders & Starr Production Supervisor: Richard Parker
BACK STREET
(C. Hatcher & B. Sharpley)
EDWIN STARR
A Solid Hitbound Production

Capitol RECORDS

LOVE AND DESIRE
(Billy Page)
PROMOTION RECORD September 11 Music BMI-2:30
NOT FOR SALE Produced by: Billy and Gene Page
PATRICE HOLLOWAY
Arranged and Conducted by Gene Page
5778 (45-56590)

JERK AND TWINE
(Smith - Davis - Allison)
Chevis Music BMI (13609) Time 2:38
CHESS
JACKIE ROSS
1920
MANUFACTURED BY CHESS PRODUCING CORP.-CHICAGO, ILLINOIS, U.S.A.

SHARE RECORDS
Van McCoy Music Inc. T.M. Music (BMI)
SR 102 A Time: 2:35
SWEET AND EASY
(J. Cobb, V. McCoy)
THE VAN McCOY STRINGS
Arr. Prod. & Cond. By Van McCoy

"HAPPY" Taken From Album "Bound To Happen" STS-2014 (B. T. Jones, W. Bell)

Stax
STA-0038 ST-0157-PL East Memphis Music, BMI Time: 2:31 June, 1969
WILLIAM BELL
Prod. by Booker T. Jones

Mirwood
Nanpra Music (BMI) (67-5091-B)
5532 Time 2:22
THAT BEATIN' RHYTHM
(Smith, Cowell, Graham, Calbert)
RICHARD TEMPLE
Produced by Leonard Jewell Smith & Sir Graham A Soundville Production

LONDON AMERICAN RECORDINGS
DEMONSTRATION SAMPLE NOT FOR SALE MADE IN ENGLAND
A 45 RPM
HL 10212
Recorded by PHIL OF SOUL Philadelphia Pedro Music TIME 2:42
(P) 1968 RELEASE DATE 26-7-68
HITCH IT TO THE HORSE
(Jesse James)
THE FANTASTIC JOHNNY C
MSC 7953

WHAT'S WRONG WITH ME BABY!
(Linzer - Randell)
dynoVoice
210 6540 Saturday Music, Inc. (BMI) Time: 2:35
PLUG SIDE
THE INVITATIONS
Arr. & Cond. By Charles Calello Prod. by Denny Randell and Sandy Linzer
DISTRIBUTED BY BELL RECORDS INC. N.Y.C.

Brunswick
MANUFACTURED BY BRUNSWICK RECORD CORP., NEW YORK, U.S.A.
FROM THE TEACHER TO THE PREACHER
(Eugene Record-Barbara Acklin-Carl Davis)
GENE CHANDLER And BARBARA ACKLIN
Vocal With Orchestra Directed by Gerald Sims PRODUCED BY Carl Davis ARRANGED by William Sanders (2:24)
MARCA REGISTRADA

MALA RECORDS
MALA 575 8283-BW Tree Publishing BMI Time: 2:17 PROMOTION COPY PLUG SIDE
A PAPA DON PRODUCTION
MY ELUSIVE DREAMS
(C. Putman - B. Sherrill)
Moses & Joshua Dillard
Arr. by Moses Dillard
A PRODUCT OF BELL RECORDS, INC. N.Y.C.

Bonatemp Pub. Co. BMI - 2:28 Arr. by Wardell Quezergue
721 171-1594 Whurley-Burley Prod.
LET'S GO BABY (Where The Action Is)
Robert Parker
ROBERT PARKER
Dist. BY DOVER RECORDS, INC. N.O.L.A.

1972 THE GOLDEN TORCH AND THE CATACOMBS - All-Nighter Fever

SLICED TOMATOES	The JUST BROTHERS	(MUSIC MERCHANT)
ONE WONDERFUL MOMENT	The SHAKERS	(ABC)
WHAT WOULD I DO	The TYMES	(MGM)
WANTING YOU	APRIL STEVENS	(MGM)
TIMES A WASTING	FULLER BROS	(SOUL CLOCK)
BOK TO BACH	FATHERS ANGELS	(MGM)
I'VE GOT SOMETHING GOOD	SAM and KITTY	(FOUR BROTHERS)
LIKE ONE	JEAN CARTER	(DECCA)
THUMB A RIDE	EARL WRIGHT	(CAPITOL)
I'M IN A WORLD OF TROUBLE	The SWEET THINGS	(DATE)

1973 THE TORCH, BLACKPOOL MECCA, WIGAN CASINO AND VA VA'S - Boom Time!

THERE'S A GHOST IN MY HOUSE	R DEAN TAYLOR	(VIP)
WHAT'S IT GONNA BE	SUSAN BARRETT	(RCA)
BABY HIT AND RUN	The CONTOURS	(TAMLA MOTOWN)
TEMPTATION IS CALLING MY NAME		
	LEE DAVID	(COLUMBIA)
TAKE AWAY THE PAIN STAIN	PATTI AUSTIN	(CORAL)
STRANGER IN MY ARMS	LYNN RANDELL	(EPIC)
I HURT ON THE OTHER SIDE	JERRY COOK	(CAPITOL)
WAIT TILL I GET TO KNOW YA	BOBBY TREETOP	(TUFF)
PUT YOUR ARMS AROUND ME	The SHERRYS	(HOT/JJ)
TAINTED LOVE	GLORIA JONES	(CHAMPION)

Left: Torch membership, basically they hoped it would last until January 31st!

Opposite: The Torch - only all-nighter in the country! And Edwin on New Year's eve - It was twenty-past twelve before people noticed it was January 1st 1973!

Inset Right: 'Show me the back street', so sad to see... The site of the Golden Torch in a Tunstall side street, awaiting demolition.

THE TORCH — TUNSTALL
Stoke-on-Trent

The Country's only...

ALL-NIGHTER

TWELVE SO FULL - SOULFUL HOURS.... 8-30 pm-8-30 am

JANUARY LINE UP...

Saturday, January 6th
"Our Thank You All-Nighter" featu...
Keith Minshull - Alan Day - Mart...
AND TO JOIN US AT THE No. 1 EVERY WE...
The North's No. 1 Spinner
TONY JEBB
Free Tickets available from pay desk on reques...

...urday, January 13th
The Kingspinners
...dmission 50p Members Guests 60p (before...

...ay, January 20th
Heat Soul Dancer '73 Competit...
...RIZE £50
...ssion 50p Members 60p Guests

... January 27th
...All-Nighter
...EEDS TO LOCAL CHARITIES
...0p Members 60p Guests

...R LANCE, ROY C, SAM...

Verve ®
SPECIAL DISC JOCKEY RECOR...

THE
SHALIMARS

STOP AND
TAKE A
LOOK AT
YOURSELF
(Jackson-Barnes)

VK-10388
(66-VK-224)

Tender Tunes/Marlinda Music
BMI
2:12
Arr., Cond. & Prod. by
Hal Wess
A Kama Sutra
Production

MGM RECORDS—A DIVISION OF METRO-GOLDWYN-MAYER INC.—MADE IN U.S.A.

THE TORCH - Tunstall - Stoke-o...

New Year's Eve All Night Ball
8-30 pm to 8-30 am
SUNDAY, DECEMBER 31st

EDWIN STARR

John McFlair Band
Keith Minshull
Martyn Ellis
Alan Day

£1-50 Members & Guests

January 13th ... A...

The Torch - Tunstall
Stoke-on-Trent

The Country's No. 1
All-Nighter

TWELVE SO-FULL SOULFUL HOURS
NOW OPEN EVERY SATURDAY
8-30 p.m. to 8-30 a.m.

341

FEBRUARY
Programme Details

RIGHT

1974 WIGAN CASINO AND BLACKPOOL MECCA - The Ultimate Year?

AFTERNOON OF THE RHINO	MIKE POST COALTION	*(WARNER BROS)*
IF THAT'S WHAT YOU WANTED	FRANKIE BEVERLY and	
	the BUTLERS	*(SASSY/GAMBLE)*
IF YOU EVER WALKED OUT OF MY LIFE		
	DENA BARNES	*(INFERNO)*
I NEVER KNEW	EDDIE FOSTER	*(IN)*
DOUBLE COOKIN	CHECKERBOARD SQUARES	*(VILLA)*
YOU DON'T LOVE ME	The EPITOME OF SOUND	*(SANDBAG)*
I GOT TO FIND ME SOMEBODY		
	The VEL-VETS	*(20TH CENTURY)*
I'LL ALWAYS NEED YOU	DEAN COURTNEY	*(RCA)*
I CAN'T HELP LOVIN YOU	PAUL ANKA	*(RCA)*
GOODBYE NOTHING TO SAY	NOSMO KING/JAVELLS	*(PYE)*

1975 WIGAN CASINO AND BLACKPOOL MECCA - More Golden Years

BETTER USE YOUR HEAD	LITTLE ANTHONY	
	and the IMPERIALS	*(VEEP)*
SEVEN DAY LOVER	JAMES FOUNTAIN	*(PEACHTREE)*
JOB OPENING	The DEL-LARKS	*(QUEEN CITY)*
COOL OFF	The DETROIT EXECUTIVES	*(PAMELINE)*
GET OUT	HAROLD MELVIN	*(LANDA)*
THE CHAMPION	WILLIE MITCHELL	*(HI)*
CASHING IN	VOICES OF EAST HARLEM	*(JUST SUNSHINE)*
LANDSLIDE	TONY CLARKE	*(CHESS)*
PLEASE OPERATOR	TONY and TYRONE	*(ATLANTIC)*
I CAN'T CHANGE	LORRAINE CHANDLER	*(RCA)*

WIGAN CASINO

Soul Club

CASINO CLUB
Station Road, Wigan
Tel. Wigan 43501

- SEP 73 **0263**
Members Name

PETER N WHITNEY

Members Signature

MEMBERS NOTE
Non-Members **MUST NOT Pay for Drinks**
This card must be produced by the
member when entering the card, and
it is strictly NOT transferable.

YEAR ENDING

BLUE ROOM

Washway Road,
Sale.
Telephone: 061-973 1508

EVERY THURSDAY 8 p.m. - 12 mid.

Featuring THE COUNTRY'S

TOP SOUL D.J's

★ IAN LEVINE & ANDY HANLEY ★

The Place to be on
Fully Licensed
This TICKET ADMITS TWO FR

ADMISSI
★
Over 18's only
before 10 p.m.

Issued subject to the

Pendulum
PASS-OUT

1976 WIGAN CASINO, BLACKPOOL MECCA AND CLEETHORPES
WINTER GARDENS - The Crowds Just Kept On Coming...

SEND HIM BACK	The POINTER SISTERS	*(ATLANTIC)*
I'M COMUN' HOME IN THE MORNUN'		
	LOU PRIDE	*(SUEMI)*
SO IS THE SUN	WORLD COLUMN	*(TOWER)*
MY WORLD IS ON FIRE	JIMMY MACK	*(PALMER)*
BURNING SENSATION	ROBBY LAWSON	*(KYSER)*
YOU DON'T KNOW WHERE YOUR INTEREST LIES		
	DANA VALERY	*(COLUMBIA)*
EVER AGAIN	BERNIE WILLIAMS	*(BELL)*
YOU GOT ME WHERE YOU WANT ME	LARRY SANTOS	*(EVOLUTION)*
COCHISE	PAUL HUMPHREY	*(BLUE THUMB)*
HEAVEN MUST BE MISSING AN ANGEL		
	TAVARES	*(CAPITOL)*

1977 WIGAN CASINO, BLACKPOOL, THE RITZ,
CLEETHORPES, ST IVES - But Will It Last?

SHAKE A TAIL FEATHER	JAMES and BOBBY PURIFY	*(BELL)*
WHEN I'M GONE	BRENDA HOLLOWAY	*(TAMLA)*
7 DAYS 52 WEEKS	CODY MICHEALS	*(MERBEN)*
IF YOU LOVED ME	PEGGY MARCH	*(RCA)*
GIVE UP GIRL	CONNIE QUESTALL	*(DECCA)*
HEY LITTLE GIRL	MISS DD PHILLIPS	*(EVOLUTION)*
THIS GETS TO ME	POOKIE HUDSON	*(JAMIE)*
YOU DON'T KNOW WHERE YOUR INTEREST LIES		
	FIVE and a PENNY	*(POLYDOR)*
A LOT OF LOVE	TAJ MAHAL	*(COLUMBIA)*
GET IT OFF MY CONSCIENCE	The LOVELITES	*(LOVELITE)*

Left: The Mecca, Colin Curtis and Ian Levine's interest in more than just stompers led to the development and change of the Blackpool sound.

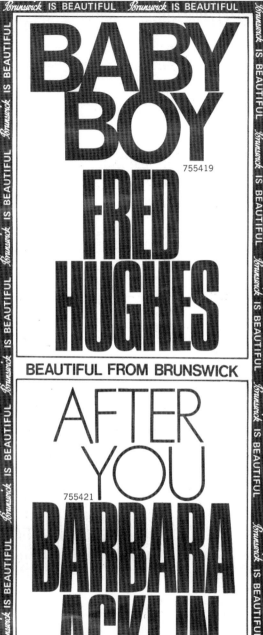

1978 WIGAN CASINO, PETERBOROUGH, THE RITZ
- Strange Times...

DO I LOVE YOU	FRANK WILSON	(SOUL)
THAT'S WHY I LOVE YOU	The PROFFESSIONALS	(GROOVE CITY)
TIME	EDWIN STARR	(GORDY)
TAKE MY HEART	MARY SAXTON	(QUALITY)
WHY DID YOU PUT IT TO ME BABY	The SHORT PEOPLE	(GUSTO)
MY LIFE WITH YOU	The TRADITIONS	(BAR CLAY)
SPRING RAIN	SILVETTI	(SALSOUL)
DON'T PITY ME	SUE LYNN	(RCA)
SAY GIRL	LONNIE RUSS	(KERWOOD)
THE ICE MAN	BILLY WATKINS	(ERA)

1979 WIGAN CASINO, MORECAMBE AND PETERBOROUGH -
The Dreaded Pop Influence!

NINE TIMES OUT OF TEN	MURIEL DAY	(PAGE ONE)
COUNTRY GIRL	VICKIE BAINES	(PARKWAY)
STOP	BOBBY DIAMOND	(COLUMBIA)
STOP AND YOU'LL BECOME AWARE	HELEN SHAPIRO	(COLUMBIA)
THIS MAN IN LOVE	The NEW WANDERERS	(READY)
THEME FROM JOE 90	RON GRAINER	(PYE)
SHE SAID GOODBYE	BILLY HAMBRIC	(DRUM)
I CAN'T STAND TO LOSE YOU	EJ CHANDLER	(SOS)
THE WHO WHO SONG	JACKIE WILSON	(BRUNSWICK)
MOVE ON UP	CURTIS MAYFIELD	(CURTOM)

Left: The Apollas who produced many Northern hits on the Warner Brothers owned Loma label, (and later for Warner themselves). Most notably the wonderful, storming 'Mr. Creator' for WB which appears in the Top 500 chart and 'I Just Can't Get Enough Of You' for Loma.

Right: David and the Giants' Mecca monster 'Superlove' was quickly followed by the popularity of 'Ten Miles High'. Though both were very poppy they at least had a Muscle Shoals pedigree - giving them a degree of credibility not shared by the likes of Muriel Day or Ron Grainer's 'Joe 90' theme.

Below and Left: The Casino just made its 500th all-nighter, but its closure in 1981 and demolition became a powerful image that symbolised the need for the scene's re-birth. Ironically this sea change had already started in the last days of Station Road.

1980 WIGAN CASINO AND ST.IVES -
A Time Of Great New Discoveries - At Last!

BORN A LOSER	DON RAY	*(RCA)*
BROKEN HEART ATTACK	The SWEET	*(SMASH)*
I DON'T LIKE TO LOSE	CECIL WASHINGTON & The GROUP	*(PROPHONICS)*
WHAT HAPPENED TO YESTERDAY	MR SOUL	*(GENUINE)*
YOU KNOW HOW TO LOVE ME	PHYLLIS HYMAN	*(ARISTA)*
I'LL PAY THE PRICE	MOSES DILLARD	*(MARK IV)*
NO SECOND CHANCE	The DEADBEATS	*(STRATA)*
I NEED MY BABY	JACKIE BEAVERS	*(REVILOT)*
RAINING TEARDROPS	The DEMURES	*(BRUNSWICK)*
YOU WON'T SAY NOTHING	TAMALA LEWIS	*(MARTON)*

1981 THE TOP OF THE WORLD, STAFFORD, THE 100 CLUB
and the death of WIGAN CASINO - The End Of The 2ⁿᵈ Era

I LOVE HER SO MUCH	The MAJESTICS	*(LINDA)*
I'M LOSING AGAIN	RAY AGEE	*(SOULTOWN)*
CAN'T GET OVER THESE MEMORIES	JON and the WEIRDEST	*(TIE)*
I HAVE A GIRL	The MAGNETICS	*(RA-SEL)*
NOTHING'S TOO GOOD FOR MY BABY		
	The SPRINGERS	*(WHALES)*
I'LL BE YOUR CHAMPION	JIMMEY 'SOUL' CLARKE	*(SOULHAWK)*
LOST AND FOUND	KENNY CARLTON	*(BLUE ROCK)*
HEARTACHE SOUVENIRS	WILLIAM POWELL	*(POWERHOUSE)*
PLEASE KEEP AWAY FROM ME	ELBIE PARKER	*(VEEP)*
LADY IN GREEN	The MAGNETICS	*(BONNIE)*

1982 STAFFORD - Birth Of A New Generation

I'D THINK IT OVER	SAM FLETCHER	(TOLLIE)
LOVE IS A SERIOUS BUSINESS	ALFIE DAVISON	(MERCURY)
I GOT A GOOD THING GOING	The EXECUTIVE FOUR	(JULMAR)
HEARTACHES I CAN'T TAKE	The GAY LETTES	(BLACK JACK)
DON'T LET HIM HURT YOU	Les CHASONETTES	(SHRINE)
UNDER YOUR POWERFUL LOVE	JOE TEX	(DIAL)
SOMETHINGS BAD	The NOMADS	(MO-GROOVE)
BABY WHAT HAPPENED TO OUR LOVE		
	The RINGLEADERS	(M-PAC)
GUESS WHO LOVES YOU	EDDIE DAYE and 4 BARS	(SHRINE)
OH YEAH YEAH YEAH	VIVIAN CAROL	(MERBEN)

Capturing perfectly Stafford's fresh new attitude, Sam Fletcher's incredible 'beat ballad' 'I'd Think It Over' would simply have never been played a couple of years earlier.

tollie
RECORDS

64-3943
VOCAL

I'D THINK IT OVER
(W. B. Willingham-A. Berry)
SAM FLETCHER
T-9012

1983 STAFFORD - A Time Of Real Innovation

SUSPICION	The ORIGINALS	*(UNISSUED MOTOWN)*
I JUST KEPT ON DANCING	DOUG BANKS	*(ARGO)*
DOWN AND OUT	GEORGE FREEMAN	*(VALIANT)*
I WON'T BE COMING BACK	JD BRYANT	*(SHRINE)*
SHOWSTOPPER	The CASHMERES	*(HEM)*
ALL OF MY LIFE	*(UNISSUED VIRTUE ACETATE)*	
I'M CATCHING ON	BETTY LLOYD	*(BSC)*
IT'S TOO LATE FOR YOU AND ME	GLADYS NIGHT and the PIPS	*(SOUL ACETATE)*
NAUGHTY BOY	JACKIE DAY	*(PHLECTRON)*
THINK SMART	The FIESTAS	*(OLD TOWN)*

1984 STAFFORD - 60's Newies - Collector's Heaven!

NO OTHER WAY	The CAUTIONS	*(SHRINE)*
LET LOVE LIVE	The VELVELETTES	*(VIP UNRELEASED)*
THE ONLY WAY IS UP	OTIS CLAY	*(ECHO)*
WHAT DIFFERENCE DOES IT MAKE	KENNY SHEPPARD	*(MAXX)*
STOP OVERLOOKING ME	The CAIROS	(SHRINE)
GIRL I LOVE YOU	The TEMPTONES	*(ARCTIC)*
JUST A FOOL	JERRY GAINEY	*(VERVE)*
I CAN'T LET YOU GO	JOHNNY SUMMERS	*(YORK TOWN)*
DON'T ACCUSE ME	The SQUIRES	*(GEE)*
LOOKY LOOKY	The BROTHERS GRIMM	*(MERCURY)*

Left: Vocal genius Emanuel Laskey, a hero to the 60's Newies scene for his variety of superlative recordings.

Opposite: A selection of Stafford sounds - though some had previously been known generally they were very different from their Wigan counterparts.

CORTLAND
SOMEBODY HELP ME
(Granger - Jenkins - Strong)
C-112 B
Robt. Catron Music
BMI - 2:29
DONALD JENKINS &
THE DELIGHTERS
112
a B.C. Production
© CORTLAND 1963

SHRINE RECORDS
Ramitary Mus. Corp.
BMI
SR 111-2
2:21
Produced by
Eddie Singleton
STOP OVERLOOKING ME
(Keni Lewis)
THE CAIROS
Arranged by
Dale Warren

TURNTABLE
RECORDING CORP. N.Y., N.Y.
LAN-6004
Benny Benjamin
Music ASCAP
Time: 2:20
45 RPM
TT-713
Produced by:
Earle Robinson
Arranged by:
Dave Ward
I'VE HAD IT
(B. Benjamin - S. Marcus)
GEORGE SMITH

TOP DOG
JUST AS MUCH
(G. Terry & M. Terry)
2:25
A - 102
Artie Fields Pub.
& LeBaron Music
BMI
KRIS PETERSON
(Producer: Artie Fields)
TOP DOG RECORD CO.
9430 Woodward Ave.
Detroit, Mich. 48202

ME-O RECORDS
M-1005-A
Recorrco Pub.
B.M.I - 2.38
45 RPM
Arranged and
Produced by
Thurman Hollis
"GIVE ME LOVE"
(Thurman Hollis)
TOOTSIE ROLLERS

PENTAGON RECORDS
447 N. 60th St.
Phila., Pa. 19151
P 1112-11
Delev & Melston
BMI
Time: 2.40
A
KLS
Production
Arr. Jos. Stevenson
I BEAR WITNESS
(J. Stevenson)
VINCE APOLLO
Vocal Assist by The Okay Sisters

GEMINI STAR RECORDS
David-Gay
BMI
8662-BW
30.005
Time: 2:34
I DIDN'T KNOW HOW TO
(David Henry)
THE CONSTELLATIONS
Produced by Pat Jaques
Arr. by Richie Tee
DISTRIBUTED BY AMY RECORDS, N.Y.C.

blue rock
LOOK AT ME
(Wright-Baxter-Hanson)
Vocal
B-4034
YW1-37267
Smashville
Music Co.
(BMI) 2:49
A Wright-Hanson
Production
R 570
FOR BROADCAST ONLY • NOT FOR SALE
VENDOR: MERCURY RECORD CORPORATION
THE DELETTS

PEAK SAINTMO
Sol: Music
16456 B
BMI
45 RPM
Time 2:53
PREMIER FILM & RECORDING CORPORATION, ST. LOUIS, MO., U.S.A.
IF I KNEW
(Arr: C. Warren)
Fabulous Four

TARX RECORDS
1639 BROADWAY, R-310, N.Y.C. 10019
45 RPM
Styletone BMI
1011-S
Benron
Productions
THAT WAS WHISKEY TALKIN'
(Ronnie McCam)
RONNIE FORTE
Arr. and Cond. by
BEN SMITH

ERA RECORDS
REG. U.S. PAT. OFF
Pattern Music,
Inc. (ASCAP)
PROMOTIONAL
COPY
(45-BSN-645)
Time 2:22
NOT FOR SALE
I'VE ARRIVED
(Steven Howard)
STEVE FLANAGAN
3186

NEW VOICE RECORDS
ISN'T IT JUST A SHAME
(G. Knight-G. Gant)
Arranged & Conducted by:
HERB BERNSTEIN
812
6789
Saturday Music,
Inc., BMI
TIME: 2.37
Promotion Copy
KENNY WELLS
A GARY KNIGHT PRODUCTION
for
BOB CREWE PRODUCTIONS
DISTRIBUTED BY BELL RECORDS, INC.

1985 STAFFORD - Still Leading The Field...

MAGIC TOUCH	MELBA MOORE	*(MUSICOR UNRELEASED)*
ENVY	The ORLONS	*(CAMEO)*
NEVER LET ME GO	MONIQUE	*(MAURCI)*
I WANNA GIVE YOU TOMORROW	BENNY TROY	*(DE-LITE)*
IT TAKES HEART	GREG PERRY	*(ALFA)*
JANICE	SKIP MAHONEY	*(SALSOUL)*
I'M COMING OVER	JOHNNY HONEYCUTT	*(TRIODE)*
TEARS OF JOY	RAY MERRELL	*(JAYBOY)*
TWO LOVES HAVE I	BIG JOE TURNER	*(BLUESTIME)*
CHEATIN KIND	DON GARDNER	*(SEDGRICK)*

1986 100 CLUB - Oldies And Newies Together

I NEED YOU LIKE A BABY	ANDREA HENRY	*(MGM)*
USE IT BEFORE YOU LOSE IT	BOBBY VALENTIN	*(FANIA)*
LONELY GIRL	ERIC MERCURY	(SACK)
SILENT TREATMENT	ARIN DEMAIN	*(BLUE STAR)*
KEEP ON LOVING ME	FRANCES NERO	*(SOUL)*
I CRIED MY LIFE AWAY	TOMMY NAVARRO	*(DE JAC)*
FIND A QUIET PLACE	MELVIN DAVIS	*(WHEEL CITY)*
PLEASE STAY	The IVORYS	*(DISPENZA)*
DON'T TURN YOUR BACK ON ME	JACK MONTGOMMERY	*(BARRACUDA)*
FOREVER IN MY HEART ('COME ON BACK TO ME BABY')		
	The TEMPTATIONS	*(MOTOWN UNRELEASED)*

Opposite and Inset: The wonderful Maxine Brown whose many Wand recordings, from 'One Step At A Time' and 'Let Me Give You My Lovin'' through to unissued material like 'It's Torture' form part of the backbone of what is the 6T's - 100 Club sound.

Police swoop on soul fans

NORTHERN SOUL fans have hit out at police who swooped on punters in a drugs blitz outside a Chesterfield nightclub last week.

More than 100 people were held for questioning, some strip-searched, during the massive operation near the Winding Wheel club. Only two people were arrested and charged under the Misuse Of Drugs Act.

Eyebrows were raised at police tactics in the area, which included stopping minibuses full of fans travelling to the all-nighter at a motorway service station.

Club promoter Danny Everard told *NME* that police also tried to block the Winding Wheel's application for an entertainment licence on the grounds that the all-nighters would encourage large scale drug abuse, and lead to more cases of missing persons. Their objections were thrown out by Chesterfield burglary, car thefts, public disorder, and lead Council's licensing committee.

"We've told the police that we've nothing to hide but they're not interested," said Everard.

"I don't want drugs in my venue, there is no dealing inside. To my knowledge, the police pulled two people out of about 350 – and they weren't even in the club! That's hardly many for a weekend."

Chesterfield police confirmed that two people were arrested for drugs-related offences. A spokesman added that the normal quota of 20 to 25 officers were on duty on the night in question, but refused to comment on the number of people searched.

"Policing was normal and necessary for the occasion. I'm not willing to define those terms."

Only three people have been arrested during the four all-nighters the Winding Wheel has held since October.

Some things never change... The rabid vendetta of the squad towards Soul fans continues. The Council owned Winding Wheel in Chesterfield was an excellent and very popular venue run by Danny Everard and Dave Thorley (Stafford promoter), it looked set to take on the torch after the closure of Stafford's legendary Top Of The World. But through the police's underhand tactics and harassment the local council was FORCED to revoke its licence.

1987 100 CLUB / CHESTERFIELD / VARIOUS

SOMETHING NEW TO DO	BOBBY SHEEN	*(WARNER BROS)*
I STILL LOVE YOU	The SEVEN SOULS	*(OKEH)*
I'LL NEVER FORGET YOU	The METROS	*(RCA LP)*
LOVED STARVED HEART	MARVIN GAYE	*(TAMLA)*
MY BABY'S GOT E.S.P.	FOUR BELOW ZERO	*(PAP)*
THE SWEETEST THING	CHANNEL 3	*(DAKAR)*
GIRLS ARE AGAINST ME	The UTOPIAS	*(LA SALLE)*
STOLEN HOURS	PATRICE HOLLOWAY	*(CAPITOL)*
WALK ON INTO MY HEART	BOBBIE SMITH	*(AMERICAN ARTS)*
WHAT MORE CAN A BOY ASK FOR	The DETROIT SPINNERS	*(MOTOWN LP)*

1988 KEELE / BLACKBURN - Big Crowds On The Horizon

LONELY FOR YOU BABY	SAM DEES	*(SSS INTERNATIONAL)*
PACKING UP	DAMON FOX	*(FAIRMOUNT)*
YOU'RE ON TOP GIRL	The EMPIRES	*(CANDI)*
ONE WAY OR ANOTHER	TINA ROBERTS	*(SECURITY)*
SAVIN' MY LOVIN' FOR YOU	The PEOPLES CHOICE	*(PALMER)*
YOU'RE MY LEADING LADY	TOMMY FRONTERA	*(ALL-RITE)*
DON'T SEND ME AWAY	GARFIELD FLEMMING	(BECKETT)
SOMEONE TELL HER	The IMPERIAL C'S	(PHIL LA OF SOUL)
I NEED LOVE	DAYBREAK	*(PAP)*
YOU HAD ME FOOLED	DANNY WOODS	*(CORREC-TONE)*

1989 KEELE - Northern Re-invents Itself

I WATCHED YOU SLOWLY SLIP AWAY		
	HOWARD GUYTON	*(VERVE)*
YOU SHOULD O' HELD ON	The 7TH AVE AVIATORS	*(CONGRESS)*
IF THIS AIN'T LOVE	JOHNNY BARTEL	*(SOLID STATE)*
I STAND ACCUSED	TONY COLTON	*(PYE)*
WELCOME TO DREAMSVILLE	SAMMY AMBROSE	*(MUSICOR)*
YOU LEFT ME	The ADMIRATIONS	*(PEACHES)*
I BEAR WITNESS	VINCE APOLLO	*(PENTAGON)*
OUR LOVE WILL GROW	The SHOWMEN	*(SWAN)*
OF HOPES AND DREAMS AND TOMBSTONES		
	JIMMY FRASER	*(COLUMBIA)*
ISN'T IT JUST A SHAME	KENNY WELLS	*(NEW VOICE)*

1990 TWISTED WHEEL REVIVIALS / BRADFORD
- The Revival About To Take Off!

I DON'T LIKE IT	TOMMY BUSH	(RIKA)
HEY GIRL	The VONDELLS	(AIRTOWN)
WHEN YOU LOSE THE ONE YOU LOVE		
	BUDDY SMITH	(BRUTE)
I'M TAKING ON PAIN	TOMMY TATE	(OKEH)
I'LL NEVER STOP LOVING YOU	CARLA THOMAS	(STAX UNISSUED)
PLEASE DON'T GO	WILLIE TEE	(GATUR)
MY FIRST LONELY NIGHT	JEWEL AKENS	(ERA)
YUM YUM TREE	BOBBY BLAND	(DUKE)
AIN'T THAT TRUE LOVE	OSCAR TONEY JUNIOR	(BELL)
I WON'T LET YOU SEE ME CRY	BIG FRANK and	
	the ESSENCE	(BLUE ROCK / PHILLIPS)

1991 BRADFORD / DROYLESDON / AVANT, OLDHAM - Revival Time

SWEET SHERRY	JJ BARNES	(VOLT)
SET MY HEART AT EASE	MIKKI FARROW	(KARATE)
PUT THAT WOMAN DOWN	JOHN LEACH	(LAWN)
QUEEN OF THE GO-GO	REX GARVIN	(TOWER)
I CAN'T HOLD ON	LORRAINE CHANDLER	(RCA)
WHAT A WONDERFUL NIGHT FOR A LOVE		
	BOBBY PATTERSON	(JET STAR)
I'VE HAD IT	LEE ANDREWS	(CRIMSON)
I STILL LOVE YOU	The 4 LARKS	(TOWER)
FRIDAY NIGHT	JOHNNIE TAYLOR	(STAX)
STORM WARNING	The VOLCANOES	(ARCTIC)

Left: During the late 80's and early 90's Brian Rae's enormously popular Twisted Wheel revivals (concentrating on the mid-60's period) at the original Whitworth Street site were a major factor in the development of today's popular R&B styled dancers.

1992 BURY / AVANT / VARIOUS - The Revival Starts To Roll

WHAT CAN I DO?	LORRAINE CHANDLER	*(GIANT)*
DO I LOVE YOU (INDEED I DO)	CHRIS CLARK	*(MOTOWN UNISSUED)*
VILLAGE OF TEARS	BENZINE	*(PARKWAY)*
NEVERTHELESS	LEE ANDREWS	*(CRIMSON)*
WAIT 'TIL I GIVE THE SIGNAL	The SHIRELLES	*(SCEPTER)*
HONEY BOY	NELLA DODDS	*(WAND)*
WISHES	The METRICS	*(CHADWICK)*
THE LIVELY ONE	BROOKS O'DELL	*(COLUMBIA)*
PRETTY AS A PICTURE	MOSES DILLARD	*(MARK IV)*
SOMETHING'S BOTHERING YOU	The DALTON BOYS	*(VIP)*

1993 THE RITZ - Rebirth of the big venue

THANKS FOR A LITTLE LOVIN'	The TRENDS	*(ABC)*
SLIPPIN' AROUND	ART FREEMAN	*(FAME)*
I GO OUT OF MY MIND	CHRIS BARTLEY	*(ACETATE)*
I WANT MY BABY BACK	EDWIN STARR	*(GORDY)*
TRIPPIN' ON YOUR LOVE	The STAPLE SINGERS	*(KENT)*
I'M THE ONE WHO LOVES YOU	DARRELL BANKS	*(VOLT)*
ASK THE LONELY	The FOUR TOPS	*(MOTOWN)*
CANDLE IN THE WINDOW	DONI BURDICK	*(UNISSUED)*
IT'S BETTER	REGGIE ALEXANDER	*(BOSS)*
I'M A BIG MAN	BIG DADDY ROGERS	*(MIDAS)*

1994 LOWTON / WINSFORD

THAT'S MY GIRL	DEE CLARK	*(CONSTELLATION)*
LOOK AT ME NOW	TERRY CALLIER	*(CADET)*
MY HEART'S BEATIN' STRONGER	ANDY FISHER	*(FAT FISH)*
ALL OVER THE WORLD	CHUCK JACKSON	*(DEBUT)*
I'M SO HAPPY	PRINCE PHILIP MITCHELL	*(ATLANTIC)*
SAY SOMETHING NICE TO ME	BOBBY KLINE	*(MB)*
COME SEE	BOBBY HUTTON	*(PHILLIPS)*
SPECIAL KIND OF WOMAN	PAUL THOMPSON	*(VOLT)*
THE WRONG GIRL	The SHOWMEN	*(MINIT)*
ABRACADABRA	ERMA FRANKLIN	*(EPIC)*

1995 NORMANTON / WINSFORD / 100 CLUB

RECONSIDER	BRENDA HOLLOWAY	(MOTOWN UNISSUED)
TOO LATE TO TURN BACK NOW	CORNELIUS BROTHERS	
	and SISTER ROSE	(UNITED ARTISTS)
REACH OUT FOR ME	LOU JOHNSON	(BIG TOP)
YOU HIT ME	KIM WESTON	(MOTOWN UNISSUED)
I CAN'T BREAK THE NEWS TO MYSELF		
	BEN E KING	(ATCO)
TUNE UP	JNR WALKER and	
	the ALLSTARS	(SOUL)
YOU AIN'T SAYING NOTHING NEW	VIRGIL HENRY	(TAMLA/COLOSSUS)
THINK IT OVER	LIZ VERDI	(COLUMBIA)
I WONDER WHY	BILLY ECKSTINE	(MOTOWN)

1996 THE RITZ

GONNA BE A BIG THING	The YUM YUMS	(ABC)
MY LOVE IS GETTING STRONGER	TOMMY RIDGLEY	(INTERNATIONAL CITY)
MAN O MAN	WALTER and	
	the ADMIRATIONS	(LA CINDY)
DON'T START NONE	MAYFIELD PLAYERS	(MAYFIELD)
I DON'T DO THIS	SYDNEY JOE QUALLS	(20TH CENTURY)
KEY TO MY HAPPINESS	The CHARADES	(MGM)
NOTHING CAN HELP YOU NOW	LENNY CURTIS	(END)
CALL ME	EDDIE BISHOP	(ABC)
TOP OF THE STAIRS	COLLINS and COLLINS	(A&M)
TOO LATE	MANDRILL	(ARISTA)

1997 WINSFORD AND THE RITZ

NO ONE CAN LOVE YOU MORE	GLADYS KNIGHT	(MOTOWN)
LUCKY NUMBER	RONNIE M^{c}NEIR	(MOTOR CITY)
HAS IT HAPPENED TO YOU YET	EDWIN STARR	(GROOVESVILLE UNRELEASED)
THAT'S NOT LOVE	HOLLY ST JAMES	(ABC)
RECIPE	LV JOHNSON	(GROOVESVILLE UNRELEASED)
LET MY HEART AND SOUL BE FREE	The TANGEERS	(OKEH)
PRESSURE	DRIZABONE	(ISLAND)
THESE MEMORIES	ALMETA LATTIMORE	(MAINSTREAM)
TAKE A GIANT STEP	The PROFILES	(GOLD TOKEN)
GETTIN' TO ME	BEN E KING	(ATLANTIC UNRELEASED)

*Yvonne Vernee, the quality of her recordings for Correc-Tone and Sonbert and a short
stint as lead singer with the Elgins have ensured her enduring popularity.*

1998 THE RITZ AND LOWTON

TRYING TO LOVE TWO	BARBARA LYNN	*(ICHIBAN)*
YOU'VE BEEN AWAY	RUBIN	*(KAPP)*
JEANETTE	WADE FLEMONS	*(RAMSEL)*
WHAT DOES IT TAKE	The BAY BROTHERS	*(MILLENNIUM)*
TOWER OF STRENGTH	GLORIA LYNN	*(EVEREST)*
I'VE HAD IT	GEORGE SMITH	*(TURNTABLE)*
I'M COMING HOME	SEPTEMBER JONES	*(KAPP)*
WHAT'S THAT ON YOUR FINGER	KENNY CARTER	*(UNRELEASED RCA)*
HE'S ALL I GOT	The SUPREMES	*(MOTOWN)*
BABY, BABY DON'T WASTE MY TIME	GLADYS KNIGHT and the PIPS	(COLUMBIA)

1999 TOGETHERNESS AND CLEETHORPES

A LOT OF LOVIN GOIN' ROUND	CLARENCE HILL	*(MAINSTREAM)*
HE WHO PICKS A ROSE	JIMMY RUFFIN	*(MOTOWN UNISSUED)*
STORMY	The SUPREMES	*(MOTOWN)*
KISS MY LOVE GOODBYE	BETTYE SWANN	*(ATLANTIC)*
TOUCH OF VENUS	BRENDA HOLLOWAY	*(MOTOWN UNISSUED)*
BABY A GO GO	BARBARA McNAIR	*(MOTOWN UNISSUED)*
PIECES OF MY BROKEN HEART	GLADYS KNIGHT and the PIPS	*(MOTOWN UNISSUED)*
I JUST WANT TO FALL IN LOVE	DETROIT SPINNERS	*(ATLANTIC)*
LOVE IS ALRIGHT	JESSE JAMES	*(VIRTUE ACETATE)*
IF YOU DON'T COME	PATIENCE VALENTINE	*(SAR)*

2000 TOGETHERNESS - Northern storms into the new Millennium

WORLD OF HAPPINESS	ARTIST UNKNOWN	*(UNISSUED HARTHON)*
POOR SIDE OF TOWN	RICHARD STREET	*(UNISSUED MOTOWN)*
KEEPS ON ROLLING	BRENDA HOLLOWAY	*(MOTOWN UNISSUED)*
HE'S THE ONE THAT RINGS MY BELL	SHERRY TAYLOR	*(GLORECO)*
THIS THING CALLED LOVE	JOHNNY WYATT	*(BRONCO)*
IT'S YOUR VOODOO WORKING	CHARLES SHEFFIELD	*(EXCELLO)*
DON'T STOP NOW	THE ORIGINALS	*(MOTOWN LP)*
MY BABY'S BEEN CHEATIN' (I KNOW)	AC REED	*(COOL)*
I JUST CAN'T SPEAK	JIMMY 'BO' HORNE	*(DADE)*
HAVE LOVE WILL TRAVEL	RICHARD BERRY	*(FLIP)*

Right: Richard Berry and the Pharoahs' 'Have Love Will Travel', one of several very different versions, it was released twice on Flip, the second issue is coupled with 'Louie Louie', the group's only real claim to musical stardom it is the original version of the Kingsmen's Doo-Wop classic.

CHARTING
HIGH... northern soul
to enter the UK pop charts

We have carefully selected the ones that charted purely due to 'Northern' demand, resulting from plays on the scene. Many, such as 'Rescue Me', 1-2-3, 'Mockingbird', 'Joe 90', 'This Old Heart Of Mine', 'Tainted Love' (by Soft Cell), 'The Only Way Is Up' (by Yazz and the Plastic Population) or 'Breakin' Down The Walls Of Heartache' have a loose connection to the Rare Soul scene and are similar sounding, but were NOT in demand on the scene from the outset. Sure, tracks such as Barry Gray's 'Joe 90' did receive minor spins but the real demand came from within the Gerry Anderson/TV 21 fan base.

The scene has direct links to the charts too with former Coventry DJ Pete Waterman peaking at no.33, 1975 as 14-18 with a song titled 'Goodbyee'. Nottingham DJ Chris King went one better than Waterman (even though the former has millions of sales as a writer/producer) by scoring with a No.1 in 1992 with 'Please Don't Go'. Arguably the strangest could be producer Simon Soussan who actually made an appearance at Wigan Casino as a DJ, and then went on to create The Sharonettes and Shalamar!

Many would argue that Freda Payne's 'Band Of Gold' is Northern, but not at the time, neither is Edwyn Collins 'A Girl Like You', although the influence is obvious (especially when you look at the picture sleeve which features Northern Soul patches and dancers). The Showstoppers' 'Ain't Nothing But A Houseparty' is an interesting call, peaking at no.11 in 1968, one could be forgiven for thinking it was born 'North of Watford', although the trademark is there, it was merely an international club record.

Northern Soul finds itself being in the frame for sampling. The dance experts have in recent years been active with 'Sliced Tomatoes', 'I'm On My Way', 'The Duck' all finding their way into other releases. TV is getting in on the act too with John E. Paul's 'I Wanna Know' and Rubin's 'You've Been Away' fronting highly original Cat food commercials!

Anyway... here's those charts!

Archie Bell and The Drells	Here I Go Again	*(Atlantic, No.11, 1972)*
George Benson	Supership	*(CTI, No.30, 1975)*
Bob and Earl	Harlem Shuffle	*(Island, No.7, 1969)*
Gene Chandler	Nothing Can Stop Me	*(Soul City, No.41, 1968)*
The Contours	Just A Little Misunderstanding	*(Tamla Motown, No.31, 1970)*
Petula Clark	A Sign Of The Times	*(Pye, No.49, 1966****)*
Guy Darrell	I've Been Hurt	*(Santa Ponsa, No.12, 1973)*
Donnie Elbert	A Little Piece Of Leather	*(London, No.27, 1972*)*
The Elgins	Heaven Must Have Sent You	*(Tamla Motown, No.3, 1971)*
The Exciters	Reaching For The Best	*(20TH Century, No. 31, 1975)*
The Fascinations	Girls Are Out To Get You	*(Mojo, No.32, 1972)*
The Flamingos	Boogaloo Party	*(Phillips, No.26, 1969)*
The Formations	At The Top Of The Stairs	*(Mojo, No.28, 1971)*
Four Seasons	The Night	*(Mowest, No.7, 1975)*
Marvin Gaye	Lucky Lucky Me	*(Motown, No.67, 1994)*
Wayne Gibson	Under My Thumb	*(Pye, No.17, 1974)*
Dobie Gray	Out On The Floor	*(Black Magic, No.42, 1975)*
Bobby Hebb	Love, Love, Love	*(Phillips, No.32, 1972)*
Tommy Hunt	Crackin' Up	*(Spark, No.39, 1975**)*
Tommy Hunt	Loving On The Losing Side	*(Spark, No.28,1976)*
Tommy Hunt	One Fine Morning	*(Spark, No.44, 1976)*
Millie Jackson	My Man Is A Sweet Man	*(Mojo, No.50, 1972)*
The Javells	Goodbye Nothin' To Say	*(Pye Disco Demand, No.26, 1974)*
L.J Johnson	Your Magic Put A Spell On Me	*(Phillips, No.27, 1976)*
Marv Johnson	I Miss You Baby	*(Tamla Motown, No.25, 1969)*
Robert Knight	Love On A Mountain Top	*(Monument, No.10, 1974)*
Gary Lewis and the Playboys	My Heart's Symphony	*(United Artists, No.36, 1975)*

Left: The Sharonettes' 'Papa Ooh Mow, Mow', a version of the Rivingtons' Doo-Wop classic became a massive hit.
'Watch Out' as the Black Magic advert says - was this intended as a warning to real Soul fans to avoid this dreadful record?

Ramsey Lewis	Wade In The Water	*(Chess, No.31, 1972)*
Little Anthony and the Imperials		
	Better Use Your Head	*(United Artists, No.42, 1976)*
Tami Lynn	I'm Gonna Run Away From You	*(Mojo, No.4, 1971)*
Harold Melvin and the Blue Notes		
	Get Out	*(Route, No.35, 1975)*
Mistura feat. Lloyd Michels	The Flasher	*(Route, No.23, 1976)*
Willie Mitchell	The Champion	*(London, No.47, 1976)*
The Newbeats	Run Baby Run	*(London, No.10, 1971)*
Dean Parrish	I'm On My Way	*(UK, No.38, 1975)*
Gene Pitney	She's A Heartbreaker	*(Stateside, No.34, 1968***)*
Mike Post Coalition	Afternoon Of The Rhino	*(Warner Bros, No.47, 1975)*
Jimmy Radcliffe	Long After Tonight Is All Over	*(Stateside, No.40, 1964****)*
San Remo Strings	Festival Time	*(Tamla Motown, No.39, 1971)*
The Sharonettes	Papa Ooh Mow Mow	*(Black Magic, No.26, 1975)*
The Sharonettes	Going To A Go Go	*(Black Magic, No.46, 1975)*
The Tams	Hey Girl Don't Bother Me	*(Probe, No.1, 1971)*
R.Dean Taylor	There's A Ghost In My House	*(Tamla Motown, No.3, 1974)*
Evelyn Thomas	Weakspot	*(20ᵀᴴ Century, No.26, 1976)*
Evelyn Thomas	Doomsday	*(20ᵀᴴ Century, no.41, 1976)*
Jamo Thomas	I Spy For The FBI	*(Polydor, No.44, 1969)*
Trammps	Hold Back The Night	*(Buddah, No.5, 1975)*
Frankie Valli	You're Ready Now	*(Phillips, No.11, 1970)*
The Velvelettes	These Things Will Keep Me Loving You	
		(Tamla Motown, No.34, 1971)
Wigan's Chosen Few	Footsee	*(Pye Disco Demand, No.9, 1975*****)*
Wigan's Ovation	Skiing In The Snow	*(Spark, No.12, 1975**)*
Wigan's Ovation	Per-so-nally	*(Spark, No.38, 1975**)*
Wigan's Ovation	Superlove	*(Spark, No.41, 1975**)*
Al Wilson	The Snake	*(Bell, No.41, 1975)*
Jackie Wilson	I Get The Sweetest Feeling	*(MCA, No.9, 1972)*
Betty Wright	Where Is The Love	*(RCA, No.25, 1975)*

Key to the above the above chart entries:

*   Re-recording of original track.

**   A cover version of the original in-demander.

***   The official B side.

****   Associated with Northern, although NOT at the time of entry into the UK charts.

*****   Based upon a 45 on US Roulette, Footsee by The Chosen Few. The track was re-created by producer Simon Soussan and retitled 'Footsee - The Sounds of Soul'. Pye records, never short on the uptake singles-wise, copied Soussan's arrangement, having obtained the rights from US label Roulette. Employee and Soul fan Dave McAleer instigated the recording, promotion and it's subsequent success. Soccer fans note: The crowd noises are actually overdubs of the 1966 FA Cup Final, Everton versus Sheffield Wednesday!

Below: 'Da, Da, Da - Da Da - Da - Da Da, La - La La'... etecetera, etcetera. The Chosen Few reworked by Simon Soussan then re-recorded by Dave McAleer, give me 'Birth Of A Playboy' any day of the week!

the strange world

Paul Humphrey
'Cochise'

For 12 months this was the scene's biggest hit!

The Playthings
'Stop What You're Doing'

A monster new release cover-up from 1973!

Johnny Jones
'Honey Bee'

A 1972 new release it had a superlative 60's sound!

Tommy Hunt
'Loving On The Losing Side'

One of the few 'tailor-mades' with real credibility!

of northern soul

Robert Knight
'Love On A Mountain Top'
Every British collector, Pop and Mobile DJ was scrambling for this one in 1971!

PJ
'TLC (Tender Loving Care)'
This lightweight 1971 release became number one in the country - for seven days!

Barnaby Bye
'Can't Live This Way'
I discovered it and passed it on to Ian Levine who made it a monster - but where's the Soul?

Jimmy Cliff 'Waterfall'
When the Casino went pop-crazy this track by the 'Rude Boy' fitted the bill perfectly! Produced by Muff Winwood, member of the Spencer Davis Group!

MAJOR LANCE
"Everybody Loves
a Good Time" 4-7233

TEACHO
"Chills and Fever"
(With The Students) c/w
"Same Old Beat"
4-7234

TED TAYLOR
"Stay Away From
My Baby" 4-7231

THE ARTISTICS
"This Heart of Mine"
4-7232

The hits are happening on OKeh

Remember when.... Whether you haven't been involved in Northern Soul for years or are a regular today, your past will be packed with special memories. The following pages are filled with some of those strange and uniquely 'Northern' people, places, records and ephemera that go to form our unique and wonderful scene...

TEN
key northern soul venues

1. **WIGAN CASINO** (1973 - 1981)
2. **BLACKPOOL MECCA** (1971 - 1980, with a short break during the days of the Torch)
3. **THE TWISTED WHEEL**, Whitworth Street, Manchester (1967 - 1971)
4. **THE GOLDEN TORCH**, Tunstall, Stoke-on-Trent (Allnighters 1972 - 73)
5. **THE RITZ**, Manchester (Alldayers 1976 - 1979, Allnighters 1993 - Present)
6. **THE CATACOMBS**, Wolverhampton (1971 - 1974)
7. **WINTER GARDENS**, Cleethorpes (1975 - 1979)
8. **KEELE**, Staffordshire (1986 - Present)
9. **KINGS HALL**, Stoke (1995 - Present)
10. **100 CLUB**, London (1981 - Present)

TEN
ultra-collectable **rare soul** labels

1. **RIC - TIC**, owned by Ed Wingate and Joanne Jackson, sold in 1966 as part of the Golden World package to Motown who continued to run it 'til 1968.

2. **SHRINE**, the ultimate 'rare' Soul label, was owned by Eddie Singleton and Raynoma Gordy, the name and logo represent a 'shrine' to the memory of John F Kenedy also closely related to the HEM and Jet Set labels.

3. **REVILOT**, formed in Detroit by the great Don Davis in partnership with Lebaron Taylor, this legendary label, home to so many classics is 'Toliver' (Taylor's real name) backwards.

4. **THELMA**, yet another Don Davis set up, this time in partnership with Hazel Coleman, based in Detroit, home to Emanuel Laskey, Joe Matthews, The Fabulous Peps, Billy Kennedy and Martha Starr.

5. **OKEH**, the oldest record label in America, had been dormant for many years before it was reactivated by Columbia records. Supported by the likes of Carl Davies, Curtis Mayfield and Van McCoy it has produced many many Northern classics from the Carstairs to the Seven Souls and Major Harris.

6. **GOLDEN WORLD**, parent company of Ric-Tic it was owned by Ed Wingate and Joanne Jackson.

7. **MOTOWN** group and SUBSIDIARIES, founded in 1959 by Berry Gordy Jnr, the group consisted of some 20 different labels, it included unlikely titles like 'Jazz Forum' and 'Weed'.

8. **CAMEO/PARKWAY**, the seminal Philadelphia labels that, with their subsidiaries, have produced countless Northern sounds from artists like Chubby Checker, Bunny Sigler, Yvonne Baker and Christine Cooper.

9. **CHESS/CADET/CHECKER/ARGO**, owned and operated by Leonard Chess and family, it was the powerhouse behind the great Chicago sound from the early Wheel sounds Ko Ko Taylor and Billy Stewart through to Terry Callier and the Dells.

10. **MIRWOOD**, operated by Randall Wood, this Los Angeles based label with close links to Keymen records boasted the writing and production talents of Len Jewell, Fred Smith, James Carmichael, Bob Relf and Earl Nelson. The label's rosta included the Olympics, Bob and Earl, Richard Temple (Jimmy Conwell) and the Belles amongst others and has produced many great Northern classics.

Opposite: Don Robey's Duke/Peacock setup, distributed by ABC, was the home to many great performers including Bobby Bland, Eddie Taylor, Buddy Lamp and Carl Carlton. It has produced many Northern classics, particularly from the days of Northern Soul at the Wheel, when many were played on UK releases like Vocallion and Sue.

TEN
collectable soul artists

Most people collect what they like, some people collect just one label, the work of only one producer or the work of only one artist. Whether you are a completeist label fanatic or simply wish to own the sounds that take your fancy, the following Soul singers would grace any record box, we've also listed some of the labels on which they produced their best work...

1. **RAY POLLARD**, Shrine, United Artists, Decca and Cub

2. **ROY HAMILTON**, RCA and MGM

3. **MAJOR LANCE**, Okeh

4. **CHUCK JACKSON**, Wand and Motown

5. **MARVIN GAYE**, Motown and CBS

6. **THE HESITATIONS**, Kapp and D-Town

7. **GENE CHANDLER**, Chess, Brunswick and Constellation

8. **JAMES CARR**, Goldwax

9. **BOBBY WOMACK**, Keyman, Liberty, Minit and Beverly Glenn

10. **JJ BARNES**, Revilot, Ric-Tic, Volt

Right: 'Nothing Can Stop' the Duke of Chicago Soul. Highly collectable Gene Chandler has produced many great Northern sounds including 'Mr. Big Shot' and 'There Was A Time'.

TEN
truly classic live performances

1. **BETTY WRIGHT** (Wigan Casino, 1975)

2. **MAJOR LANCE** (The Torch, 1972

3. **JIMMY RUFFIN** (The Wheel, 1970)

4. **RIC - TIC Revue** (Hinkley, 1983)

5. **JACKIE WILSON** (Wigan Casino, 1975)

6. **JJ BARNES** (The Torch, 1972)

7. **RAY POLLARD** (100 Club, 1988)

8. **EDWIN STARR** (The Wheel last night, January 1970)

9. **BARBARA LYNN** (Togertherness Weekender, September 1999)

10. **TAVARES** (The Ritz, 1976)

Everybody's favourite lady - with everybody's favourite doorman. Bubbly Brenda Holloway having a laugh with Big Ron at Blackpool's Togetherness Weekender in September 1998.

At their specific request, Brenda toured with the Beatles in 1964. Watching footage of her Shea stadium performance the power of her voice is staggering.

TEN
four figure classics

1.	**MR. SOUL/AL SCOTT**	What Happened To Yesterday	*(GENUINE)*	£1,500
2.	**FRANK WILSON**	Do I Love You (Indeed I Do)	*(SOUL)*	£15,000
3.	**DON GARDNER**	Cheatin Kind	*(SEDGRICK)*	£3,000
4.	**THE BUTLERS WITH FRANKIE BEVERLY**			
		Because Of My Heart	*(ROUSER)*	£5,000
5.	**BERNIE WILLIAMS**	Ever Again	*(BELL)*	£1,500
6.	**INSPIRATIONS**	No One Else Can Take Your Place		
			(BREAKTHROUGH)	£4,000
7.	**JD BRYANT**	I Won't Be Coming Back	*(SHRINE)*	£3,000
8.	**JACKIE DAY**	Naughty Boy	*(PHLECTRON)*	£1,500
9.	**THE MASQUERADERS**	(Mis-spelt as Masquaders on label)		
		That's The Same Thing	*(SOUL TOWN)*	£2,000
10.	**DENNIS EDWARDS**	Johnny On The Spot	*(SOULVILLE)*	£2,000

Damned expensive it may be, and very popular amongst collectors, but JD Bryant's Shrine rarity 'I Won't Be Coming Back' won't be making it into our all time Top 500!

TEN
current in-demand singles
that **nobody** wanted in the 70's

1.	**CELESTE HARDIE**	You're Gone	(REYNOLDS)
2.	**HANK JACOBS**	Elijah Rockin' With Soul	(CALL ME)
3.	**CONNIE LAVERNE**	Can't Live Without You	(GSF)
4.	**NOLAN PORTER**	If I Could Only Be Sure	(ABC)
5.	**SEVEN SOULS**	I Still Love You	(OKEH)
6.	**GENE TOONES**	What More Do You Want	(SIMCO)
7.	**TOMMY RIDGLEY**	My Love Is Getting Stronger	(INTERNATIONAL CITY)
8.	**THE DYNELLS**	Call On Me	(ATCO)
9.	**ROY HAMILTON**	The Panic Is On	(MGM)
10.	**CLAUDE 'BABY' HUEY**	Why Did You Blow It	(GALAXY)

Right: Though popular for a while during the 80's amongst Scooter riding Soul fans 'Elijah Rockin' With Soul' was never a big mainstream sound in the 70's. However recent years have seen it become sought after and prices have risen accordingly.

TEN
in-demanders from the 70's that **nobody** wants today!

Lloyd Michels

Left: Lloyd Michels, the man behind Mistura.

Their 'Flasher' on Fusion or Route in the UK, once incredibly popular, is now very rarely played and is today a perennial inhabitant of the '50p Cheapies Box' alongside the likes of James Coit, Joe Frazier and Jimmy Cliff.

1.	**T.D VALENTINE**	Love Trap	(EPIC)
2.	**MISTURA**	The Flasher	(FUSION)
3.	**REPARATA AND THE DELRONS**		
		Panic	(MALA)
4.	**JAMES COIT**	Black Power	(PHOOF)
5.	**JIMMY CLIFF**	Waterfall	(A&M)
6.	**AL FOSTER BAND**	The Night Of The Wolf	(ROULETTE)
7.	**JOE FRAZIER**	First Round Knockout	(MOTOWN)
8.	**BABE RUTH**	Elusive	(CAPITOL)
9.	**SNOOPY DEAN**	Shake 'N' Bump	(TK)
10.	**BAJA MARIMBA BAND**	Along Comes Mary	(A&M)

TEN
worst records EVER - my choice!

Take note that our old friend the Soul Fox features in almost EVERY case. Simon Soussan had an incredible gift when it came to tracking down new discoveries, unfortunately it didn't extend to a talent for making NEW vinyl (for Black Magic, Soul Galore and Soul Fox, though his work with Shalimar and Casablanca records did produce some passable disco sounds).

1.	THE FLOORSHAKERS	Six by Six	*(SOUL FOX)*
2.	SOUL FOX STRINGS	Mountain Top Theme	*(SOUL FOX)*
3.	THE DYNAMITES	Ain't No Soul	*(SOUL GALORE)*
4.	THE TERRIFICS	I Can't Get Enough	*(SOUL GALORE)*
5.	THE DYNAMITES	Bok To Bach	*(SOUL GALORE)*
6.	THE HOTSHOTS	Run Baby Run	*(SOUL GALORE)*
7.	LESTER LANIN	Dizzy	*(METROMEDIA)*
8.	HUGO MONTENEGRO	Sherry	*(TIME)*
9.	RAIN	Out Of My Mind	*(BELL)*
10.	THE SHARONETTES	Papa Oom - Mow Mow	*(BLACK MAGIC)*

You would undoubtedly do yourself an injury if you attempted to dance to Lester Lanin's insanely fast instrumental take on Tommy Roe's 60's hit. Also featured 'Oh Bla De, Oh Bla Da' on the reverse!...

It was quite literally 'Mad, Bad and Dangerous to Know' - DREADFUL!

TEN
legendary cover-ups

Over the years our scene has been much criticised for the practice of 'covering-up' records, outsiders often see it as some form of arrogant elitism. However over the years this practice has been important in maintaining exclusivity for a certain DJ which has paradoxically improved the longevity of many records by saving them from mass over-playing.

Where tracks are unissued or 'one-offs' this has not been a problem, but for a relatively easy record to track down like the Coaster's 'Crazy Baby' on Atco which was covered-up for some years as Freddie Jones it has been an important factor in raising the record to the status of respected classic that it holds today before it was swamped out by a flood of copies from the States.

Little Ann whose unissued Topper cut 'When He's Not Around' remains very popular today. It was a particularly long-lived cover-up as 'Rose Valentine'.

1. **ROSE VALENTINE**   WHEN HE'S NOT AROUND   *(actually by LITTLE ANN, unissued Topper)*

2. **PHANTOM JANITOR**   NO SECOND CHANCE   *(actually by THE DEADBEATS on Strata)*

3. **FREDDIE JONES**   MY HEARTS WIDE OPEN   *(actually by THE COASTERS on Atco)*

4. **JOE MATTHEWS**   I DON'T LIKE TO LOSE   *(actually by THE GROUP feat. CECIL WASHINGTON on Prophonics)*

5. **MICKY VALVANO**   SHE'S FIRE   *(actually by THE C.O.D.'s on Kellmac)*

6. **CHRISTINE COOPER** COUNTRY GIRL   *(actually by VICKIE BAINES on Parkway)*

7. **HB BARNUM**   THE ICE MAN   *(actually by BILLY WATKINS on Era)*

8. **JAMES LEWIS**   THAT'S THE WAY   (actually by THE Q on Hound)

9. **MAURICE McCALLISTER**
WHAT HAPPENED TO YESTERDAY   (actually by MR. SOUL/AL SCOTT on Genuine)

10. **GENE McDANIELS**   SLEEPLESS NIGHTS   (actually by PARIS on Doc)

TEN
northern soul 'buzz' words

In common with every underground scene Northern Soul has developed its own langauge to describe our special interests, differing terms come and go ('dubes' and 'circles', 60's terms for pills would be met with blank faces today!), there are many more but here are a few commonly used ones.

1. **GEAR** — Drugs, usually amphetamines (bombers, blues, dexies etc - uppers, downers - the addictive opiates and barbiturates - are generally frowned upon).

2. **COVER-UP** — A ficiticious title and/or artist attributed to a record to protect its exclusivity (and therefore usually longevity) for a particular DJ.

3. **NEWIE** — A recent discovery, usually from the 60's, hence the term '60's Newie'.

4. **SMASHED** — The desirable/undesirable (depending on your viewpoint) effect of too much amphetamine ('blocked' is ideal, the next stage is 'hammered' - too wrecked to do anything).

5. **THE SCENE** — Definitive term given to the Northern Soul culture - a hang-over from Mod days, an allnighter regular (ie weekly adherent) often being termed as 'on the scene'.

6. **BACK DROP** — One of the acrobatic dance moves, literally dropping back onto your hands, others include 'Russian Rolls', 'Swallow Dives', 'Back Springs' and of course assorted high kicks, somersaults and splits.

7. **SHUFFLING** — An excruciatingly difficult dance (usually to fast 70's sounds) where the feet move at great speed as if bearing no body weight, incredible to see - but **very few** can do it well!

8. **OLDIES** — A movement started in 1974 when Dave Evison did a short spot at Stafford (courtesy of yours truly locking my record box and leaving the stage mid-spot). Dave quickly joined Wigan on the opening of the now legendary Mr. M's, essentially concentrating on long-gone cheapies his 'Oldies' spots fulfilled the need to hear the sounds of our past (primarily those of the Wheel) - at this time the scene was obsessed with rapid turnover of new sounds. Today variants include 'forgotten oldies' (usually referred to by people arguing for their reactivitation) and 'overplayed oldies' (condemned by most regulars, though they usually still love them and just want them to get a rest!).

9. **MODERN** — More recent Soul releases, ranging from 70's to 90's, but usually refering to sounds released post - the late 70's.

10. **CROSSOVER** — Late 60's/early 70's down tempo, frequently collector oriented sounds.

TEN
venues with **amazing** attendences

Although many bemoan the passing of the glory days of Northern Soul in the 70's and whilst it is true that the average attendence at an allnighter today is around 500 it is interesting to note that some of the big attendences listed below are from more recent years. All night venues like Manchester's Ritz and Togetherness' events at the King's Hall Stoke regularly play host to 1,000 or more Souls. Today Soul nights in Blackburn and Prestwich, Manchester expect a minimum of 600 for the evening, whilst the weekenders in Blackpool and Cleethorpes both sell out weeks or even months in advance!

1.	**QUEENS HALL (Allnighter)**	Leeds	(1974)	7,000
2.	**WIGAN CASINO (Allnighter)**	Wigan	(1974/75)	2,500
3.	**TOGETHERNESS (Allnighter)**	Stoke-on-Trent	(1998)	1,700
4.	**THE RITZ (Alldayer)**	Manchester	(1977)	1,500
5.	**THE RITZ (Allnighter)**	Manchester	(1998)	1,200
6.	**THE MECCA (Alldayer)**	Blackpool	(1976)	1,400
7.	**THE TORCH (Allnighter)**	Tunstall, Stoke-on-Trent	(1973)	1,300
8.	**THE PALAIS (Alldayer)**	Nottingham	(1975)	1,200
9.	**THE PIER (Allnighter)**	Morecambe	(1984)	1,300
10.	**THE WIRRINA STADIUM (Alldayer)**	Peterborough	(1978)	1,100

Tram Lines (!) in the flagstone floor, loose boards put down to dance on, nowhere to sit and a dreadful sound system...

In 1974 the Queens Hall in Leeds had it all, plus Major Lance live on stage and SEVEN THOUSAND PUNTERS!

Opposite: The International Soul Club put on many well attended events around the UK during the 70's.

TEN
gone but not forgotten venues

Every all-nighter goer will remember names like The Twisted Wheel, Wigan Casino, The Torch and Blackpool Mecca, but there have been countless other clubs that have each had their own input to the scene, in the 60's clubs like Derby's Blue Orchid had their own adherents who were equally into soul as those who attended the Wheel.

In the 70's there were countless other venues like the Winter Gardens in Cleethorpes and the Ivo Centre in St Ives, whilst the 80's saw a massive shake-up from Stafford's Top Of the World... All were important to the scene, here are a few more key venues that are gone, but certainly NOT forgotten...

1. **STARS AND STRIPES,** Yate

2. **THE HOWARD MALLETT,** Cambridge

3. **THE ASSEMBLY ROOMS,** Derby

4. **VA-VA'S,** Bolton

5. **SAMANTHAS,** Sheffield

6. **THE 76 CLUB,** Burton-on-Trent

7. **THE CROMWELIAN,** Bolton

8. **CENTRAL,** Leeds

9. **THE KING MOJO,** Sheffield

10. **THE CHATEAU IMPNEY,** Droitwich

CATACOMBS **CATACOMBS CLUB** **Wolverhampton** **28682**	LEADING R & B SOUL DISCOTHEQUE			
	WEDNESDAY	**THURSDAY**	**FRIDAY**	**SATURDAY**
	BLUE MAX Members Only 12p	**CARL DENE** Members FREE	**BARMY BARRY** Members 30p Name D.J's once a month	**ALAN DAY BLUE MAX PEP** Members 40p

TEN
gone and **sadly missed** characters

1.	**Les Cokell**	(The last DJ at the Twisted Wheel)
2.	**Andy Lee**	(Collector)
3.	**Nev Wherry**	(DJ and collector)
4.	**The Mighty Bub**	(DJ, character - comedian!)
5.	**Roger Eagle**	(The first DJ at the Twisted Wheel)
6.	**Pete Lawson**	(Key collector, legendary for having the words to Jerry Williams' classic 'If You Ask Me' tattooed on his chest!)
7.	**'Flash' Atkinson**	(Collector)
8.	**Kenny Spence**	(Mr M's and allnighter character)
9.	**Mick Kowalski**	(Early allnighter character and collector)
10.	**Mike Walker**	(Casino Manager - known by everyone as a 'nice' guy)

TEN
influential promoters
of the golden era and beyond!

1. **CHRIS BURTON**   The Torch, Queens Hall - Leeds, International Soul Club

2. **TERRY SAMSON**   KGB, Sheffield

3. **MARY CHAPMAN**   Winter Gardens, Cleethorpes

4. **NEIL RUSHTON**   The Ritz Alldayers

5. **MICK FLELLO**   West Midlands Soul Club

6. **NITA ANDERSON**   Wulfrun/Civic Hall, Wolverthampton

7. **CHRIS KING**   Hinckley, Loughborough, Bretby and many live acts

8. **ADY CROASDELL**   The 100 Club, London/Cleethorpes Weekender

9. **DAVE THORLEY**   Top Of The World, Stafford

10. **ALAN SENIOR**   Clifton Halls, Rotherham

insatiable record hounds

1. **JOHN ANDERSON** — Soul Bowl and Grapevine Records

2. **MARTIN KOPPEL** — Kopp's Collectables, Anglo American, an ex-Pat. based in Canada

3. **JOHN MANSHIP** — Record Dealer

4. **ADY PIERCE** — Record Collector and Dealer

5. **DAVE RAISTRICK** — Record Collector and Dealer

6. **PAT BRADY** — DJ, Record Collector and Dealer

7. **TIM BROWN** — Anglo American and the Collector to end them all!

8. **GARY CAPE** — Record Dealer

9. **MARK DOBSON** — The DJ 'Butch', Record Collector and Dealer

10. **TIM ASHIBENDE** — Occasional DJ, Record Collector and Dealer

Right: Toronto based ex-pat Martin Koppel, the North American partner in Anglo-American Records. Martin was on the UK scene in the late 60's before moving to Canada in 1971. Together with British associate Tim Brown he has been responsible for supplying UK based collectors with some staggering rare vinyl - including a copy of Frank Wilson's 'Do I Love You (Indeed I Do)'.

TEN
venues to hear the top 500

1. **THE RITZ,** Manchester
2. **THE RITZ,** Brighouse
3. **SAMANTHAS,** Sheffield
4. **LEISURE CENTRE,** Alfreton
5. **GRASSHOPPERS,** Preston
6. **THE PALAIS,** Nottingham
7. **TOGETHERNESS,** Fleetwood Weekender/Stoke Allnighter
8. **KEELE UNIVERSITY,** Newcastle Under Lyme
9. **CIVIC HALL,** Winsford
10. **LEISURE VILLAGE,** Kettering

COLUMBIA
Recording Artists

THE SPELLBINDERS

DOSHAWNS Mgt. Inc.
BU-8-1375 UN-5-9795
NEW YORK CITY

TEN
old monsters **out of step today**

1. **TRAVIS WAMMACK**   Scratchy   *(ARA)*

2. **PAUL HUMPHREY**   Cochise   *(BLUE THUMB)*

3. **WIGAN'S CHOSEN FEW**   Footsee   *(PYE DISCO DEMAND)*

4. **THE HOLIDAYS**   Makin' Up Time   *(GOLDEN WORLD)*

5. **JAMES COIT**   Black Power   *(PHOOF)*

6. **MOOD MOSAIC**   A Touch Of Velvet - A Sting Of Brass
                                                 (UK COLUMBIA)

7. **REX GARVIN AND THE MIGHTY CRAVERS**
                             Sock It To 'Em JB   *(LIKE)*

8. **BOBBY GOLDSBORO**   Too Many People   *(UK UNITED ARTISTS)*

9. **AUGUST AND DENEEN**   WE GO TOGETHER *(ABC)*

10. **KIKI DEE**   ON A MAGIC CARPET RIDE
                                                 (PHILIPS)

Right: Alice Clarke whose classic Warner Brothers recording 'You Hit Me' remained popular for many years. It is largely forgotten today NOT because the sound ha become unpopular but simply because Kim Weston's incredible original unissued version (unearthed in the Motown vaults by Chris King) has totally overshadowed it!

*Pictured: Nolan Porter whose 'Keep
On Keeping On' on Lizard and
'If I Could Only Be Sure' for ABC
have both been important musical
groundbreakers on the scene.*

TEN
northern ground breakers

1.	CARSTAIRS	It Really Hurts Me Girl	(RED COACH)
2.	JAMES FOUNTAIN	Seven Day Lover	(PEACHTREE)
3.	MIKE POST COALITION	Afternoon Of The Rhino	(MERCURY)
4.	MR. FLOODS PARTY	Compared To What	(GM)
5.	NOLAN PORTER	If I Could Only Be Sure	(ABC)
6.	TOMMY NAVARRO	I Cried My Life Away	(DEJAC)
7.	TERRY CALLIER	Look At Me Now	(CADET)
8.	CHARLES SHEFFIELD	It's Your Voodoo Working	(EXCELLO)
9.	N F PORTER	Keep On Keeping On	(LIZARD)
10.	JAMES LEWIS AND THE CASE OF TYME		
		Manifesto	(LEGEND)

TEN
interesting lines of **northern** trivia

1. Newsreader **ANNA FORD**, was a regular visitor to WIGAN CASINO

2. Former soccer sensation **GEORGE BEST** was spotted at THE TWISTED WHEEL

3. **ROB DICKENS**, Warner Music Chief and close friend to CHER,
    acquired the publishing rights to 'THE FLASHER' in 1976.

4. **'REACHING FOR THE BEST'** was originally a ficticious title of a 'single' by BOB RELF, before
    becoming a reality for THE EXCITERS

5. **PETE WATERMAN** once had a hit as 14/18, while still playing Northern in Coventry.

6. **PATRICE HOLLOWAY** of 'LOVE AND DESIRE'/'ECSTACY' fame was the lead singer of 70's
    Hanna - Barbara cartoon girl group 'Josie and the Pussycats'.

7. **CAROL DECKER**, singer with T'PAU was a regular at the Whitchurch Alldayers in the 70's.

8. **ROBERT PALMER** was an occasional visitor Wolverhampton's Catacombs, so it's unsurprising
    to hear his obsession with Soul coming out in all those cover versions of Marvin Gaye.

9. **FRANK WILSON**, Northern Soul legend, has sold over 35 million
    singles worldwide as a writer and producer.

10. **STUART COSGROVE** former Wigan Casino regular and
    occasional DJ at venues like Peterborough's Fleet
    Allnighter is now a senior executive at Channel 4.

'No Honest Bob mate, I've got a copy!'
over the years Simon Soussan's capers
have become legendary, Exciters eat your
heart out! Here's one we 'made earlier'!

It's been around for nigh-on twenty five years, but there's still ONLY ONE COPY!

The wonderful 'No One Else Can Take Your Place' by the Inspirations - AS RARE AS IT GETS!

BREAKTHROUGH

Little Jeff
Time: 1:52

100
(01

NO ONE ELSE
CAN TAKE YOUR PLACE
(L. Ivey - L. Bell - H. Bell - J. Gibson)
INSPIRATIONS
Prod. by Joey Jefferson

TEN
planet northern rarities

1.	**FRANK WILSON**	Do I Love You (Indeed I Do)	*(Soul)*
2.	**INSPIRATIONS**	No One Else Can Take Your Place	*(Breakthrough)*
3.	**THE BUTLERS WITH FRANKIE BEVERLY**		
		Because Of My Heart	*(Rouser)*
4.	**THE ANDANTES**	Like A Nightmare	*(VIP)*
5.	**DON GARDNER**	Cheatin' Kind	*(Sedgrick)*
6.	**UNKNOWN**	A World Of Happiness	*(Virtue Acetate)*
7.	**JD BRYANT**	I Won't Be Coming Back	*(Shrine)*
8.	**THE PROPHETS**	One Gold Piece	*(Shrine)*
9.	**NATHAN WILLIAMS**	What Price	*(Tru-Gems)*
10.	**BUDDY SMITH**	When You Lose The One You Love	*(Brute)*

TEN
unlikely northern soul hitmakers

1. **GARY LEWIS AND THE PLAYBOYS**
2. **PAT WILLIAMS ORCHESTRA**
3. **MIKE POST COALITION**
4. **AL DELORY**
5. **BOBBY GOLDSBORO**
6. **PAUL ANKA**
7. **PEGGY MARCH**
8. **SPIRAL STARECASE**
9. **LEN BARRY**
10. **THE VENTURES**

Left: Dusty Springfield, we tend to forget that her Colonial upbringing as a wealthy Irish Catholic was a particulalry unlikely route into Soul music.

However alongside her version of 'What's It Gonna Be' which is of course well known on the scene and a host of Motown covers, she also recorded some more unlikely tracks including 'Bring Him Back' and 'Long After Tonight Is All Over'.

The 'Dusty In New York' EP featured here contains another great forgotten nighter sound - 'Live It Up'.

TEN
famous rare soul fans

1. **PETE WATERMAN**
   Ex-Coventry area DJ, now record mogul
   behind PWL and acts such as Steps.

2. **BELLE AND SEBASTIAN**
   A massive indie-pop act.

3. **PAUL WELLER**
   Top pop star.

4. **ERIC KNOWLES**
   Antiques Roadshow presenter.

5. **PETER STRINGFELLOW**
   Ex-Promoter and DJ of the Mojo,
   now Nightclub Owner.

6. **STEVE DAVIES**
   Snooker and Pool legend.

7. **JOHN SMITH**
   A prominent football agent.

8. **TREVOR EAST**
   Key SKY TV Sports executive.

9. **DALE WINTON**
   TV personality/presenter.

10. **NORMAN COOK**
    DJ, mixer and artist Fatboy Slim.

*Below: Pete Waterman, pop-hit production supremo -
and Northern Soul DJ! Pete and I worked together
regularly in and around Coventry during the 70's.*

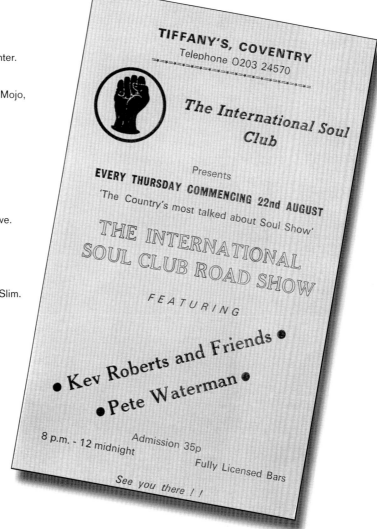

TIFFANY'S, COVENTRY
Telephone 0203 24570

The International Soul
Club

Presents

EVERY THURSDAY COMMENCING 22nd AUGUST
'The Country's most talked about Soul Show'

THE INTERNATIONAL
SOUL CLUB ROAD SHOW

FEATURING

● Kev Roberts and Friends ●
● Pete Waterman ●

8 p.m. - 12 midnight   Admission 35p

Fully Licensed Bars

See you there ! !

great **blue eyed northern** tracks

PAUL ANKA	I Can't Help Lovin' You	RCA
BOBBY GOLDSBORO	Too Many People	United Artists (UK)
RUFUS LUMLEY	I'm Standing	Holton
THE CROW	Your Autumn Of Tomorrow	Right On
THE CONSTRUCTION	Hey Little Way Out Girl	Sync 6
LYNNE RANDELL	Stranger In My Arms	Epic
BOBBY PARIS	I Walked Away	Capitol
TONI BASIL	Breakaway	A&M
HELEN SHAPIRO	Stop And You'll Become Aware	Columbia (UK)
BARBARA MILLS	Queen Of Fools	Hickory

Like a cross between Val Doonican and Billy Idol! Rufus Lumley is best known for 'I'm Standing' recorded for Holton records. Nice pullover by the way!

TEN
quality uk only northern

1.	**CARL DOUGLAS**	Serving A Sentence Of Life	(*UNITED ARTISTS*)
2.	**KENNY BERNARD**	What Love Brings	(*PYE*)
3.	**JIMMY THOMAS**	The Beautiful Night	(*PARLOPHONE*)
4.	**TIMI YURO**	It'll Never Be Over For Me	(*LIBERTY*)
5.	**RAY MERRELL**	Tears Of Joy	(*JAY BOY*)
6.	**JACKIE EDWARDS**	I Feel So Bad	(*ISLAND*)
7.	**LEVI JACKSON**	This Beautiful Day	(*COLUMBIA*)
8.	**KENNY BERNARD**	Pity My Feet	(*PYE*)
9.	**MARK LLOYD**	When I'm Gonna Find Her	(*PYE*)
10.	**KENNY LYNCH**	Movin' Away	(*HMV*)

Right: British artist Carl Douglas' 'Serving A Sentence Of Life' very rare, it was only released in the UK unlike his 'Marble And Iron' which only came out Stateside!

TEN major northern soul cities or areas

1. STOKE ON TRENT	3. GREATER MANCHESTER
3. WOLVERHAMPTON / BLACK COUNTRY	6. LONDON
6. NOTTINGHAM / THE EAST MIDLANDS	7. NORTHAMPTONSHIRE
5. SOUTH /WEST YORKSHIRE	8. BEDFORDSHIRE
9. COUNTY DURHAM	10. CAMBRIDGESHIRE

TEN ★ important northern soul towns

1. BOLTON	2. DUDLEY
3. PONTEFRACT	4. MANSFIELD
5. BURNLEY	6. BURY/RADCLIFFE
7. NEWTON AYCLIFFE	8. WIGAN
9. PRESTON	10. KETTERING

Though traditionally associated with the North West, Northern Soul has many centres around Britain. Though they have never had big Soul venues of their own, towns like Kettering in Northamptonshire and Newton Aycliffe in the North East have been the homes of large and dedicated groups of Soul fans who have had to habitually travel some way to the great Allnighter venues around Manchester and along the M6. Conversly a town like Dudley has very few nighter goers today (Dave Rimmer of Soulful Kinda Music fame - and that's about it!), but boasts long standing Soul venues like Dudley Zoo.

TEN
essential Northern questions

1. **GOT ANY GEAR?** / KNOW ANYONE WHO'S GOT ANY GEAR? / IS IT ANY GOOD?

2. **IF THE CLOCKS GO BACK, DOES IT STILL FINISH AT 8?**
   (MAY BE FOLLOWED BY THE HAPPY REALISATION THAT THE CLOCKS HAVE
   ACTUALLY GONE FORWARD AND ITS GOING TO BE A 9 HOUR NIGHTER!)

3. **HAVE YOU GOT A PEN?** / HAVE YOU SEEN WHAT HAPPENED TO MY PEN?

4. **HAVE YOU SEEN** (INSERT NAME)**?** (BEST ASKED WHEN YOU CAN'T REMEMBER THE NAME)

5. **IS IT** (INSERT NAME) **NEXT WEEK?** (USUALLY SEVERAL WEEKS EARLY/LATE)

6. **WHERE'S THE CLOAKROOM?** (WATCH IT! THIS IS JUST A RUSE TO START VERBALLING!)

7. **WILL YOU TAKE £30?** (FOR THE £50 RARITY ON SALE FOR ONLY £40)

8. **DO YOU NEED ANYTHING?** (IF THEY OFFER IT THEY'RE PROBABLY SQUAD - OR IT'S CRAP!)

9. **WHAT TIME DOES THE BAR SHUT?** (WHETHER OR NOT THE VENUE HAS A LICENSE
   - SEE NUMBER 6 - REFERENCE THE DREADED VERBALS)

10. **CAN YOU LOOK AFTER MY COAT, OH AND PLAY SOMETHING GOOD!**
    (TO THE DJ, PUTTING IN REQUESTS 2 RECORDS FROM THE END OF A SPOT IS
    ALSO A POPULAR, IF POINTLESS PASS TIME)

*Opposite: The brilliant Isley Brothers,
artists behind such Northern greats as
'Why When Love Is Gone', 'Tell Me It's
Just A Rumour' and 'My Love Is Your
Love', all recorded during their period
with Motown.*

TEN
classic re-issue labels

1. **ACE/KENT**
2. **RHINO**
3. **WESTSIDE**
4. **SEQUEL**
5. **GOLDMINE/SOUL SUPPLY**
6. **CHARLY**
7. **MOTOWN**
8. **CONNOISSEUR COLLECTION**
9. **EXPANSION**
10. **DEMON/EDSEL**

TEN
great dancers

1. **FRANK BOOPER**
2. **ANGELA LAWRENCE**
3. **MATCHIE**
4. **SOULIE**
5. **SNOWY**
6. **SANDY**
7. **JC**
8. **PHIL WALMSLEY**
9. **CRAIG WESTWOOD**
10. **GIGSY**

Picture: Drilling a hole in the dancefloor at Blackpool Weekender!... Spinning's easy, it's not falling over that's the hard bit!

TEN
innovative dj's of the 60's

1. **LES COKELL**
   The Twisted Wheel

2. **'FARMER' CARL DENE**
   Catacombs, Chateau Impney.

3. **BRIAN PHILLIPS**
   The Twisted Wheel

4. **GUY STEVENS**
   The Scene, London

5. **BRIAN WALKER**
   The Twisted Wheel

6. **PETE STRINGFELLOW**
   The Mojo

7. **TONY BANKS**
   Leeds Central

8. **JEFF KING**
   Leicester Area

9. **BRIAN RAE**
   The Twisted Wheel

10. **BARRY TASKER**
    Various , later Pendulum

Right: JJ Barnes whose 'Please Let Me In' was a major ground breaker at the Wheel, it was first played by Les Cokell who had borrowed it off a young Blackpool collector called Ian Levine.

TEN
giant **dj's** of the 70's

Above: Wigan anchormen;
Russ, Kev and Richard in
the early days of the Casino.

1. **IAN LEVINE**

2. **COLIN CURTIS**

3. **RICHARD SEARLING**

4. **MARTYN ELLIS**

5. **RUSS WINSTANLEY**

6. **PEP**

7. **SOUL SAM**

8. **ALAN DAY**

9. **TONY JEBB**

10. **KEITH MINSHULL**

Right: Messing about at the Mecca, Judith Searling,
Ian Levine, Bernie Golding, Len Glab and the late
Les Cokell (crouched) in a light hearted mood.

TEN
movers and dj's of the 80's

1. **CHRIS KING**	2. **DAVE EVISON**
3. **GUY HENNIGAN**	4. **KEB DARGE**
5. **SHAUN GIBBONS**	6. **DAVE THORLEY**
7. **PAT BRADY**	8. **TED MASSEY**
9. **ALAN SENIOR**	10. **ADEY CROASDELL**

TEN
turntable terrors of the 90's

1. **GINGER TAYLOR**

2. **BOB HINSLEY**

3. **TERRY DAVIES**

4. **DEREK ALLEN**

5. **SHIFTY**

6. **KENNY BURRELL**

7. **TOT JOHNSON**

8. **KEV MURPHY**

9. **CARL WILLINGHAM**

10. **BARRY MALEADY**

*Right: Dancefloor terrorist,
the much loved Ginger Taylor.*

TEN

north american record dealers

The Northern Soul scene has long honored the talents of the legendary DJs for breaking classic vinyl at allnighters like Wigan, the Torch and the Wheel, but these great spinners have had to track down that vinyl. In many cases key figures like John Anderson have been the supplier but they in turn have had to obtain the vinyl as have those intrepid characters who trawl the States for new vinyl. Whilst America is looked upon as largely ignorant of Rare Soul there are a number of key dealers across America have turned up some of the great finds going right back to the earliest days of imports. Here are ten key figures in the search for elusive vinyl.

1. **VAL SHIVELY** (Philadelphia)

2. **SIMON SOUSSAN** (Los Angeles)

3. **JOHN LAMONTE** (Philadelphia)

4. **MARTIN KOPPEL** (Toronto)

5. **FRED KAPLAN** (New York)

6. **RAY AVERY'S** (Los Angeles)

7. **RADIO CENTRE** (Baltimore)

8. **BERNIE BINNICK** (Philadelphia)

9. **RICH ROSEN** (Las Vegas)

10. **DOWNSTAIRS** (New York)

TEN
essential 70's northern accessories

1. **HOLDALL,** big, shapeless and ideal for dumping in a corner to be left untouched all night.

2. **BOWLING SHIRT,** big, baggy and light in colour to show off the stains from dripping condensation!

3. **FLARED SKIRT,** flared skirts or box skirts look dead good for spinning in, just like those enormous 40" Spencer baggies we like to forget about!

4. **DISCATRON,** the potable 45 player that was perfect for ruining your newly purchased vinyl before you even got it home!

5. **SPEED,** bombers, dexies, blues, daps, green and clears, red and browns but not powder or pondies - unless you'd been let down, or you were a 'div'!

6. **TALCUM POWDER,** Brut was the powder of choice - in a bag hanging from your belt.

7. **BEER TOWEL,** hanging next to your talc bag, additional tennis sweat bands and a couple of strategically placed plasters to stop 'jogger's nipple' were optional!

8. **SEW ON PATCHES,** anniversary patches, label patches, Soul Shetland patches (?) you name it!

9. **FORD CAPRI,** 'cos you couldn't afford a tan Scimitar!

10. **WIGAN CASINO MEMBERSHIP CARD,** older the better! Always in your wallett and preferably next to a gold Torch card, a round Wheel 'beer mat' and a couple of choice others like the Va-Va or Mecca.

Opposite and right:
'Get them while they're hot - they're lovely'... The massive explosion in Northern of the mid-70's kicked of a frenzy of commercialisation.

From a new take on traditional anniversary patches to the more bizarre 'Fully Adjustable' belts (ONLY £1 - and ideally suited for holding up those 40" baggies) it was easy to become a 'bona-fide' Soul fan (just like that 'Wigan's Ovation') by mail order - without ever going to an allnighter!

Today thankfully all the tourists are long-gone!

The INTERNATIONAL SOUL CLUB

2 Marsh Parade
Newcastle
Staffs ST5 1BT

Over 40,000 Members

BADGES
Due to increase in manufacturing costs all badges are now **35p**

1. INTERNATIONAL SOUL CLUB
2. SOUL STOKE-ON-TRENT
3. SOUL LINCOLN
4. SOUL LEEDS
5. NORTHERN SOUL HUMBERSIDE
6. SOUL LONDON
7. SOUL GLOUCESTER
8. THE YOGI BEAR CLUB
9. SOUTH WEST INTERNATIONAL SOUL CLUB
10. SOUL BIRMINGHAM
11. RIGHT ON J.J. BARNES
12. SOUL WARWICKSHIRE
13. DETROIT EMERALDS FEEL THE NEED IN ME
14. SOUL WOLVERHAMPTON
15. SOUL BLACKPOOL
16. RIGHT ON THE TORCH
17. SOUL NORTH WALES
18. SOUL YORKSHIRE
19. SOUL LANCASHIRE
20. OKeh
21. THE TWISTED WHEEL LIVES ON
22. INTERNATIONAL SOUL CLUB 1974 LEEDS FESTIVAL
23. SOUL NOTTINGHAMSHIRE
24. VA VA LIVES ON THE N1 ALL NIGHTER BOLTON
25. FOREVER THE TORCH
26. SOUL
27. THE TORCH STOKE-ON-TRENT
28. SOUL U.S.A.
29. TORCH FOREVER NORTHERN SOUL
30. THE TORCH RULES
31. KEEP THE FAITH
32. THE DRIFTERS
33. KEEP THE FAITH THE CATACOMBS
34. SOUL STAFFORD
35. SOUL DERBY
36. SOUL CHESHIRE
37. SOUL LEICESTER
38. SOUL SCOTLAND

BADGES Each **35p** + S.A.E.

MEMBERS NOTICE

SATURDAY, 24th MAY

THE EVENT AT THE
NORBECK CASTLE HOTEL,
QUEENS PROMENADE,
BLACKPOOL

IS **POSTPONED**
UNTIL FURTHER NOTICE

DUE TO THE NEW MANAGEMENT OF THE HOTEL,
WILL NOT PERMIT EVENT TO TAKE PLACE

VOUCHER HOLDERS RETURN TO I.S.C. HEAD OFFICE
FOR FULL REFUND

---

1. INTERNATIONAL SOUL CLUB

2. KEEP THE FAITH SOUL WIGAN

CAR STICKERS

A great offer – Still only **15p** Each + S.A.E.

MAIL ORDER DEPARTMENT

ORDER FORM

Print clearly your name, address, requirements, enclosing cheque/P.O. for correct amount to :
I.S.C. Mail Order Dept. 2 Marsh Parade, Newcastle, Staffs. ST5 1BT. remember your s.a.e.

Name: _____

Address: _____

_____

Please send me :-
Badges No's. _____

Key Ring No's. _____

_____ Car Stickers _____

1975 MEMBERSHIP RENEWAL !!!
put cross in box and send 10p   plus S.A.E.

TEN
venues that are very busy TODAY

Northern Soul is very much alive and kicking! Not only on the traditional home turf, but throughout the UK a wide range of promoters old and new are finding that their venues are regularly full to capacity. Even in London Capitol Soul Club's Friday night Soul Night expects attendences of 650 for an event that finishes at 1.00am! If you're not back on the scene yet you'd better get your dancing shoes polished quick - you may not be able to get in!

1. **TOGETHERNESS EVENTS**   Blackpool Weekender and the King's Hall, Stoke, Allnighter

2. **CLEETHORPES WEEKENDER**   Run by Ady Croasdell and the 6T's crew

3. **THE RITZ,** MANCHESTER   Cellar Full of Soul Bank Holiday Allnighters run by Richard Searling

4. **LOWTON CIVIC HALL**   Soul Nights/occasional Allnighters run by Kev Murphy

5. **PRESTON GRASSHOPPERS**   Classic Soul Nights

6. **100 CLUB,** LONDON   The longest running allnighter by far run under the 6T's banner by Adey Croasdell

7. **ALBRIGHTON**   Soul Nights and occasional Allnighters

8. **LONGFIELD SUITE,** PRESTWICH   Terry Davies promoted Soul Nights and occasional Allnighters

9. **THE RITZ,** BRIGHOUSE   Classic Soul Nights

10. **THE DOME,** LONDON   Soul Nights run by the Capitol Soul Club

TEN
journalists to chronicle our scene

Over the years there have been many fanzines to cover Northern Soul, today there are perhaps more than ever, they have all had writers who have captured our scene in print, both as fans and journalists. Here are a selection of influential writers, though the Number 1 slot could go to only one man - Dave Godin. Father of British Soul, he of course christened our unique brand of dance music.

1. **DAVE GODIN**
2. **FRANK ELSON**
3. **RICHARD SEARLING**
4. **NEIL RUSHTON**
5. **PAUL PHILIPS**
6. **TONY CUMMINGS**
7. **MARK BICKNELL**
8. **DAVE RIMMER**
9. **CHRIS SAVOURY**
10. **DAVE NOWELL**

TEN
northern soul fanzines

There have been many fanzines to cover Northern Soul. Though they are not necessarily entirely devoted to Northern (usually including Deep or Modern Soul) the following, which are mostly still in print, have been particularly long running, informative and influential.

1. **TOGETHERNESS**
2. **SOULFUL KINDA MUSIC**
3. **SOUL UNDERGROUND**
4. **IN THE BASEMENT**
5. **ECHOES**
6. **BLUES AND SOUL**
7. **SHADES OF SOUL**
8. **SOUL SURVIVOR**
9. **VOICES FROM THE SHADOWS**
10. **SOUL UP NORTH**

Right: Edited by Russ Winstanley, the short-lived Wigan Casino fanzine 'Northern Noise' ran to just 4 issues.

SIXTIES
northern soul producers - a selection

Here are a selection of important producers and their 60's addresses, it is interesting to note that many producers were officially based in New York even though they may have worked in Detroit, Philadelphia or the like...

Herb Bernstein Enterprises
39 West 55th Street, New York, New York

Quinton Claunch & Rudolph Russell
2445 Chelsea Avenue, Memphis, Tennessee

Tommy Coghill & Chips Moman
827 Thomas Street, Memphis, Tennessee

Bob Crewe
1841 Broadway, New York, New York

Steve Cropper
926 East McLemore Street, Memphis, Tennessee

Don Davis
13640 Pembroke, Detroit, Michigan

Fame Productions (Rick Hall)
603 East Avalon, Muscle Shoals, Alabama

GWP Productions
210 East 55th Street, New York, New York

Marc Gordon Productions Inc.
1022 North Palm Avenue, Los Angeles, California

Ellie Greenwich & Mike Rashkow
1414 Avenue Of the Americas, New York, New York

HB Barnum Productions
1239 North Highland Avenue, Hollywood, California

Leon Haywood
2426 1/2 Lucerne Street, Los Angeles

Quin Ivy & Marlin Breene
101 East 2nd Street, Sheffield, Alabama

Just Productions (Lorraine Chandler)
6097 Whitewood Street, Detroit, Michigan

Kama Sutra Productions Inc. (Phil Steinberg, Arie Ripp)
1650 Broadway, New York, New York

Levine - Resnick Productions
1619 Broadway, New York, New York

John Madara Productions
250 South Broad Street, Philadelphia, Pennsylvania

Jessie Mason - Willie Hutch
8350 Wilshire Boulevard, Los Angeles, California

Curtis Mayfield
8543 Stoney Island Avenue, Chicago, Illinois

Van McCoy Music Inc.
1619 Broadway, New York, New York

Lizard Productions
1826 Canyon Boulevard, Hollywood, California

Mira Productions (Randall Wood)
9025 Sunset Boulevard, Hollywood, California

Willie Mitchell
306 Poplar Street, Memphis, Tennessee

Jerry Murray (Jerryo)
1830 South Karlov, Chicago, Illinois

Music Enterprises (Huey P Meaux)
PO Box 206, Winnie, Texas

Bobby Paris
8358 Sunset Boulevard, Los Angeles, California

A. Mike Terry - Joe Armstead Productions
5622 South Maryland Avenue, Chicago, Illinois

Johnny Rivers - Marc Gordan
8923 Sunset Boulevard, Los Angeles, California

Sidrian Productions
18292 Wyoming, Detroit, Michigan

Shelby Singleton Productions
1817 16th Avenue South, Nashville, Tennessee

Fred Smith
7400 Fountain Avenue, Los Angeles, California

Soulville Records (Horace Parks, James Frazier)
1640 Broadway, Gary, Indiana

Tangerine Records
2107 West Washington Boulevard, Los Angeles, California

Tran-San Productions (George Kerr)
66 Telford Street, East Orange, New Jersey

Teddy Vann Productions
1619 Broadway, New York, New York

Andre Williams
67412 Cornell, Chicago, Illinois

Jimmy Wisner
888 8th Avenue, New York, New York

Charles Wright - Fred Smith
4219 Normal Street, Los Angeles, California

Richard 'Popcorn' Wylie
3044 Taylor Avenue, Detroit, Michigan

*Laura Lee the 'Rip Off' girl who recorded a number of Northern tracks including 'To Win Your Heart', vocal to
'Festival Time' and an influential Ric-Tic recording that was very popular in the early 70's.*

TEN
wonderful motown non-hits

1.	**KIM WESTON**	HELPLESS	Gordy
2.	**THE SPINNERS**	WHAT MORE CAN A BOY ASK FOR	Motown
3.	**BARBARA RANDOLPH**	I GOT A FEELING	Soul
4.	**THE ORIGINALS**	SUSPICION	Unreleased Soul
5.	**THE CONTOURS**	BABY HIT AND RUN	UK Tamla Motown /MFP
6.	**JUNIOR WALKER AND THE ALLSTARS**	I AIN'T GOING NOWHERE	Motown
7.	**BRENDA HOLLOWAY**	RECONSIDER	Unreleased Tamla
8.	**GLADYS KNIGHT AND THE PIPS**	JUST WALK IN MY SHOES	Soul
9.	**ISLEY BROTHERS**	TELL ME IT'S JUST A RUMOUR BABY	UK Tamla Motown only on 45
10.	**FRANCES NERO**	KEEP ON LOVIN' ME	Soul

Opposite: Remember? Most of us on the Soul scene started at Youth Clubs and small local halls. The sounds we heard were the 'cheapies', frequently reissues or bootlegs, they were the ones which we ourselves would go on to buy when we first started collecting.

Gladys Knight and the Pips, despite their now superstar status, found 'Just Walk In My Shoes' sold very poorly at the time of release.

TEN
northern soul favourites of the author

1.	**JOHNNY WYATT**	THIS THING CALLED LOVE	Kapp
2.	**JOHNNY TAYLOR**	FRIDAY NIGHT	Stax
3.	**EDDIE FOSTER**	I NEVER KNEW	In
4.	**RUBIN**	YOU'VE BEEN AWAY	Kapp
5.	**BOBBY FREEMAN**	I'LL NEVER FALL IN LOVE AGAIN	Autumn
6.	**ERNEST MOSELY**	STUBBORN HEART	La Cindy
7.	**TAMALA LEWIS**	YOU WON'T SAY NOTHING	Marton
8.	**LOU JOHNSON**	UNSATISFIED	Big Top
9.	**PATTI AND THE EMBLEMS**	I'M GONNA LOVE YOU A LONG, LONG TIME	Kapp
10.	**SANDY WYNNS**	THE TOUCH OF VENUS	Doc

Left: The author's all-time favourite, Johnny Wyatt's 'This Thing Called love' which also came out on UK President and was covered by Danny Wagner on his 'Kindred Soul' album.

416

TEN
chart hits played
first on the **northern scene**

1	**TAVARES**	HEAVEN MUST BE MISSING AN ANGEL	*Capitol '76*
2.	**VICKI SUE ROBINSON**		
		TURN THE BEAT AROUND	*RCA '76*
3.	**ESTHER PHILLIPS**	WHAT A DIFFERENCE A DAY MAKES	*Kudu '75*
4.	**BETTY WRIGHT**	WHERE IS THE LOVE	*RCA '75*
5.	**TAVARES**	DON'T TAKE AWAY THE MUSIC	Capitol '76
6.	**GEORGE BENSON**	SUPERSHIP	*CTI '75*
7.	**THE MOMENTS**	I'VE GOT THE NEED	*All Platinum '75*
8.	**SILVETTI**	SPRING RAIN	*Salsoul '77*
9.	**THE O'JAYS**	I LOVE MUSIC	*PIR '75*
10.	**THE MIRACLES**	LOVE MACHINE	*Tamla '76*

Right: Betty Wright's chart topper 'Where Is the Love' - (here on the US release) despite essentially having only this one biggie to sing, her performance at Wigan is considered one of the great live shows of the Northern scene.

TEN
chart hits played
later on the **northern scene**

1.	**CURTIS MAYFIELD**	MOVE ON UP	*Buddah '71*
2.	**THE SHOWSTOPPERS**		
		AIN'T NOTHING BUT A HOUSEPARTY	*Beacon '68*
3.	**FONTELLA BASS**	RESCUE ME	*Chess '65*
4.	**DON COVAY**	IT'S BETTER TO HAVE	*Mercury '74*
5.	**THE MIRACLES**	GOING TO A GO-GO	*Tamla '66*
6.	**THE MIRACLES**	COME ROUND HERE I'M THE ONE YOU NEED	
		/SAVE ME	*Tamla '66*
7.	**GRAHAM BONNEY**	SUPER GIRL	*Columbia '66*
8.	**JNR. WALKER**	HOW SWEET IT IS	*Soul '66*
9.	**GENE MCDANIELS**	TOWER OF STRENGTH	*Liberty '61*
10.	**JIMMY RADCLIFFE**	LONG AFTER TONIGHT IS ALL OVER	*Musicor '64*

Below Right: James 'Jimmy Mac' (NO not THAT Jimmy Mack!)' McKeachin, manager and producer of the Furys - a great yet sadly unsuccessful group, he was also responsible for production on Alexander Patten's legendary 'A Little Lovin' Sometimes' - another criminal failure.

TEN
most hyped tracks that never made it!

1. **REACHING FOR THE BEST**   BOB RELF   *
2. **SIX BY SIX**   TONY TURNER   *
3. **MESSING WITH MY MIND**   BARBARA CARR   (BARR-CARR)
4. **HUNG UP ON YOU**   ROY ORBISON   (MERCURY)
5. **OUR LOVE IS IN IN THE POCKET** INSTRUMENTAL   *
6. **LANDSLIDE**   INSTRUMENTAL   *
7. **SHERRY**   HUGO MONTENEGRO   (TIME)
8. **DIZZY**   LESTER LANIN   (METROMEDIA)
9. **SOCIAL TRAGEDY**   DAUGHTERS OF EVE   (CHECKER)
10. **MR MISERY**   PADDED CELL   (TODDLIN' TOWN)

*These records do NOT exist!... Despite being MEGA-HYPED in the 70's!

Right: Perhaps it's the relative obscurity of most Northern sounds and therefore information about them, perhaps it's just the gear... But the Northern scene has always been rife with stories of records that just don't exist.

Tony Turner's 'Six By Six' vocal - supposedly on Musicor is a prime example. Much talked of in the 70's - for some unknown reason no-one ever managed to track down a copy - I wonder why?!!! Anyway for all you frustrated would be owners - here at last it is (we'll also be glad to supply a copy of the label of Elvis' version of 'My Sugar Baby' to anyone interested! (please specify preferred label)).

TEN
brilliant tracks that never really made it!

1.	**LOOK AT ME LOOK AT ME**	VERNON GREENE	*(MINIT)*
2.	**AIN'T GONNA DO YOU NO HARM**	NEW WANDERERS	*(READY)*
3.	**WISHES**	The METRICS	*(CHADWICK)*
4.	**CAN YOU REMEMBER**	RHONDA DAVIES	*(DUKE)*
5.	**I MUST LOVE YOU**	TIMOTHY WILSON	*(SKY DISC)*
6.	**I DON'T WANNA GET AWAY FROM YOUR LOVE**		
		YVONNE DANIELS	*(STERLING SOUND)*
7.	**JUST DO THE BEST YOU CAN**	DUKE and LEONARD	*(STOMP TOWN)*
8.	**HEY GIRL**	The TOPICS	*(CHADWICK)*
9.	**WISHIN' AND HOPIN'**	BILLY KEENE	*(PAULA/VAULT)*
10.	**I KNOW I'M IN LOVE WITH YOU**	GEORGE 'JUKE' BYRD	*(PAY-TONS)*

'Not the kind of guy to give in and give up', a young Ian Levine, already established as one of the scene's most important DJs, with Mirwood Soul man Jimmy Thomas on a 'Beautiful Night' at Tunstall's legendary Torch club in 1972.
Ian's unparalleled knowledge of Soul music and personal vision for the development our scene not only resulted in his launching a staggeringly high proportion of the greatest Northern classics, but was also responsible for the introduction of almost brand new 70s releases. In the heyday of the screaming stomper these new and utterly different shuffling Mecca sounds were so opposed to the norm that it is hard to appreciate their shattering impact and the controversy surrounding them. Today our scene would be almost unrecognisable without their pervasive and, in retrospect, highly positive influence.

and finally...

For over 30 years Northern Soul has remained a unique form of youth culture that continues to unearth many superb and totally unknown 60s and 70s dance sounds from the States even after so many years of searching. Today many Soul fans who started 'Living The Nightlife' in the scene's earliest days are still regulars on the scene - after 30 years only wishing they had started going sooner! Whether you are a past member of the Soul fraternity, or are just starting to learn about our music, remember that the incredible vinyl featured throughout this book is on the turntables at at least one Allnighter and dozens of Soul Nights every week throughout the country, you'll find there's a space reserved for you on the dancefloor!

togetherness

the magazine... love soul? subscribe now

From the earliest sounds to all our tomorrow's, building bridges in the Soul scene. Each big issue is packed with the latest news, reviews of top venues, new discoveries, hot new releases, imports and authoritative contributions from the leading names in Northern, Modern and Deep Soul. PLUS FREE with every issue an **EXCLUSIVE TOGETHERNESS** CD featuring top current Northern sounds from Goldmine Soul Supply and the cream of Modern from Expansion records. Togetherness magazine is total coverage for the UK Soul scene in one essential publication.

ONLY £10.00 incl. P&P for a yearly two-issue subscription (Europe £14.00, Worldwide £15).

Send your details with a cheque a P/O or your credit card details (Visa, Switch, Mastercard or Solo) today: **KRL, PO Box 909, Worksop, Nottinghamshire S80 3YZ, UK.** Tel: 01909 515150 Fax: 01909 774200

You can now order TOGETHERNESS MAGAZINE online too: www.firstnet.co.uk/goldsoul or e-mail: goldsoul.firstnet.co.uk.

Soul for the Soulful

Covering the full spectrum of Deep, Modern and Northern Soul from the latest dancefloor monsters to in-demand connoisseur classics, Goldmine Soul Supply are the leading music, video and book publishers working exclusively in the Soul music field. Send your address and £1.50 to the above address for your copy of our comprehensive Millennium Soul Catalogue.

Available through all good record stores, or direct from the Goldmine Soul Supply website, www.firstnet.co.uk/goldsoul/.

Goldmine Soul Supply Limited, PO Box 4, Todmorden OL14 6DA, UK

Trade enquiries ONLY to Vital Distribution, 01454 886423.

index